THE HISTORY OF AL-ṬABARĪ

AN ANNOTATED TRANSLATION

VOLUME XXIX

Al-Manṣūr and al-Mahdī

A.D. 763–786/A.H. 146–169

SUNY

SERIES IN NEAR EASTERN STUDIES

Said Amir Arjomand, Editor

The preparation of this volume was made possible in part by a grant from the National Endowment for the Humanities, an independent federal agency.

Bibliotheca Persica
Edited by Ehsan Yar-Shater

The History of al-Ṭabarī
(Ta'rīkh al-rusul wa'l mulūk)

VOLUME XXIX

Al-Manṣūr and al-Mahdī

translated and annotated
by

Hugh Kennedy

University of St Andrews

State University of New York Press

Published by
State University of New York Press, Albany

Printed in the United States of America

For information, address State University of New York Press, State University Plaza, Albany, N.Y., 12246

Library of Congress Cataloging-in-Publication Data

Ṭabarī, 838?–923.
Al-Manṣūr and al-Mahdī.
(The history of al-Ṭabarī = Ta'rīkh al-rusul wa'l mulūk; v. 29) (Bibliotheca Persica) (SUNY series in Near Eastern studies)
Translation of extracts from: Ta'rīkh al-rusul wa-al-mulūk.
Bibliography: p.
Includes index.
1. Islamic Empire—History—750–1258. 2. Manṣūr, Abū Ja'far, Caliph, ca. 712–775. 3. Mahdī, Caliph, d. 785. I. Kennedy, Hugh (Hugh N.) II. Title. III. Series: Ṭabarī, 838?–923. Ta'rīkh al-rusul wa-al-mulūk. English; v. 29. IV. Series: Bibliotheca Persica (Albany, N.Y.) V. Series: SUNY series in Near Eastern studies.
DS38.2.T313 1985 vol. 29 909'.1 s 88–35573
[DS38.6] [909'.097671]
ISBN 0-7914-0142-1
ISBN 0-7914-0143-X (pbk.)
10 9 8 7 6 5 4 3 2 1

Preface

THE HISTORY OF PROPHETS AND KINGS (*Ta'rīkh al-rusul wa'l-mulūk*) by Abū Ja'far Muḥammad b. Jarīr al-Ṭabarī (839–923), here rendered as the *History of al-Ṭabarī*, is by common consent the most important universal history produced in the world of Islam. It has been translated here in its entirety for the first time for the benefit of non-Arabists, with historical and phiological notes for those interested in the particulars of the text.

Ṭabarī's monumental work explores the history of the ancient nations, with special emphasis on biblical peoples and prophets, the legendary and factual history of ancient Iran, and, in great detail, the rise of Islam, the life of the Prophet Muḥammad, and the history of the Islamic world down to the year 915. The first volume of this translation will contain a biography of al-Ṭabarī and a discussion of the method, scope, and value of his work. It will also provide information on some of the technical considerations that have guided the work of the translators.

The *History* has been divided here into 38 volumes, each of which covers about two hundred pages of the original Arabic text in the Leiden edition. An attempt has been made to draw the dividing lines between the individual volumes in such a way that each is to some degree independent and can be read as such. The page numbers of the original in the Leiden edition appear on the margins of the translated volumes.

Al-Tabarī very often quotes his sources verbatim and traces the chain of transmission (*isnād*) to an original source. The chains of transmitters are, for the sake of brevity, rendered by only a dash (—) between the individual links in the chain. Thus, "According to Ibn Ḥumayd—Salamah—Ibn Isḥāq" means that al-Ṭabarī received the report from Ibn Ḥumayd, who said that he was told by Salamah, who said that he was told by Ibn Isḥāq and so on. The numerous subtle and important differences in the original Arabic wording have been disregarded.

The table of contents at the beginning of each volume gives a brief survey of the topics dealt with in that particular volume. It also includes the headings and subheadings as they appear in al-Ṭabarī's text, as well as those occasionally introduced by the translator.

Well-known place names, such as, for instance, Mecca, Beghdad, Jerusalem, Damascus, and the Yemen, are given in their English spellings. Less common place names, which are the vast majority, are transliterated. Biblical figures appear in the accepted English spelling. Iranian names are usually transcribed according to their Arabic forms, and the presumed Iranian forms are often discussed in the footnotes.

Technical terms have been translated wherever possible, but some, such as dirham and imām, have been retained in Arabic forms. Others that cannot be translated with sufficient precision have been retained and italicized as well as footnoted.

The annotation aims chiefly at clarifying difficult passages, identifying individuals and place names, and discussing textual difficulties. Much leeway has been left to the translators to included in the footnotes whatever they consider necessary and helpful.

The bibliographies list all the sources mentioned in the annotation.

The index in each volume contains all the names of persons and places referred to in the text, as well as those mentioned in the notes as far as they refer to the medieval period. It does not include the names of modern scholars. A general index, it is hoped, will appear after all the volumes have been published.

For further details concerning the series and acknowledgments, see Preface to Volume I.

Ehsan Yar-Shater

Contents

The Caliphate of al-Manṣūr

The Caliphate of al-Mahdī

Abbreviations

EI[1]: *Encyclopaedia of Islām*, first edition
EI[2]: *Encyclopaedia of Islām*, second edition

Translator's Foreword

This volume is a translation of the part of Ṭabarī's *History* that deals with the period from 145/762 to 169/786. It begins immediately after al-Manṣūr's defeat of the ʿAlid rebellion of Muḥammad the Pure Soul and his brother Ibrāhīm and deals with the rest of al-Manṣūr's reign until his death in 158/775. Much of the material is simply administrative detail, government appointments, and the travels of the caliph, but two important subjects are dealt with: the foundation of Baghdad, on which Ṭabarī provides some valuable information to supplement the well-known accounts of the geographers, and the caliph's efforts to force ʿĪsā b. Mūsā to renounce his right to the caliphate in favor of his own son al-Mahdī. Much of the anecdotal material here reveals the caliph in a distinctly unfavorable light. The climax of this section is the extraordinarily detailed and vivid account of al-Manṣūr's death, plainly showing the awe and fear with which he was regarded.

The next section is a series of anecdotes about his behavior and appearance. These are not arranged in chronological order but read rather as isolated narratives that Ṭabarī could not fit into the main run of the text but felt were too good to miss out. There are some general themes here: the caliph's determination to uphold his authority, the contrast between his frugality and al-Mahdī's easy going generosity, his eloquence and the effectiveness with which he dealt with hecklers in the mosque, and his relations with the wild and unruly Maʿn b. Za'idah. Despite the random nature of much of this material, we get a very clear idea of al-

Manṣūr's personality, and even after twelve hundred years he seems a powerful, individual, rounded character. It says much for the immediacy of the narrative that such a lively impression survives.

The third section deals with the reign of his son, al-Mahdī. Compared with the upheavals and struggles of his father's life, al-Mahdī's caliphate was altogther quieter. Much emphasis is laid on his pious works, his building of mosques, his encouragement of the holy war against the Byzantines, and his persecution of the Manichaean Zindiqs. We are also given detailed accounts of government appointments. The major political events were, once again, the removal of ʿĪsā b. Mūsā from his position in the succession in favor of al-Mahdī's own son al-Hādī and the meteoric rise and sudden fall of the vizier Yaʿqūb b. Dāwūd, who was originally appointed as the caliph's intermediary with the ʿAlid family but who went on to become his all-powerful minister. This section also ends with an account of the caliph's death and sundry anecdotes about his behavior. Unlike the accounts of al-Manṣūr's death, which are generally consistent, these accounts are directly contradictory, and it is impossible to decide which if any is true. From the point of view of assessing the accuracy of Ṭabarī's work as a whole, it is interesting to note that it is not only in the earlier parts on the life of the Prophet and the early caliphs that such contradictory accounts survive side by side but even of events that took place well after the establishment of the ʿAbbāsids and within the lifetimes of such authorities as al-Wāqidī and al-Madā'inī.

In terms of literary approach, the early ʿAbbāsid parts of the history are transitional between the *akhbār* narratives of the early parts and the more linear official narratives of the third century. The use of classical Muslim historiographical technique, the individual *akhbar*, each supported by its own *isnād*. becomes much less common after the death of al-Saffāḥ in 136/754, and much more of the material is unattributed or consists of no more than laconic notes about appointments and dismissals. The latest major work that seems to have used the classical canons was ʿUmar b. Shabbah's account of the rebellion of Muḥammad the Pure Soul, which finishes immediately before the beginning of the section translated here. Those narratives, still large in number, that are attributed are often attached to isolated individuals, many of whom contribute no more than one or two accounts and few of whom are known to have composed books. Many of them are eyewitnesses or sons of eyewitnesses, and it is quite unclear in what form these accounts reached Ṭabarī more than a century later. The established compilers like al-Madā'inī and al-Wāqidī are relied on for points of detail, rather than substantial narratives.

Of the sources that can be identified, many are closely linked to Baghdad and the caliphal court and bureaucarcy, like the Qurashī 'Alī b. Muḥammad al-Nawfalī, whose father was an important courtier and Yaḥya b. al-Ḥasan b. 'Abd al-Khāliq, a relative of the ubiquitous chamberlain al-Rabī' b. Yūnus. This means that we have very little information from provincial sources. There are virtually no extended narratives dealing with Syria or Egypt. Even Khurāsān, which looms so large in earlier parts of the *History*, is largely neglected. Historical writing, like politics and administration, was becoming more centralized in the 'Abbāsid period.

At their best, the accounts collected by Ṭabarī and translated here are interesting and lively; at their worst they are obscure and monotonous. But whatever their literary merit, there can be no doubt that they form by far the most important historical source for the early 'Abbāsid caliphate.

It remains a pleasure to thank those who have helped me in the preparation of his translation and generously given of their time, patience, and erudition: Dr. David Jackson and Richard Kimber of the Department of Arabic Studies in the University of St Andrews and especially Judy Ahola, whose aid and encouragement were invaluable. I must also express by thanks to Dr. E. Whelan of the Ṭabarī project for her help. Most of all, I would like to thank Professor Ihsan Abbas, whose patient editing of my typescript and immense knowledge of classical Arabic literature notably improved the readability of the text and saved me from numerous errors. Such mistakes as may remain are, of course, entirely my responsibility.

Hugh Kennedy

The Caliphate of al-Manṣūr

The Events of the Year 146 [319]

(March 21, 763–March 9, 764)

The events of this year:

Among these was Abū Ja'far's[1] completion of his city, Baghdad.

According to Muḥammad b. 'Umar:[2] Abū Ja'far moved from Madīnat Ibn Hubayrah[3] to Baghdad in Ṣafar 146 (April 20–May 18, 763) and settled in it and built his city.

Information about the description of the building.

We have mentioned before the reason that impelled Abū Ja'far to build it and the reason why he chose the site on which he built his city, and we will now describe the building of it.

According to Rashīd Abū Dāwūd b. Rashīd: Abū Ja'far set out for al-Kūfah when he received news of the rebellion of Muḥammad b. 'Abdallāh. He had prepared the necessary wood and teak

---

1. The caliph al-Manṣūr. In contrast to other 'Abbāsid caliphs, he was frequently known by his *kunyah*, Abū Ja'far, perhaps because his *ism* (first name), 'Abdallāh, and his father's name, Muḥammad, were so common.

2. The well-known historian al-Wāqidī, d. 207/823, author of the surviving *Kitāb al-Maghāzī* and other, lost works; see *EI*[1], s v. "al-Wāḳidī." Al-Ṭabarī frequently quotes him for exact dates but rarely for extended narrative.

3. Between Baghdad and al-Kūfah, near modern Hillah: Le Strange, *Lands*, 71.

and other things, for the building of the city of Baghdad and when he set out he left his freedman Aslam in charge of completing what he had prepared. Aslam heard that Ibrāhīm b. ʿAbdallāh had defeated the army of Abū Jaʿfar, and he burned the teak and wood [320] that Abū Jaʿfar had left him in charge of, for fear that that might be taken from him if his master was defeated. When Abū Jaʿfar heard what his freedman Aslam had done, he wrote to him, censuring him for that, and Aslam wrote to him, informing him that he had feared that Ibrāhīm would be victorious over them and take it, and he did not say anything to him.

According to Isḥāq b. Ibrāhīm al-Mawṣilī—his father[4]: When al-Manṣūr wished to build his city of Baghdad, he asked the advice of his companions, and and one of those whose advice he sought was Khālid b. Barmak,[5] and he gave him advice.

According to ʿAlī b. ʿIṣmah: Khālid b. Barmak laid out the city of Abū Jaʿfar for him and gave him advice about it. When he needed rubble he said to him, "What do you think about demolishing the city of the *īwān* of Chosroes at al-Madā'in[6] and taking the rubble from it to this city of mine?" He replied, "I do not think that [is a good idea] O Commander of the Faithful," and he asked him why, and he answered, "It is one of the proofs of Islam by which the observer is convinced that people like its (the palace's) lords were not swept away by the power of this world but only by the power of religion. Furthermore, O Commander of the Faithful, there is in it a place where ʿAlī b. Abī Ṭālib prayed." The caliph said, "How wrong you are Khālid; you did not agree because of your partiality for your friends the Persians."

---

4. Ibrāhīm al-Mawṣilī, d. 188/804, was a famous poet and singer at the ʿAbbāsid court, and his son Iṣḥāq succeeded him. Al-Ṭabarī uses them as a source for much incidental detail and anecdotal information. See *EI*[2], s.v. "Ibrāhīm al-Mawṣilī."

5. The founder of the fortunes of the Barmakid family. Khālid's ancestors were hereditary guardians of a Buddhist shrine at Balkh in northern Afghanistan, but the family converted to Islam in the Umayyad period. Khālid joined the ʿAbbāsid movement early and distinguished himself in an administrative role. He was employed by al-Saffāḥ and al-Manṣūr in the financial administration and as governor of Fārs. He died in 163/780: Sourdel, *Vizirat*, I, 129–34. See Crone, *Slaves*, 176–77; Kennedy, *Abbasid Caliphate*, 101–2.

6. Al-Madā'in was the ancient Ctesiphon, the Sasanian capital, southeast of Baghdad; see Yāqūt, *Muʿjam*, V, 74–75; Le Strange, *Lands*, 33–35. The *īwān* of Chosroes is the giant arch of the royal palace, part of which still survives to this day.

He ordered that the white palace be demolished, and a section of it was and the materials were brought. He investigated the amount it cost them to demolish and transport it, and they found that that would be more expensive than it would be if it were newly made. This was reported to al-Manṣūr, and he summoned Khālid b. Barmak and told him what it cost them to demolish and transport and asked him for his opinion. He said, "O Commander of the Faithful, I thought before that you should not do it, but since you have done it I think that you should demolish it now down to the foundations because, if you do not, it will be said that you failed to demolish it." Al-Manṣūr rejected that advice and [321]
ordered that it should not be demolished.

According to Mūsā b. Dāwūd al-Muhandis (engineer): Al-Ma'mūn told me this story, "If you build me a building, make it impossible to demolish so that its remains and traces may last."

It is said: Abū Ja'far needed gates for the city and Abū 'Abd al-Raḥmān al-Humānī alleged that Sulaymān b. Dāwūd had built a city called Zandaward near the site on which al-Ḥajjāj[7] had built Wāsiṭ. The devils had made five doors of iron for it the likes of which people today could not make, and he set them up in it. They remained there until al-Ḥajjāj built Wāsiṭ and this city was in ruins. Al-Ḥajjāj transported its doors and used them in his city of Wāsiṭ. When Abū Ja'far built the city, he took those doors and used them for his city, and they are there until today. The city has eight doors, four inside and four outside, and four out of these five doors were used on the inside ones and the fifth on the outside gate of the palace.

On the outside Khurāsān gate he used a door that was brought from Syria, of pharaonic workmanship. On the outside Kūfah gate, he used a door brought from al-Kūfah, which had been made by Khālid b. 'Abdallāh al-Qasrī.[8] He ordered that a door be produced for the Syrian gate, so one was made in Baghdad, and it was the weakest of all the gates.

---

7. Al-Ḥajjāj b. Yūsuf al-Thaqafī, d. 95/714, the celebrated governor of Iraq and the east for the Umayyads who founded the city of Wāsiṭ. Sulaymān b. Dāwūd is the biblical King Solomon, who is credited with numerous building achievements in the Muslim tradition. For Zandaward, see Yāqūt, *Mu'jam*, II, 154, where he explains that the city fell into ruins with the foundation of Baghdad.

8. Governor of Iraq for the Umayyads, 105–20/723–38.

The city was built round so that, if the king settled in the middle of it, he was not nearer one place of it than another. He set up four gates on the model of military camps in war, and he built two walls, the inside wall being higher than the outside one. He built his palace in the middle of it and the congregational mosque next to (*ḥawla*) the palace.[9]

It is said that al-Ḥajjāj b. Arṭāh[10] was the man who laid out the
[322] plan of the congregational mosque on the orders of Abū Ja'far and laid its foundations. It is said that its *qiblah* was not in the right direction and that anyone praying in it had to turn a little toward the Baṣrah Gate and that the *qiblah* of the mosque of al-Ruṣāfah[11] was more correct than the *qiblah* of the mosque of the city because the mosque of the city was built onto the palace, while the mosque of al-Ruṣāfah was built before the palace and the palace was built onto it and it happened because of that.

According to Yaḥyā b. 'Abd al-Khāliq[12]—his father: Abū Ja'far appointed a commander to every quarter of the city to hurry the completion of the building of that quarter.

According to Hārūn b. Ziyād b. Khālid b. al-Ṣalt—his father: Al-Manṣūr appointed Khālid b. al-Ṣalt in charge of the expenses of one of the quarters of the city when it was being built. Khālid said: When I had finished the building of that quarter, I brought him all the expenses on it, and he added them up with his own hand, and I still owed fifteen dirhams, and he imprisoned me in the Sharqiyyah prison for some days until I paid it. The mud bricks that were made for the building of the city were each a cubit by a cubit.

---

9. For the design of the Round City and the problems it raises, see Le Strange, *Baghdad*; Creswell, *Early Muslim Architecture*, II, 1–38; and Lassner, *Baghdad*.

10. Al-Nakha'ī: Having served the Umayyads, he went over to the 'Abbāsid cause and became *qāḍī* of al-Baṣrah and later a secretary to Abū Ja'far. He died in al-Rayy, where he had gone with al-Mahdī, probably in 150/767 (Crone, *Slaves*, 157). For his role in planning the northern suburbs of Baghdad, see Ya'qūbī, *Buldān*, 241, where he is described as a *muhandis* or engineer. His obituary is given by al-Dhahabī, *Tārīkh*, VI, 51–53.

11. The settlement founded by al-Mahdī on the east bank of the Tigris at Baghdad. The *qiblah* is the direction of prayer and should be oriented toward Mecca.

12. Yaḥyā was a maternal uncle of al-Faḍl, son of al-Manṣūr's chamberlain al-Rabī' b. Yūnus. Al-Ṭabarī draws on him extensively for inside information on court and bureaucratic intrigues.

According to one source: He demolished a section of the wall on the Muḥawwal Gate side and found in it a mud brick on which was written in red its weight, 117 *raṭls*,[13] and he said, "We weighed it, and we found it was the weight that was written on it." The doors of the chambers of the mass of the military commanders and secretaries of Abū Ja'far opened onto the courtyard of the mosque.

According to Yaḥyā b. al-Ḥasan b. 'Abd al-Khāliq, the maternal uncle of al-Faḍl b. al-Rabī': 'Īsā b. 'Alī[14] complained to Abū Ja'far, "O Commander of the Faithful, it is tiring for me to walk from the gate of the courtyard to the palace, for I have become [323] weak," and he replied, "Have yourself carried in a litter," but he responded, "I am embarrassed because of the people." Al-Manṣūr said, "Is there anyone who continues to be embarrassed because of them?" but 'Īsā continued, "Allow me, O Commander of the Faithful, what is allowed, one of the water-carrying camels." He said, "Does any water-carrying or riding animal enter the city?" Thus he ordered that everyone move their doors to the intervalla (*fuṣlān*) of the arcades and that no one should enter the courtyard except on foot. When al-Manṣūr ordered that the doors that led into the courtyard should be blocked and opened to the intervals of the arcades, the markets were established in the four arcades of the city, each one having a market. This continued until one of the *patrikioi*[15] of Byzantium came as an ambassador, and he ordered al-Rabī'[16] to take him on a tour of the city and its sur-

13. A *raṭl* was a dry measure that varied from place to place but was usually between 2 and 4 kg.

14. One of al-Manṣūr's paternal uncles. In 132/750, immediately after the 'Abbāsid revolution, he had been sent by al-Saffāḥ to Fārs as governor. It seems that he was worsted in an unsuccessful struggle for power there with Abū Muslim's nominee, Muḥammad b al-Ash'ath al-Khuzā'ī, after which, unlike his brothers, he never held a governorate. He remained at court, an influential adviser and promoter of the interests of his brothers and their children. He acquired extensive properties in Baghdad on the west bank and was the first member of the 'Abbāsid family to build a palace there. He died in Baghdad in 163/780.

15. For the most recent discussion of the interior of the Round City and the problems raised by this text, see Lassner, *'Abbasid Rule*, 184–97, where the role of the intervalla between different rings of the Round City is explained. A Patrikios, or patrician: a Byzantine official title. The Arab transliteration *biṭrīq* is used to designate Byzantine officials in general, see *EI*², s.v. Biṭrīḳ."

16. A man of obscure origin, apparently a freed slave, who rose to great impor-

roundings to see the development and the building. Al-Rabīʿ took him on a tour, and when it was finished he asked, "What do you think of my city?" He had gone up on the walls of the city and in the domes of the gates, and he said, "I saw a beautiful building, but I saw your enemies with you in the city." The caliph asked him who they were, and he replied, "The market people." Abū Jaʿfar was silent about it and, when the *patrikios* had gone, he ordered that the market be sent out of the city. He appointed Ibrāhīm b. Ḥubaysh al-Kūfī and attached Jawwās b. al-Musayyab al-Yamānī, his freedman, and ordered the two of them to build the markets in the Karkh area and ordered them to make booths (*ṣufūf*, lit: rows or ranks) and houses for every trade and to hand them over to the people. When they had done this, he moved the market there from the city and imposed rents on them according to size.

When the number of people grew, they built markets on sites Ibrāhīm b. Ḥubaysh and Jawwās had not sought to build on because they were unable (to construct) the booths from their resources.
[324] They were charged less in rents than was collected from those who settled in the buildings of the authorities.

One of them said: The reason Abū Jaʿfar moved the merchants from the city to al-Karkh and the nearby areas outside the city was that it was said to Abū Jaʿfar that foreigners and others stayed the night in it and that it was not safe because there might be spies and intelligence agents among them or they might open the gates of the city by night because of the position of the markets. So he ordered that the market be removed from the city and he established the *shurṭah* and *ḥaras*[17] in it and for the merchants,

---

tance in the service of al-Manṣūr and al-Mahdī. He was officially *ḥājib*, or chamberlain, but he used this position to become one of the most powerful men at court, masterminding the succession of al-Mahdī. He became leader of the *mawālī* (freedmen) at court and a bitter opponent of the *kuttāb* (secretaries) and their leaders, like Abū ʿUbaydallāh Muʿāwiyah and the Barmakid family. He had very extensive properties in Baghdad, notably in the market area of al-Karkh to the south of the Round City. He died c. 169/786 after the death of al-Mahdī, but his position was inherited by his son al-Faḍl, who became the chief rival of the Barmakids during Hārūn's reign. On al-Rabīʿ, see Crone, *Slaves*, 193–94; Kennedy, *ʿAbbasid Caliphate*, 103–4.

17. "Police" is the conventional translation of the Arabic *shurṭah*. In fact, the *shurṭah* seems to have been a small, elite military force attached to a ruler or governor to maintain order in peacetime and to act as a stiffening to other military

built at the Gate of the Ḥarrānī Arch, the Syrian Gate, and in al-Karkh.

According to al-Faḍl b. Sulaymān al-Hāshimī—his father: The reason for the removal of the markets from the City of Peace and the City of al-Sharqiyyah to the Karkh Gate, the Barley Gate, and the Muḥawwal Gate,[18] was that al-Manṣūr had appointed a man called Abū Zakkariyyā' Yaḥyā b. ʿAbdallāh in charge of the *ḥisbah* (accounts) of Baghdad and the markets in the year 157 (November 21, 773–November 10, 774), when the market was in the city. Al-Manṣūr was pursuing those who had rebelled with Muḥammad and Ibrāhīm sons of ʿAbdallāh b. Ḥasan.[19] This *muḥtasib*[20] had some connection with them, and he gathered a group against al-Manṣūr and led the lower classes of them astray, and they caused a commotion and gathered together. Al-Manṣūr sent Abū al-ʿAbbās al-Ṭūsī[21] to them, and he calmed them down and took Abū Zakariyyā' and put him in in his custody. Abū Jaʿfar ordered him to kill him, so a chamberlain of Abū al-ʿAbbās al-Ṭūsī, called Mūsā, killed him with his own hands at the Golden Gate in the courtyard on the order of al-Manṣūr. Abū Jaʿfar ordered that those houses that extended into the street of the city be destroyed and that the street be forty cubits wide. He demolished whatever had been extended into that width and ordered that the markets be removed to al-Karkh.

According to Abū Jaʿfar: When he ordered the removal of the [325]
merchants from the city to Karkh, Abān b. Ṣadaqah spoke[22] to

---

forces in war. The *shurṭah* referred to here is the caliph's *shurṭah* in Baghdad, but it seems that most provincial governors also had such forces at their disposal. The guard (*ḥaras*) seems to have been a personal bodyguard attached to the caliph.

18. For the geography of these areas, see Le Strange, *Baghdad*, pp. 57–80.

19. The ʿAlid rebels of 145/762.

20. An official responsible for maintaining law, order, and fair trading in the market.

21. Al-Ṭā'ī. a Khurāsānī officer, who participated in the wars of the ʿAbbāsid Revolution, notably the siege of Wāsiṭ. He seems to have remained in Iraq until 166/782–83, when he was appointed governor of Khurāsān. In 171/787–88 he returned to the west to take control of the *khātam*, the caliph's official seal, but he died shortly afterward. He was responsible for dividing up land on the west bank in Baghdad and kept extensive properties for himself (Crone, *Slaves*, 174)

22. Originally a secretary (*kātib*) to al-Manṣūr's *wazīr* Abū Ayyūb al-Mūryānī, he later became secretary and *wazīr* to Hārūn and then Mūsā, sons of al-Mahdī, during their father's reign. He died in 167/783–84, while in service with Mūsā b. al-Mahdī in Jurjān (Sourdel, *Vizirat*, I, 97–98).

him on behalf of a vegetable seller and he consented on the condition that he should sell vinegar and greens alone. Then he ordered that in each quarter one vegetable seller should be established following that example.

According to ʿAlī b. Muḥammad[23]—al-Faḍl b. al-Rabīʿ: When al-Manṣūr had finished building his palace in the city, he entered it and toured it and approved of it and examined it and admired what he saw in it, except that he thought he had spent too much money on it.

He looked at one part of it and thought it excellent, and he said to me, "Go out to al-Rabīʿ and tell him to go out to al-Musayyab[24] and tell him to bring me a competent builder immediately." I went out to al-Musayyab and told him, and he sent for the chief of the builders and summoned him and sent him in to Abū Jaʿfar, and when he stood before him he said to him, "How did you work for our overseers on this palace, and how much did you take in wages for each thousand baked bricks and sun-dried bricks?" The builder stood and was not able to make any reply, and al-Musayyab was afraid of him. Al-Manṣūr said to him, "What is the matter with you that you do not speak?" and he said, "I do not know, O Commander of the Faithful," and he said, "Damn you! tell me! You are safe from everything you are afraid of." He replied, "O Commander of the Faithful, I do not concern myself with it, and I do not know it." He took his hand and said, "Come, may God not teach you the right thing!" He took him into the room he admired and showed him a *majlis*[25] that was in it and said, "Look at this

23. Probably the historian al-Madāʾinī. Al-Ṭabarī uses three sources he refers to as ʿAlī b. Muḥammad in this period, ʿAlī b. Muḥammad al-Madāʾinī, ʿAlī b. Muḥammad al-Nawfalī, and ʿAlī b. Muḥammad b. Sulaymān al-Hāshimī. It is often difficult to know which source is being referred to. The problem is mitigated by the fact that al-Nawfalī's information is obtained from his father, whereas al-Madāʾinī does not quote his father at all. Al-Hāshimī also received information from his father, the important ʿAbbāsid Muḥammad b. Sulaymān. Al-Madāʾinī's information tends to be matters of fact and date, whereas both al-Nawfalī and al-Hāshimī retell court gossip and circumstantial eyewitness accounts.

24. B. Zuhayr al-Ḍabbī: a long serving Khurāsānī officer. He had participated in the early stages of the ʿAbbāsid Revolution in Khurāsān and come to Iraq with the ʿAbbāsid army. He was at various times chief of police for al-Saffāḥ, al-Manṣūr and al-Rashīd, as well as being governor of Khurāsān from 163/780 to 166/782–83 (Crone, *Slaves*, 186–88).

25. *Majlis* is used in two senses by al-Ṭabarī and his sources, as an assembly of

majlis, and build an arch next to it so that it will be similar to the house, and do not use any wood in it." The builder said, "Yes, O Commander of the Faithful," and the builder and all those who were with him began to marvel at his understanding of building and engineering. The builder said to him, "I am not expert enough to construct it in this way and cannot do it as you want," and he [326] said, "I will help you."

He ordered baked bricks and plaster, and these were brought, and then he began to calculate the amount of baked bricks and plaster involved in the construction of the arch, and he continued doing it for the rest of that day and part of the next. He called al-Musayyab and said to him, "Give him his pay for the amount of his work with you." Al-Musayyab calculated it and reached five *dirhams*, and al-Manṣūr thought that was too much and said, "I am not satisfied with that," and he went on until he had reduced it by a *dirham*. Then he took the measurements and looked into the measurement of the arch of the room so that he understood it. He obliged the agents and al-Musayyab to take the expenses and with him took reliable builders and engineers, who told him the value of the work. He went on adding one thing after another and charged them what he had calculated the cost of the building of the arch to be. He demanded from al-Musayyab more than six thousand *dirhams* of the money he had, and he arrested him for it and interned him, and he did not leave the palace until he had paid it to him.

According to ʿĪsā b. al-Manṣūr: I found in the treasuries of my father, al-Manṣūr, among the papers that he spent on the City of Peace and its mosque and the Palace of Gold in it and the markets and the intervals and the trenches and its domes and its gates, four million eight hundred and thirty three *dirhams*. The equivalent in *fulūs* was 100,023,000. that was when a master mason was paid a *qīrāṭ* of silver a day and a laborer (*rūzgārī*) two or three *ḥabbah*.[26]

---

people or audience and also as the setting in which such an assembly takes place, either a building or a tent. See *EI*², s.v. "*Madjlis*."

26. Baghdad was officially known as Madīnat al-Salām, the City of Peace, and I have translated it as such when it is used. The old name, Baghdad, remained more common. *Fulūs* were small copper coins of differing values; see *EI*² s.v. "Fals." *Ḥabbah* and *qīrāṭ* were fractions of a *dirham* and units of account, not minted coins, a *ḥabbah* being 1/160 *dirham* and a *qīrāṭ* 4 *habbahs*.

In this year al-Manṣūr deposed Salm b. Qutaybah[27] from al-Baṣrah and appointed as governor[28] Muḥammad b. Sulaymān b.
[327] ʿAlī.[29] The reason for his deposition:

According to ʿAbd al-Malik b. Shaybān—Yaʿqūb b. al-Faḍl b. ʿAbd al-Raḥmān al-Hāshimī: Abū Jaʿfar wrote to Salm b. Qutaybah when he appointed him governor of al-Baṣrah, "To continue: demolish the houses and destroy the palm trees of those who rebelled with Ibrāhīm,"[30] and Salm wrote back, "With which of those shall I begin, the houses or the palm trees?" and Abū Jaʿfar wrote, "To continue: if I had written ordering you to destroy their dates, you would have written asking me whether you should begin with the *barnī* dates or the *shahrīz* dates," and he deposed him and appointed Muḥammad b. Sulaymān as governor. He arrived and caused havoc.

According to Yūnus b. Najdah: Salm b. Qutaybah came to us as governor after the rout with Abū Barqah Yazīd b. Salm[31] in charge of his police. Salm remained there five months; then he was deposed, and Muḥammad b. Sulaymān was appointed governor over us.

According to ʿAbd al-Malik b. Shaybān: When Muḥammad b. Sulaymān arrived, he destroyed the houses of Yaʿqūb b. al-Faḍl and Abū Marwān in the quarter of the Banū Yashkūr and those of

---

27. Son of the celebrated Qutaybah b. Muslim al-Bāhilī, conqueror of much of Transoxiana for the Muslims. He himself was governor of al-Baṣrah for the Umayyads at the time of the ʿAbbāsid Revolution and thereafter lived in retirement in al-Rayy until he was summoned by al-Manṣūr, who needed his support in al-Baṣrah when the city was taken by the ʿAlid rebel Ibrāhīm b. ʿAbdallāh in 145/762. He died in 149/766–67 (Crone, *Slaves*, 136–38).

28. Al-Ṭabarī uses the word *wallāhu* for the appointment. The two words commonly used for provincial governors are *wālī* and *ʿāmil*. Although the former is slightly more common and occurs also in the verbal forms *wallā* or the passive *wulliya*, there is no discernible distinction between the two terms. The office of governor is also frequently indicated by the preposition *ʿalā*, which I have translated as "in charge of."

29. Muḥammad b. Sulaymān b. ʿAlī was the able and most important of the younger generation of the ʿAbbāsid family at this time. His father, Sulaymān, uncle of al-Manṣūr, had been governor of al-Baṣrah. He died in 142/759–60, and Muḥammad inherited his status. He was at times governor of al-Baṣrah and al-Kūfah and a firm opponent of the claims of ʿĪsā b. Mūsā to the succession. He died as governor of al-Baṣrah in 173/789–90, and al-Rashīd's agents confiscated much of his vast wealth.

30. See note 19 above.

31. Salm's son.

ʿAwn b. Mālik, ʿAbd al-Wāḥid b. Ziyād and al-Khalīl b. al-Ḥuṣayn in the quarter of the Banū ʿAdī and the house of ʿAfw Allah b. Sufyān and destroyed their palm trees.[32]

In this year Jaʿfar b. Ḥanẓalah al-Bahrānī[33] led the summer expedition against the Byzantines.

In this year ʿAbdallāh b. al-Rabīʿ[34] was deposed from Medina, and Jaʿfar b. Sulaymān[35] was appointed in his place, and he arrived there in the month of Rabīʿ I (May 19–June17, 763).

In this year also al-Sariyy b. ʿAbdallāh[36] was deposed from Mecca, and ʿAbd al-Ṣamad b. ʿAlī[37] was appointed governor. [328]

The leader of the pilgrims in this year was ʿAbd al-Wahhāb b. Ibrāhīm b. Muḥammad b. ʿAlī b. ʿAbdallāh b. ʿAbbās,[38] as is said by Muḥammad b. ʿUmar and others.

---

32. ʿAlid supporters in al-Baṣrah.

33. A long-time supporter of the Umayyads, who served on the Byzantine frontier in the early ʿAbbāsid period. Al-Manṣūr sought his advice at the time of the ʿAlid rebellion in 145/762. This is his last appearance in the historical record, and we must assume that he died soon after.

34. Al-Ḥārithī. The Ḥarithīs had no record of service in the ʿAbbāsid cause but became important because of their kinship with the mother of al-Saffāḥ. ʿAbdallāh b. al-Rabīʿ, who was an intimate of al-Manṣūr, had been appointed governor of Medina the previous year. This is his last datable appearance in the historical record. In the treasury of St. Germer in Cologne, West Germany, there is an ivory box with an inscription saying that it was made for him in Aden (Crone, *Slaves*, 149).

35. Less successful brother of Muḥammad b. Sulaymān (see note 29). He was later absentee governor of al-Baḥrayn in 157/773–74 and of Mecca and Medina in the reign of al-Mahdī, c. 166/782. Apart from these, he held no high office and died in 177/793–94.

36. B. al-Ḥārith b. ʿAbdallāh b. al-ʿAbbās, hence a distant relative of al-Manṣūr. He was with al-Mahdī in Khurāsān in 141/758–59 and had been governor of Mecca since 143/760–61. According to al-Yaʿqūbī, *Taʾrīkh*, II, 470, he led the summer expedition against the Byzantines in 147/764.

37. The youngest of the Banū ʿAlī, al-Manṣūr's uncles. He was in some ways the black sheep of the family, joining the unsuccessful rebellion of his brother ʿAbdallāh against al-Manṣūr in 137/754 and being deposed from the governorate of al-Jazīrah and imprisoned for insulting al-Mahdī (see below p. 214). He also emerged as spokesman for the family interests against the power of the freedmen (*mawālī*) at this time. He was briefly governor of Damascus, where he caused trouble by favoring the Yamāniyyah, and al-Baṣrah, at the beginning of al-Rashīd's reign. He survived until 185/801.

38. Despite the fact that he was the son of the martyred Ibrāhīm b. Muḥammad, the ʿAbbāsid pretender killed by the Umayyads shortly before the ʿAbbāsid Revolution, he never became a political figure of consequence. He spent most of his time in Syria and the Byzantine frontier areas, where he led the summer raid at least twice, and he died as governor of Syria or Palestine, c. 157/774.

The Events of the Year 147

(March 10, 764–January 28, 765)

The events of this year:

Among these was the attack by Istarkhān al-Khwārazmī[39] with a body of Turks on the Muslims in the area of Armenia and his taking of many of the Muslims and the *ahl al-dhimmah*[40] prisoner, their entry into Tiflīs,[41] and their killing of Ḥarb b. ʿAbdallāh al-Rāwandī after whom the Ḥarbiyyah in Baghdad is named.[42] It is said that this Ḥarb was stationed in Mosul with 2,000 soldiers because of the Khārijites in al-Jazīrah.[43] When Abū Jaʿfar heard

---

39. The invaders were Khazars from north of the Caucasus. Barthold reads the name as Tarkhān and suggests that he came from the Muslim bodyguard of the Khazar Khaghans, who were recruited in Khwārazm: *EI*², s.v. "Khazar."

40. Protected people; the name given to Jews or Christians who lived under Muslim rule but were free to practice their own religion: See *EI*², s.v. "Dhimma."

41. Tblisi, capital of Georgia, strategically located where the Kura river emerges from the northern Caucasus mountains into the broad plains of Azerbaijān; it was the farthest outpost of Muslim rule in this direction.

42. A Khurāsānī officer who served in Baghdad before being posted to Mosul. The Ḥarbiyyah quarter was situated immediately northwest of the Round City (Le Strange, *Baghdad*, 122–33) and was the area of western Baghdad where most of the Khurāsānī soldiers settled.

43. See Azdī, *Tārīkh al-Mawṣil*, 194–95, Kennedy, *Provincial Elites*, 30–31.

about the gathering of the Turks in those areas, he sent Jibra'īl b. Yaḥyā[44] to fight them, and he wrote to Ḥarb ordering him to go with him. He went with him, and Ḥarb was killed and Jibra'īl was put to flight, and those Muslims whom I have mentioned were killed.

In this year the death of 'Abdallāh b. 'Alī b. 'Abdallāh b. 'Abbās occurred.[45] Opinions differ as to the cause of his death, and some follow 'Alī b. Muḥammad al-Nawfalī from his father: Abū Ja'far [329]
went on the pilgrimage in the year 147 some months after he had given al-Mahdī precedence over 'Īsā b. Mūsā.[46] He had deposed 'Īsā b. Mūsā from al-Kūfah and its territory and appointed Muḥammad b. Sulaymān b. 'Alī as governor in his place. He sent 'Īsā to the City of Peace and al-Manṣūr summoned him and handed 'Abdallāh b. 'Alī over to him secretly in the depths of the night. Then he said, "O 'Īsā, this man wishes to remove God's favor from you and from me. You are my heir apparent after al-Mahdī, and the caliphate will pass to you, so take this man and behead him without being weak or half-hearted. You must do this, or the power that I have built up will be weakened and destroyed." He then set off on his way and wrote to him three times on the road asking him what he had done in the matter that he had been

44. Al-Bajalī: a Khurāsānī officer who had previously been stationed on the Byzantine frontier. He survived this defeat and later served in his native Khurāsān, being governor of Samarqand in 159/775–76 (see below, pp. 45, 171; Crone, *Slaves*, 179–80)

45. One of al-Manṣūr's paternal uncles, the Banū 'Alī, he had led the 'Abbāsid armies in pursuit of Marwān, the last Umayyad caliph. He then became governor of Syria and attracted the support of many cadres of the Umayyad regime. With their encouragement, he launched a rebellion against al-Manṣūr immediately after his accession but was defeated and forced to take refuge with his brother Sulaymān in al-Baṣrah After Sulaymān's death in 142/759–60 his position became increasingly exposed, but he continued to enjoy the support of his surviving brothers. See Kennedy, *'Abbasid Caliphate*, 59–61; Lassner, *'Abbasid Rule*, 39–57.

46. 'Īsā b. Mūsā b. Muḥammad b. 'Alī b. 'Abdallāh b. al-'Abbās. He had participated in the defeat of the Umayyad forces in Iraq at the time of the 'Abbāsid Revolution and was rewarded with the governorate of al-Kūfah, which he held for the next fifteen years. He also played a major part in the defeat of the 'Alid rebellion of 145/762. On his deathbed al-Saffāḥ had been concerned that his heir, al-Manṣūr, then on the pilgrimage, might not return alive, so as a precaution he had stipulated that al-Manṣūr should be succeeded in turn by 'Īsā b. Mūsā The oath of allegiance was then taken to both of them. By this time al-Manṣūr was trying to revise the succession so that it would pass directly to his own son Muḥammad, but 'Īsā was resisting stubbornly.

instructed in, and he wrote to him, "I have executed what you ordered," and Abū Jaʿfar had no doubt that he had done what he had ordered him to do and that he had killed ʿAbdallāh b. ʿAlī. When he had been handed over to him, ʿĪsā had hidden him, and he called his secretary Yūnus b. Farwah and said to him, "This man has handed over his paternal uncle to me and ordered me to do such and such to him," and he replied, "He wants to kill you and kill him. He ordered you to kill him secretly, and he will claim him from you openly and then he will retaliate on you for his death." ʿĪsā asked for his advice, and he said, "I think that you should hide him in your house and do not let anyone know about his affair. If he seeks him openly from you, then hand him over openly but do not ever hand him over secretly, for, although he had entrusted him secretly to you, his affair will be produced in public." ʿĪsā did this.

Al-Manṣūr came and conspired with his paternal uncles, urging them to ask him to give ʿAbdallāh b. ʿAlī to them, and he gave them hope that he would do that.[47] They came to him and spoke to him and aroused his compassion and reminded him of their
[330] kinship and showed their good will to him, and he said, "Yes, bring me ʿĪsā b. Mūsā." So he came to him, and he said, "O ʿĪsā, you know that I handed over to you my paternal uncle and your paternal uncle, ʿAbdallāh b. ʿAlī, before I set out on the pilgrimage and I ordered you to keep him in your house," and he replied, "You did that, O Commander of the Faithful," and he went on, "Your paternal uncles have spoken to me on his behalf, and I have decided to pardon him and release him. Bring him to me!" He said, "O Commander of the Faithful, did you not order me to kill him so I killed him?" but al-Manṣūr replied, "I only ordered you to imprison him in your house," but he insisted, "You ordered me to kill him." Then al-Manṣūr said, "You have lied; I did not order you to kill him." He said to his paternal uncles, "This man has confessed to you that he has killed your brother and claims that I ordered him to do that, but he has told a lie."

They said, "Hand him over to us so that we can kill him in

47. ʿAbdallāh was, of course, brother to these paternal uncles, who seem to have been led at this time by ʿĪsā b. ʿAlī and Muḥammad, son of the dead Sulaymān b. ʿAlī, and they are seen acting together to protect ʿAbdallāh.

retaliation," and he said, "Do as you like with him!" and they sent him out to the courtyard. People gathered, and the matter became widely known. One of them stood up and drew his sword and advanced on ʿĪsā to strike him, and ʿĪsā said to him, "Are you going to do it?" and he said, "Yes by God!" and ʿĪsā said, "Do not be hasty but send me back to the Commander of the Faithful," and so they returned him to him, and he said, "You only wanted me to kill him so that you could kill me. Your paternal uncle is alive and well, and, if you order me to hand him over to you, I will do so." Al-Manṣūr said, "Bring him to us," so he brought him to him, and ʿĪsā said to him, "You schemed against me something toward which I was suspicious and my suspicion was right. Deal with your paternal uncle as you like." He said, "Let him enter so that I can consider my opinion." Then they left, and he ordered him to be put in a house with salt in the foundations and that water be poured into the foundations, and it collapsed on him and he died, and it happened to him as it happened.

ʿAbdallāh b. ʿAlī died in this year, and he was buried in the cemetery at the Syrian Gate, and he was the first person to be buried there.[48]

According to Ibrāhīm b. ʿĪsa b. al-Manṣūr Ibn Burayh: ʿAbdallāh [331]
b. ʿAlī died in prison in 147 at the age of 52.

According to Ibrāhīm b. ʿĪsā: When ʿAbdallāh b. ʿAlī died, al-Manṣūr was riding one day, and ʿAbdallāh b. ʿAyyāsh was with him, and he said to him as he was alongside him, "Do you know that three caliphs whose name began with *ʿayn* killed three rebels whose names began with *ʿayn*?" He replied, "I only know that the common people say that ʿAlī killed ʿUthmān, and they lie, and ʿAbd al-Malik b. Marwān killed ʿAbd al-Raḥmān b. Muḥammad b. al-Ashʿath and ʿAbdallāh b. al-Zubayr and ʿAmr b. Saʿīd[49] and a house collapsed on ʿAbdallāh b. ʿAlī." Al-Manṣūr said, "Am I to blame if the house collapsed on ʿAbdallāh b. ʿAlī?" and he replied, "I never said you were to blame."

In this year al-Manṣūr deposed ʿĪsā b. Mūsā and had the oath of allegiance taken to his son al-Mahdī and appointed him heir apparent after him and, some say, ʿĪsā b. Mūsā after him.

---

48. Le Strange, *Baghdad*, 130–49.

49. All these names begin with the Arabic letter *ʿayn*. The caliph ʿUthmān

The reasons for his deposition and how the matter happened:

Opinions differ as to what brought al-Manṣūr to the point of deposing him. Some say the reason that brought al-Manṣūr to do that was that Abū Ja'far confirmed 'Īsā b. Mūsā, after the death
[332] of Abū al-'Abbās, in what Abū al-'Abbās had appointed him to, the governorship of al-Kūfah and its Sawād. He honored him and treated him with respect, and when he came in to him he sat him on his right hand and sat al-Mahdī on his left. This was his attitude to him until al-Manṣūr decided to give al-Mahdī precedence over him in the caliphate. Abū al-'Abbās had decided that the succession after him should pass to Abū Ja'far and then after Abū Ja'far to 'Īsā b. Mūsā.

When al-Manṣūr decided on that he spoke to 'Īsā b. Mūsā about giving his son precedence over him with kind words, and 'Īsā replied, "O Commander of the Faithful, what about the oaths and agreements that bind me and bind the Muslims in my favor and the freeing and divorcing and other guarantees of the oaths?[50] There is no way to that, O Commander of the Faithful."

When Abū Ja'far saw his refusal, his mood (color) changed, and he became rather estranged from him. He ordered that al-Mahdī be given permission[51] (to enter) before him, and he used to come in and sit on al-Manṣūr's right hand in 'Īsā's seat. Then he gave 'Īsā permission, and he entered and sat beyond al-Mahdī on al-Manṣūr's right as well, and nobody sat on his left on the seat that al-Mahdī used to sit on. Al-Manṣūr was furious about that, and matters were coming to a head. He used to order that al-Mahdī be given permission, then that 'Īsā b. 'Alī be given permission after him. Then he waited a little while and ordered that 'Abd al-Ṣamad b. 'Alī be given permission, and then he waited a little while

---

was murdered in 35/656 by insurgents from Iraq and Egypt. 'Alī b. Abī Ṭālib, who succeeded him, was not directly involved. The Umayyad caliph 'Abd al-Malik b. Marwān was responsible for the deaths of the rebels Ibn al-Ash'ath (85/704) and Ibn al-Zubayr (72/792). 'Amr b. Sa'īd al-Ashdaq was an Umayyad rival to 'Abd al-Malik, executed by him in 70/689–90.

50. He had sworn oaths with the condition that his slaves would be freed and his wives divorced if he broke them.

51. Allowing people to enter the caliph's audience was the function of the *ḥājib* (chamberlain), and the order in which people were admitted was an important indication of status.

before ordering that ʿĪsā b. Mūsā be given permission. After that he always gave al-Mahdī permission first on every occasion, but he mixed up the rest, giving precedence to some who had been kept waiting and keeping waiting some who had been given precedence, letting ʿĪsā b. Mūsā think that he gave them precedence only because of some business that had cropped up and to discuss his affair with them. Then he used to give ʿĪsā b. Mūsā permission after them, and he was silent about all that and did not complain at all and did not criticize.

Then he moved on to harsher measures. There were with ʿĪsā in the audience some of his children, and he heard digging at the foot of the wall and feared that the wall would fall down on top of him. Dust was scattered on him, and he looked up to the wood of the ceiling of the audience room and saw that one of its sides had been dug out to be removed from its place, and dust fell on his *qalansūwah*[52] and his clothes. He ordered those of his children who were with him to move, and he stood up to pray. Then permission came to him, so he stood up to go in in that state with the dust on him and he did not shake it off. When al-Manṣūr saw him, he said, "O ʿĪsā, no one ever comes in to me in a state like yours with so much dirt and dust on you. Does all this come from the street?" He replied, "I suppose so, O Commander of the Faithful." Al-Manṣūr had only spoken to him like that because he wanted him to complain to him about something. Al-Manṣūr had sent ʿĪsā b. ʿAlī to him about the matter that he wanted from him, and ʿĪsā b. Mūsā did not appreciate his visit to him, for it was as if he were provoking him. [333]

It is said that he administered to ʿĪsā b. Mūsā something that would make him perish, and he rose up from the audience and al-Manṣūr said, "Where are you going, O Abū Mūsā?" and he replied, "I have a stomach ache, O Commander of the Faithful." "Then retire to the house." He replied, "The ache that I have is more severe than I can bear in the house." "Where are you going to?" "To the (my) lodging." So he got up from the audience and went to his river boat and al-Manṣūr got up after him and followed in his tracks to the river boat, pretending alarm for him. ʿĪsā asked

52. The *qalansūwah* was a tall hat in the shape of a cone or truncated cone. See Ahsan, *Social Life*, 30–31.

him for permission to go to al-Kūfah, but he said, "Stay rather, and be treated here." He refused and pressed him, and he gave him permission. The person who encouraged him to do that was his doctor Bukhtīshū' Abū Jibra'īl,[53] who said, "I, by God, would not venture to treat you at court, and my soul would not be safe." Al-Manṣūr gave him permission and said, "I am going on the
[334] pilgrimage in this year of mine, and I will stay with you in al-Kūfah until you recover, if God wills."

When the time of the pilgrimage approached, al-Manṣūr set out and reached a place outside al-Kūfah called al-Ruṣāfah,[54] and he stayed there for several days. He held horse races there and visited 'Īsā more than once. Then he returned to the City of Peace and did not go on the pilgrimage, giving the shortage of water on the road as an excuse. 'Īsā b. Mūsā's illness reached such a point that his hair fell out, and then he recovered from that illness. Yaḥyā b. Ziyād b. Abī Ḥuzābah al-Burjumī Abū Ziyād[55] said about this:

You escaped from the medicine of the doctor as
    the gazelle escapes well-aimed arrows.
From a hunter whose arrow penetrates *al farīṣ* (the flesh
    behind the shoulder blades) when
    he prepares the arrow of death in his bowstring.
God defended you from the assault of a lion
    who wants (to hunt) lions inside his thicket.
That is why he came to us carrying within him a hidden
    (illness)[56]
    made known through hearing and seeing him,
A man with little hair, for from his head
    the thick black hair has gone away.

It is said that 'Īsā b. 'Alī used to say to al-Manṣūr that 'Īsā b. Mūsā refused to take the oath of allegiance to al-Mahdī only

---

53. Well-known physician, d. 185/801.

54. Near al-Kūfah, not to be confused with al-Ruṣāfah of Baghdad or Ruṣāfat Hishām. For the numerous al-Ruṣāfahs scattered through the Muslim world from Cordova to Nīshāpūr, Yāqūt, *Mu'jam*, III, 46–50. The word means a causeway or bank of masonry.

55. Grandson of the poet Abū Ḥuzābah al-Walīd b. Ḥanafiyyah; *Aghānī*, Būlāq XIX, 152, Beirut, XXII, 273.

56. Referring to 'Īsā.

because he was looking after this matter for his son Mūsā,[57] and it was Mūsā who was preventing him. Al-Manṣūr said to ʿĪsā b. ʿAlī, "Speak to Mūsā b. ʿĪsā and make him afraid for his father and for his son." ʿĪsā b. ʿAlī spoke to Mūsā about that, made him give up hope, threatened him, and warned him of the wrath of al-Manṣūr. When Mūsā was filled with fear and became apprehensive [335] and feared that something dreadful would happen to him, he came to al-ʿAbbās b. Muḥammad[58] and said to him, "O my paternal uncle, I am speaking to you with speech that no one, by God, has ever heard from me before, nor will anyone ever hear again and only my position of trust and confidence in you has extracted it from me. It is entrusted with you and I am putting my life in your hands." He replied, "Speak, O son of my brother, you appreciate my feelings toward you." He said, "I can see what my father is facing in order to resign this matter and have it transferred to al-Mahdī. He is treated with different sorts of harm and evil. Once he is threatened and once his permission to enter is delayed, once the walls are demolished on him, once death is plotted for him. My father will not give in because of this. That will never be. But here is an idea according to which he may give up if ever he will." He said, "What is it, O my brother's son? You are certainly correct and have earned my sympathy." Mūsā continued, "Let the Commander of the Faithful speak to him in my presence and say to him, 'O ʿĪsā, I know that you are not withholding this matter from al-Manṣūr for yourself because of your advanced age and your nearness to death, and indeed you know that you do not have a long span, but you are withholding it because of the position of your son Mūsā. Do you think that I should allow your son to survive you and my son to survive with him, so that he can have

57. He survived to be restored to his father's old office of governor of al-Kūfah in 167/783–84 by al-Mahdī. In Hārūn's reign he was serveral times governor of al-Kūfah, as well as of Syria and Egypt. He never made any attempt to claim the caliphate and died in 183/799–800.

58. Brother of the caliphs al-Saffāḥ and al-Manṣūr. He spent much of his time leading expeditions on the Byzantine frontier and does not seem to have played an important role in politics. He was, however, immensely wealthy, being the owner and developer of the ʿAbbāsiyah Island in Baghdad, among other properties: see Yaʿqūbī, *Buldān*, 243, 252; Le Strange, *Baghdad*, 142, 148. He is last recorded at the court of al-Hādī in 170/786–87.

power over him? Absolutely not, by God, that would never be! I would fall upon your son with you watching until you despaired for him and I was safe from him dominating my son. Do you think that your son is preferable to me than my son?' Then he would order either that I was suffocated or that the sword was drawn on me. If he ('Īsā) will agree to anything, then perhaps he will do it for this reason and not for any other."

[336] Al-'Abbās said, "May God reward you well, O son of my brother! You have sacrificed your life for your father, and you have preferred his survival to your own fortune. You have had the best opinion and followed the best of paths." Then he came to Abū Ja'far and told the news, and al-Manṣūr rewarded Mūsā well and said, "He has acted well and decently, and I will do as he has advised me, if God wills." When they gathered and 'Īsā b. 'Alī was there, al-Manṣūr turned to 'Īsā b. Mūsā and said, "O 'Īsā, I am not ignorant of the motive that you harbor nor of the aim you have pursued in this matter that I asked of you; you wanted this affair only for your son, who has been an evil omen both for you and for himself."

'Īsā b. 'Alī said, "O Commander of the Faithful, I need to relieve myself," and he said, "We will call for a receptacle so that you can urinate in it." He said, "In your audience, O Commander of the Faithful? That cannot be, but let me be guided to the nearest latrine to get to it." He ordered a man to guide him, and there he went.[59] 'Īsā b. Mūsā said to his son Mūsā, "Get up with your paternal uncle and gather his garments up behind him and give him a cloth if you have one so that he can wipe himself with it." When 'Īsā squatted down to urinate, Mūsā gathered his clothes up behind him, and he did not see him and he said, "Who is that?" and he replied "Mūsā b. 'Īsā." 'Īsā said, "May you be saved with my father and may the father who begot you be saved with my father! By God, I know that there will be no good in this matter after you two have departed, and I know that you two have the best right to it, but man is fond of what he can get soon!" Mūsā said to himself, "By God, this man has exposed his vulnerable

59. The story suggests that 'Īsā b. 'Alī, an old man at this date, was blind, but there is no other evidence for this in the sources.

spot to me, and it is he who urged (al-Manṣūr) on against my father. By God I will kill him because of what he said to me. I don't care if the Commander of the Faithful kills me after him, but there would be consolation for my father in his killing, and he would forget that I had been killed."[60]

When they returned to their positions, Mūsā asked, "O Commander of the Faithful, may I say something to my father?" and that pleased him, and he thought that he wanted to discuss some [337] of their affair with him. So he said, "Go on," so he went to him and said, "O my father, ʿĪsā b. ʿAlī has killed you and me many times because of what he has said about us. He has exposed his vulnerable spot to me." His father asked, "How?" and he replied, "He said to me this and that, and if I tell the Commander of the Faithful he will kill him, and you will satisfy your thirst for revenge and kill him before he kills you and me. We don't care what happens afterwards." His father said, "Damn this thought and opinion! Your paternal uncle said words to you in confidence that he hoped would please you, and you have made them into a reason for doing him evil and annihilating him! Keep silent and do not let anyone hear this from you and go back to your place." He stood up and returned to his place, and Abū Jaʿfar waited to see if he could see any result from his going to his father and speaking with him, and when he saw nothing he went back to his original threats and tried to intimidate him. "By God, I will swiftly do to you what harms you and what will make you despair of his surviving after you! O Rabīʿ, go up to Mūsā and strangle him with his sword belt!"[61] Al-Rabīʿ came up to him and gathered his sword belt and began to strangle him slowly.

Mūsā shouted out, "O Commander of the Faithful, (fear) God in killing me and shedding my blood! I am not in the position you imagine, and ʿĪsā will not care if you kill me, for he has more than ten male children, all of whom are like me or have precedence over me." The caliph said, "Tighten more, O Rabīʿ; finish him off!" Al-Rabīʿ made as if he were going to annihilate him and

60. ʿĪsā b. ʿAlī admits that ʿĪsā b. Mūsā is in the right, and so Mūsā b. ʿĪsā could have accused him of disloyalty to al-Manṣūr.

61. The strap by which the wearer hangs a sword around his neck; see Lane, s.v. *miḥmal.*

undid the belt and Mūsā cried out, and when ʿĪsā saw that he said, "By God, O Commander of the Faithful, I did not think that the affair would go as far as all this. Order him to leave him alone, for I could not go back to my family if one of my slaves had been killed because of this affair, never mind my son. I give you witness that my wives will be divorced, my slaves free, and what I own spent in the path of God among whomever you wish, O Commander of the Faithful. Here is my hand for the oath of allegiance to al-Mahdī."

He took the oath of allegiance to him as he wanted, and then he
[338] said, "O Abū Mūsā, you have answered this request of mine in hate, and I have a request I would like you to answer in obedience so that you expunge with it your feelings toward me concerning the first request." ʿĪsā asked, "What is that, O Commander of the Faithful?" and he replied, "That this affair will pass to you after al-Mahdī." ʿĪsā said, "I cannot enter into it after I have gone out from it." The caliph and those of his family who were present did not stop pressing him until finally he said, "O Commander of the Faithful, you know best."

One of the people of al-Kūfah said, when ʿĪsā passed by him with retinue: "This is the man who was tomorrow and became the day after tomorrow." This story, it is said, is attributed to the family of ʿĪsā, who told it.

According to those who relate this matter from other sources: Al-Manṣūr wanted the oath of allegiance for al-Mahdī and he spoke to the army about that and when they saw ʿĪsā riding they made him hear what he did not like and he complained to al-Manṣūr and he said to the soldiers, "Do not annoy my brother's son for he is the skin that lies between my eyes, and, if I come closer to you, I would cut off your heads" and they used to stop and then begin again and continued with it for some time. Then he wrote to ʿĪsā:

> In the Name of God, the Merciful, the Compassionate.
>
> From the slave of God ʿAbdallāh al-Manṣūr, Commander of the Faithful, to ʿĪsā b. Mūsā: peace be upon you. I praise to you God, beside Whom there is no other god.
>
> To continue: praise be to God of ancient grace, great

kindness and magnificent blessing who began creation with His knowledge and puts the decree into effect by His order. No creature reaches the end of His justice or attains the end of describing His glory. He arranges affairs as He wishes with His power and dispatches according to His will and there is no judge in them except Him and no executing of them except through Him. He carries them through with ease and He consults no *wazīr* about them [339] nor asks the advice of any helper. He is not confounded about anything He wishes and its completion comes to pass whether the worshippers like it or hate it. They are unable to protect themselves from Him nor do they have any defense for themselves against Him. He is the Lord of the earth and what is on it. To Him belong creation and affairs, may God be blessed, the Lord of the universe.

You know the position we were in during the rule of oppressors and the state of our power and our expedients against what the cursed house[62] inflicted on us whether we liked it or not. So we patiently accepted having to give up things to those [rulers] to whom they committed our affairs and whose opinions were unanimously agreed upon. We were unjustly treated and downtrodden by oppression, not resisting tyranny, not preventing injustice, not giving right nor forbidding wrong. We were unable to accomplish it or to benefit ourselves until what was ordained came to pass and the affair reached its allotted span. God allowed the destruction of His enemy and blessed with compassion the people of the family of His Prophet. God sent helpers (*anṣār*)[63] for them to seek to avenge them and to strive against their enemies, to summon to support them and to give victory to their state from scattered lands and different reasons but united wishes. God gathered them in obedience to us and formed in their hearts affection for us to give us victory and made them glorious through our

62. The Umayyads.
63. The term *anṣār* (helpers) was used for the people of Medina who supported the Prophet Muḥammad. 'Abbāsid propaganda often drew parallels between them and the Prophet and referred to the Khurāsānīs as their *anṣār*.

victory. We would not have met many of them, nor drawn a sword with them if God had not affected their hearts and sent them to us from their countries with committed enthusiasm and pure obedience to meet victory and to return victorious and to win victory by fear. They did not meet anyone without putting him to flight nor any offender without killing him so that God brought to us by
[340] that the end of our waiting, the limit of our affliction, the fulfillment of our hopes, the manifestation of our right, the slaughter of our enemies through the blessing of God, great and glorious, as a favor from Him to us without any effort or power from us.

After that we remained in the blessing of God and His favor until this young man[64] grew up and for him God worked on the hearts of the helpers of the Faith whom he had sent to us as He had done to us at the beginning of our power. He filled their hearts with affection for him and spread love of him in their breasts. They got to the point where they could only talk of his virtue, only gave praise to his name and only recognized his right.

Then when the Commander of the Faithful saw how God had filled their hearts with affection for him (al-Mahdī) and put his name on their tongues and (saw) their recognition of him by his characteristics and his name and the demand of the common people that he should be obeyed, the Commander of the Faithful became certain that this was a matter that God had decreed and wrought. His servants had no authority or power or counsel or discussion about it because of what the Commander of the Faithful saw of the consensus of opinion and attachment of the people. The Commander of the Faithful thought that even if al-Mahdī was not recognized by right of descent, power would pass to him. The Commander of the Faithful was not preventing what the people had agreed on and was not seeking to avoid granting what they claimed for him.

64. Al-Manṣūr's son al-Mahdī.

The most pressing of the people on the Commander of the Faithful in that were the very closest of his courtiers and the trustworthy men of his Guard and Police. The Commander of the Faithful saw no alternative to approving of and following them. The Commander of the Faithful and the people of his family were the most justified of those who hastened to that and strove for him and desired him and recognized his virtue and hoped for his blessing and told true reports about him and thanked God if He [341]
put in his offspring what the Prophets asked for before him when the true servant said, "Lord give me an heir as from Thyself, one that will truly represent me, and represent the posterity of Jacob; and make him, O my Lord! One with whom Thou art well pleased!"[65] God gave to the Commander of the Faithful an heir and made him God fearing, blessed and rightly guided (*mahdī*) and a namesake of the Prophet.[66] He seized those who assumed this name and claimed that resemblance, which confused the people of that intention about it and stirred up strife among the people of that misery. He removed that from them and put upon them the calamity that befalls.[67] He established the right firmly and raised up to al-Mahdī his splendor and to the Faith its supporters.

The Commander of the Faithful wanted to inform you what the subjects had agreed. You were like a child of his to him and he wants to protect you and guide you and make you glorious, as he would himself and his children. He thinks about you that if you hear about what you see the people have agreed on concerning the position of your cousin (al-Mahdī) you will take the start unurged, so that our helpers, the people of Khurāsān and others come to know that you will be more speedy than themselves in doing what they would like according to their opinion about their own well-being; that for any merit they rec-

65. Zacharias, father of John the Baptist. *Qur'ān*, XIX: 5–6.
66. A play on the name of al-Mahdī, whose name was Muḥammad and whose title, al-Mahdī, means "rightly guided."
67. Cf. *Qur'ān*, IX: 99 and XLVIII: 66.

ognize in al-Mahdī or hope from him, you would still be the most happy of men over that and delighted about it because of his position and kinship. Accept the advice of the Commander of the Faithful to you, for through it you get better and are guided. Peace be upon you and the mercy of God.

So ʿĪsā b. Mūsā wrote to him in reply:

In the name of God, the Merciful, the Compassionate.

To the servant of God ʿAbdallāh Commander of the Faithful from ʿĪsā b. Mūsā: Peace be upon you, O Com-
[342] mander of the Faithful, and the Mercy of God. I praise to you God, other than Whom there is no god. To continue: Your letter has reached me in which you mention what you have decided on in contradicting the law and committing sin in the cutting off of your kin and violating the pact that God has accepted from the people about faithfulness to the caliphate and to my inheriting it after you in order to cut off what God made close by bonds of affection and to split up what God joined together and join together business that God separated in defiance of God in His heaven and turning from God in His decree and following Satan in his desire.

Whoever defies God He throws him down and whoever goes against Him He subdues and whoever tries to deceive Him about anything He requites, but whoever puts his trust in God He protects and whoever humbles himself before God He raises up. The rule on which the building was founded and that should be followed is that there is an inheritance to me from the last Caliph from God and a command before which we are the same and no one Muslim has more right to change than another. The fulfillment of it is obligatory and the first has no more right to change it than the last and if something is legal for the second then it cannot be forbidden for the first. The first who followed information about it and recognized its sign and revealed what he thought about it and hoped from it has precedence. He who wished to work first was more entitled to the right.[68] Neither being made negligent by God nor giving license to the people to abandon fulfillment (of the oath) will get you safety from affliction. Anyone who answered you in abandoning anything that was due to me and considered that legal against me would not feel embarrassed when opportunity enabled him and license tempted him to be more hasty in finding it licit against you also and to be more destructive to what you have established.

So accept the consequence and be pleased with God for what He has done, take what you were given strongly and be among those who are grateful (to God) for God, Great and Glorious, increases him who gives Him thanks as a just promise from Him with no breaking in it. Whoever fears God He protects and whoever decides to oppose Him He turns away from, for God "knows of (the tricks) that deceive with the eyes and all that the hearts (of men) conceal."[69] [343]

In addition to that, we are not safe from disasters or sudden death before (the completion of) what you have begun in cutting me out. If death comes quickly to me, you will have been saved the trouble and you would have hidden the ugliness of what you wished to make open. And if I survive after you, you would not have put my back up (lit: aroused my bitter feelings) and severed relationships with me and helped my enemies to follow in your traces, accept your tutelage and act according to your examples.

You mentioned that all affairs are in the hands of God and He is their organizer and measurer and executor according to His wish. You are right. Affairs are in the hands of God, and he who knows this fact and can define it should accomplish it and try to reach it (as a goal). Know that we ourselves did not acquire any benefit to ourselves or push away any mischief and we did not obtain what you know by our own power or by our own strength. If we

68. ʿĪsā being the first, al-Mahdī the second.
69. *Qur'ān*, XX:19.

had been left to depend on our own efforts and desires, our power would be weakened and our ability diminished to seek what God brought us. But God, if He wishes firmly to execute His order and carry out His promise and complete His covenant and make certain His pact, decides His conclusion and concludes His decision and gives light to his announcement and establishes His pillars when He founds His building, and (His) servants are not able to delay what He is hastening or to hasten what He is delaying. But Satan, the beguiling and obvious enemy, whom God has warned against obeying and made clear his enmity, causes disputes among the agents of the right and the people of His obedience so that they divide their community and scatter their gathering. He sows discord and
[344] hatred among them and washes his hands of them when the realities of affairs and the straits of tribulation become conspicuous.

God, Great and Glorious, has said in His Book, "Never did We send an apostle or a prophet before thee, but, when he framed a desire, Satan threw some (vanity) into his desire: but God will cancel anything (vain) that Satan throws in and God will confirm (and establish) His signs: for God is full of knowledge and wisdom."[70] and He described those who fear (Him) and said, "When a thought of evil from Satan assaults them, bring God to remembrance, when lo! they see (aright)!"[71]

So I ask God's protection for the Commander of the Faithful, lest his intentions and the innermost part of his soul are in opposition to what God, Great and Glorious, granted to those who were before him. Indeed their sons asked them and their desires had led them to a similar position to what the Commander of the Faithful was considering, but they preferred the right over its opposite and they knew that nobody overcomes the decree of God, nor turns away His gifts. And beside that, they did not feel

70. *Qur'ān*, XXII: 52.
71. *Qur'ān*, VII: 200.

secure from the change of fortune and the hastening of afflictions. So they chose the life to come and accepted the consequences and hated change and feared alteration. They showed fine conduct and God brought their affairs to completion and sufficed for what concerned them and protected their authority and glorified their helpers and honored their supporters and made their buildings noble so the prosperity was completed and the blessings became apparent and they felt obliged to give thanks. So the order of God was completed, even if they did not like it.

Peace be upon the Commander of the Faithful and the mercy of God.

When his letter reached Abū Jaʿfar al-Manṣūr, he kept aloof from him and was exceedingly angry. The army renewed what they had been doing more violently. Among them were Asad b. al-Marzbān, ʿUqbah b. Salm, Naṣr b. Ḥarb b. ʿAbdallāh[72] with a group, and they came to ʿĪsā's door and prevented anyone from going in to him and when he rode out they walked behind him [345] and said, "You are the cow of which God said, "They offered her in sacrifice, but not with good will.""[73] He returned and complained about them, and al-Manṣūr said to him, "O son of my brother, I am afraid what they might do to you and me. Their hearts are full of the love of this young man,[74] but if you give him precedence before you so that he is between you and me, they will refrain." ʿĪsā agreed to do it.

According to Isḥāq al-Mawṣilī—al-Rabīʿ: When ʿĪsā's answering letter reached al-Manṣūr, as we have described, he wrote on

72. Asad, a soldier presumably of Persian origin, Marzbān being a Persian title given to military officials in frontier districts of the Sasanian Empire. For his subsequent relations with ʿUqbah and his death, see below p 60. ʿUqbah was from Hunāʾah of Azd (Caskel, table 211). He is first recorded in Sind with ʿUyaynah b. Mūsā in 142/759–60 (Yaʿqūbī, *Tārīkh*, II, 448). For his subsequent role in al-Baḥrayn, see below p. 60. He was assassinated in 167/783–84, apparently in revenge for a man he had killed in al-Yamāmah (below p. 238; Yaʿqūbī, *Tārīkh*, II, 478). Naṣr, a Tamīmī and a member of Abū Jaʿfar's guard, was subsequently appointed to the frontiers of Fārs (below p. 85). He was probably the son of Ḥarb b. ʿAbdallāh al-Rāwandī (see note 42 above).

73. *Qurʾān*, II 71.

74. Al-Mahdī.

it "If you accept its loss, you may obtain compensation for it in this world, and you may be secure from it responsibilities in the next."

There has been given on the subject of al-Manṣūr's deposition of ʿĪsā b. Mūsā a version other than these two, which is the one which Abū Muḥammad known as al-Aswārī recounted on the authority of al-Ḥasan b. ʿĪsā the secretary;[75] Abū Jaʿfar wanted to depose ʿĪsā b. Mūsā from his position as heir apparent and to give al-Mahdī precedence over him, but he refused to agree to that. The affair defied all Abū Jaʿfar's efforts so he sent for Khālid b. Barmak and said to him, "Speak to him, O Khālid. You have seen his refusal to give the oath of allegiance to al-Mahdī and what we have done before about his affair. Do you have any stratagem for it? All sorts of tricks have exhausted us, and our ideas have come to nothing." He replied, "Yes, O Commander of the Faithful. Choose thirty senior men of the party[76] and attach them to me." Khālid b. Barmak rode out, and they rode with him and reached ʿĪsā b. Mūsā and brought him Abū Jaʿfar's message. He replied, "I will not depose myself for God, Great and Glorious, has entrusted this matter to me." Khālid worked on him with every sort of warning and desire, but he refused (to change his mind).

Khālid left him and the members of the party left after him, and
[346] Khālid said to them, "What is your advice in this matter?" and they said, "Let us bring the Commander of the Faithful his message and tell him what we did and what he did," but Khālid said, "No, we will tell the Commander of the Faithful that he has agreed and we will bear witness against him if he denies it." They replied, "Do it and we will do our part," and he said, "It is the right course," and he informed the Commander of the Faithful about what he attempted and wished.

They went to Abū Jaʿfar, and Khālid was with them, and told him that he had agreed so he issued the document for the oath of allegiance to al-Mahdī and wrote all areas.

When the news reached ʿĪsā b. Mūsā, he came to Abū Jaʿfar

75. Nothing seems to be known of these.

76. The word *shīʿah* here, and elsewhere in al-Ṭabarī's work, applies to the ʿAbbāsid party; only later does it come to be applied exclusively to the pro-ʿAlid party in the modern sense.

denying the claim that he had agreed to giving al-Mahdī precedence over himself and he reminded him of God in what he had intended. Abū Jaʿfar summoned them and asked them, and they said, "We bear witness against him that he did agree and he should not go back on it." Abū Jaʿfar carried the matter through and thanked Khālid for what he had done and al-Mahdī was aware of what had happened and praised the excellence of his opinion in this affair..

According to ʿAlī b. Muḥammad b. Sulaymān—his father—ʿAbdallāh b. Abī Sulaym, freedman of ʿAbdallāh b. al-Ḥārith b. Nawfal:[77] I was traveling with Sulaymān b. ʿAbdallāh b. al-Ḥārith b. Nawfal when Abū Jaʿfar had decided to give al-Mahdī precedence over ʿĪsā b. Mūsā in the oath of allegiance. We met Abū Nakhīlah the poet[78] with his two sons and two slaves, both of them carrying some of the luggage of their people. Sulaymān b. ʿAbdallāh stopped by them and said, "Abū Nakhīlah, what is this I see and what position are you in?" He replied, "I was staying [347] with al-Qaʿqāʿ, who was a man of the family of Zurārah who was in command of ʿĪsā b. Mūsā's *shurṭah*, and he said, "Leave me, for this man has done good to me, and it has reached my notice that you composed a poem about this oath of allegiance to al-Mahdī. I am afraid that he will hear of it and I will be exposed to reproach because you stayed with me," and he pestered me until I left.

He said to me, "O ʿAbdallāh, go with Abū Nakhīlah and give him a safe place to spend the night in my house and treat him and those with him well. Then Sulaymān b. ʿAbdallāh told Abū Jaʿfar about the poem of Abū Nakhīlah in which he says,

ʿĪsā let it slide to Muḥammad (al-Mahdī)
so that it may be passed from hand to hand
Among you, and it rests there while it is increasing.
We are delighted with the beardless youth (al-Mahdī).

---

77. See note 23 above.

78. Abū Nakhīlah (his *ism*, not his *kunyah*) b. Ḥazn al-Tamīmī was court poet to the Umayyads from the time of Maslamah b. ʿAbd al-Malik, his first patron. He transferred his allegiance to the ʿAbbāsids and became their panegyrist, styling himself the "poet of the Banū Hāshim" (*Aghānī*, Būlāq, XVIII, 139; Beirut, XX, 361.) For the family of Zurārah, see Crone, *Slaves*, 121–23.

When it was the day on which Abū Ja'far had the oath of allegiance taken to his son al-Mahdī and gave him precedence over 'Īsā, he summoned Abū Nakhīlah and ordered him to recite the poem. Sulaymān b. 'Abdallāh spoke to Abū Ja'far and advised him in what he said to give him the most magnificent reward. He said, "It is something that will remain about you in books and people will talk about it at the time and for eternity," and he continued until Abū Ja'far ordered that he be given ten thousand *dirhams*.

According to Ḥayyān b. 'Abdallāh b. Ḥibrān al-Ḥimmānī—Abū Nakhīlah: I came to Abū Ja'far and waited for a month at his gate and did not reach him until the day when 'Abdallāh b. al-Rabī' al-Ḥārithī said to me, "O Abū Nakhīlah, the Commander of the Faithful has nominated his son for the caliphate and the oath of
[348] allegiance (*'ahd*), and he is giving him precedence before 'Īsā b. Mūsā. If you said something encouraging him in that and mentioning the virtue of al-Mahdī, you would be likely to receive some favor from him and from his son," so I said:[79]

Take care, 'Abdallāh, who is worthy of it,
(I mean) the caliphate of God, which He has given you.
He has chosen you, he has chosen you for it, He has chosen you.
We had looked for a time to your father,
Then we looked to you for it.
We were among them,[80] but our longing was for you.
Yes, we shelter in your protection.
Rest your staff on Muḥammad,
Your son, who, whatever you entrust to him, can bear the responsibility.
The best man to protect it (the caliphate) is the nearest kin to you.
I fatigued my legs and thighs,
I roamed until I found no place to go,
I turned here and there and everywhere,

79. For a variant version of this poem, *Aghānī*, Būlāq, XVIII, 152; Beirut, XX, 391.

80. Supporters of the Umayyads. Much of the poem is concerned with the author's attempt to excuse his support of the previous dynasty.

and every word I spoke except about you
Was a lie, and this has done penance for that.

I also recited my poem in which I said:[81]

To the Commander of the Faithful betake yourself, O my she-camel,
traveling to the foamy sea of seas (or to the most generous of men).
You are he, O son of the namesake of Aḥmad,[82]
O son of the noble Arab house,
Yes, the trustworthy of the Eternal One,
it is you who was appointed by the Lord of the mosque.
The heir apparent to it (the caliphate) most fortunately
was ʿĪsā, and he let it slide to Muḥammad
And before ʿĪsā it was gradually surrendered from one to one,
so that it may be passed from hand to hand
Among you, and it rests there while it is increasing [349]
and we are delighted with the beardless youth.[83]
We have arrived to witness, but we did not,
the pact has not been confirmed.
So, if we hear the clamor "Stretch out! Stretch out!" (your hand),
it will be for us like the torrent of rain for a thirsty horse.
So call to the oath of allegiance the surging crowds.
It will become clear to you today or tomorrow.
It is he (al-Mahdī) who has become perfect, and no obstacle [stands in his way].
He has increased as you wish, so give him more, that he may increase further.
Clothe him yourself in the mantle you choose and he is ready to wear,
for it is the mantle of the garlanded horse that goes before.
It had been related that it was as if it (the caliphate)
had returned, and when it did it was not rejected.
For it used to wander from one wilderness to another

81. For a variant, see *Aghānī*, Būlāq, XVIII, 151; Beirut, XX, 288–89.
82. Muḥammad al-Mahdī was the namesake of the Prophet.
83. Al-Mahdī.

for some time. So, when the time for the drinkers to gather around the spring has arrived,
And the time of turning the vile seducer (into a man of virtue) has also arrived
God would say to it, "Come along quickly and be rightly guided!"
Then it is settled in the right place,
in the best lineage, in the best lineage,[84] in the most glorious lineage.
The loud complaint of jealous souls has not been silenced by better than a firm and reliable lord.
When they started striking fire by unsparkling firesteel,
they were tested with the extremely firm and powerful
Who increases in watchfulness against threats.
So they changed to compliance and supplication
Toward a determined sword, which eats up every file.

This was recited and spread through the mouths of the servants
[350] and reached Abū Ja'far, who asked who the author was. He was informed that it was a member of the Banū Sa'd b. Zayd Manāt and he was pleased. He called me and I was brought into his presence. 'Īsā b. Mūsā was on his right-hand side, and the people were with him with the chiefs of the commanders and the army. When I was in a place he could see me, I cried out, "O Commander of the Faithful, bring me near you so that I can make you understand and you can listen to what I have to say." He beckoned with his hand, and I came near until I was closed to him. When I was in front of him I spoke and raised my voice and recited to him from this position. Then I returned to the beginning of the *urjūzah*,[85] and I recited it from the beginning to this place also. I repeated it a second time until I came to its end. The people were listening, and he was delighted with what I recited to him when he was listening to it. When we left him, there was a man putting his hand on my shoulder, and I turned and there was 'Iqāl b. Shabbah saying, "As for you, you have delighted the Commander of the Faithful and, if the affair is resolved as you wish and you said, by

84. That is, the caliphate was settled on al-Mahdī.
85. A poem in the *rajaz* meter.

my life you will be well rewarded by him, but, if it is otherwise, then look for a tunnel in the earth or a ladder to the sky."[86]

Al-Manṣūr wrote to him at al-Rayy that he be given a reward, and 'Īsā sent men after him and he was intercepted on his way and he had his throat cut and the skin stripped off his face. It is said that he was killed after he left al-Rayy and he had taken his reward.

According to al-Walīd b. Muḥammad al-'Anbarī: The reason why 'Īsā gave Abū Ja'far his consent for giving al-Mahdī precedence over him was that Salm b. Qutaybah said to him, "O man, take the oath of allegiance and give him precedence over yourself. If you resign from the affair, he will assign it to you ('Īsā) after him (al-Mahdī), and you will please the Commander of the Faithful." He said, "I will succeed him?" and he replied, "Yes," and 'Īsā said, "I will do it." Salm came to al-Manṣūr and told him of 'Īsā's reply, and he was pleased about that and Salm's status with him increased, and the people took the oath of allegiance to [351]
al-Mahdī and to 'Īsā b. Mūsā after him. Al-Manṣūr preached the sermon in which was the announcement of the precedence of al-Mahdī over 'Īsā, and 'Īsā preached after that and gave precedence to al-Mahdī over himself, and al-Manṣūr fulfilled what he had promised him.

According to some of the companions of Abū Ja'far: We were reminiscing about the affair of Abū Ja'far and 'Īsā b. Mūsā and the oath of allegiance and his resigning of it and giving precedence to al-Mahdī, and one of the commanders, whose name he gave, said, "By God, other than Whom there is no god, the deposition of 'Īsā from it happened only with 'Īsā's consent, his dependence on *dirhams*, and his failure to appreciate the importance of the caliphate and his desire to escape it. When the day came when he went out to the deposition and resigned, I was in the *maqṣūrah*[87] (of the mosque) in the City of Peace when Abū 'Ubaydallāh,[88]

86. That is, if al-Mahdī is made heir apparent.

87. An enclosure in the mosque, usually to separate the ruler and his entourage from the people.

88. Abū 'Ubaydallāh Mu'āwiyah b. 'Ubaydallāh was vizier and secretary to al-Mahdī. Originally from Palestine, his father had served the Umayyads (Jāḥiẓ, 126; *'Uyūn*, 281). He was attached to al-Mahdī when he was sent to al-Rayy and continued as his vizier after he became caliph. He aroused the jealousy of Ya'qūb

secretary to al-Mahdī, with a group of people of Khurāsān came out and ʿĪsā spoke and said, "I have handed over the position of heir apparent to Muḥammad, son of the Commander of the Faithful, and have given him precedence over me." Abū ʿUbaydallāh said, "It was not like that, may God glorify the Amīr, but tell it in truth and honesty and say what you wanted for it and what you were given." ʿĪsā replied, "Yes, I sold my rights of precedence in the position of heir apparent to ʿAbdallāh, Commander of the Faithful, to his son Muḥammad al-Mahdī for ten million *dirhams* and three hundred thousand to be divided among my children such and such and such (and he named them) and seven hundred thousand to so-and-so (one of his wives, and he named her), with a good heart on my part and desire that it might pass to him because he is most worthy of it and has the most right and strongest claim to
[352] it and to undertake it. I do not have any right to precedence over him in big or in little. If ever I claim anything after this day of mine, then I am in the wrong and have no rights in it, no claim and no demand."

He said: Sometimes he forgot one thing or another about that and Abū ʿUbaydallāh reminded him until he finished up. Abū ʿUbaydallāh only sought confirmation and sealed the document and the witnesses witnessed it. I was present until ʿĪsā put his own handwriting and seal on it with the people gathered there. Then they went in from the *maqṣūrah* to the palace.

He said: The Commander of the Faithful robed ʿĪsā and his son Mūsā and other children of his with robes to the value of over one million, two hundred thousand *dirhams*.

The governorship of ʿĪsā b. Mūsā over al-Kūfah and its Sawād and the area around it lasted thirteen years[89] until al-Manṣūr deposed him and appointed Muḥammad b. Sulaymān b. ʿAlī as governor when he refused to give al-Mahdī precedence over himself.

---

b. Dāwūd and of al-Rabīʿ and the *mawālī*, which eventually led to his fall; he lost his post as vizier in 163/779–80 and as *ṣāḥib al-rasāʾil* (in charge of correspondence) in 166/782–83. He survived into the reign of Hārūn, when Yaḥyā b. Khālid invited him to return to government, but he declined because of his great age. See below, pp. 199–202, al-Jahshiyārī, 141–57, 179; Sourdel, *Vizirat*, I, 94–103.

89. According to al-Ṭabarī, III, 72, ʿĪsā had been appointed governor of al-Kūfah in 132/750. This would have given him fifteen years as governor.

It is said: Al-Manṣūr only appointed Muḥammad b. Sulaymān as governor when he did because he wanted to humiliate ʿĪsā, but Muḥammad did not do that and continued to treat him highly and to show him respect.

In this year Abū Jaʿfar appointed Muḥammad b. Abī al-ʿAbbās, his brother's son, as governor of al-Baṣrah, but he asked to be excused, so he was, and he left there for the City of Peace and died there. His wife al-Baghūm b. ʿAlī b. al-Rabīʿ shrieked and lamented him. One of the guards struck her with a bridle rein on the posterior, and the servants of Muḥammad b. Abī al-ʿAbbās took turns in beating him until he was killed, and his blood was unavenged. When Muḥammad b. Abī al-ʿAbbās set out from al-Baṣrah he left ʿUqbah b. Salm as his deputy over it, and Abū Jaʿfar confirmed him in charge of it until 151 (January 26, 768–January 13, 769).

Al-Manṣūr led the pilgrimage in this year. In this year his governor of Mecca and al-Ṭā'if was his paternal uncle ʿAbd al-Ṣamad b. ʿAlī, over Medina Jaʿfar b. Sulaymān, over al-Kūfah and its territory Muḥammad b. Sulaymān, over al-Baṣrah ʿUqbah b. Salm with Sawwār b. ʿAbdallāh in charge of the judiciary there, and Yazīd b. Ḥātim was in charge of Egypt.[90] [353]

---

90. B. Qabīṣah b. al-Muhallab: He had been governor of Egypt since 143/760–61. A descendant of the famous al-Muhallab b. Abī Ṣufrah, he is said to have been instrumental in saving Abū Jaʿfar's life before the ʿAbbāsid revolution. He was governor of Azerbaijān, Egypt, and, in 154–70 (771–786/7), of Ifrīqiyah, where he died. See also his brother Rawḥ and cousin ʿUmar b. Ḥafṣ (al-Ṭabarī, III, 68, 142, 370, 372, 373, 569; al-Kindī, *Governors*, 111–15; Ibn Idhārī, *Bayān*, 78–82). Ibn Idhārī gives his date of death as Ramaḍān 171/February–March 788. For the Muhallabids in the early ʿAbbāsid period, see Kennedy, *ʿAbbasid Caliphate*, 82–83; Crone, *Slaves*, 133–35.

The Events of the Year

148

(February 27, 765–February 15, 766)

The events of this year:

In this year Al-Manṣūr sent Ḥumayd b. Qaḥṭabah[91] to Armenia to make war on the Turks who had killed Ḥarb b. ʿAbdallāh and ravaged Tiflīs. Ḥumayd went to Armenia and found that they had gone, so he left without meeting a single one of them.

In this year Ṣāliḥ b. ʿAlī[92] made camp at Dābiq,[93] it is said, and did not go on a raid.

---

91. Son of Qaḥṭabah b. Shabīb, who had led the ʿAbbāsid armies from Khurāsān at the time of the revolution. He had initially supported the rebellion of ʿAbdallāh b. ʿAlī against al-Manṣūr in 137/754 but was restored to favor, serving briefly as governor of Egypt in 143–45/761–63 and, from 151 until his death in 159 (768–76), as governor of Khurāsān. See al-Ṭabarī, III, 15, 21, 48, 55, 92–93, 369, 459; al-Kindī, *Governors*, 110; Ḥamzah, 141. For the role of his family in the early ʿAbbāsid state, see Kennedy, *ʿAbbasid Caliphate*, 79–80; Crone, *Slaves*, 188–89.

92. Paternal uncle of al-Saffāḥ and al-Manṣūr. He had been active in the ʿAbbāsid conquest of Syria and was the leader of the ʿAbbāsid force that killed Marwān, the last Umayyad caliph in Egypt. He was briefly in charge of Egypt on two occasions, but most of his career was spent in Syria, where he took over many former Umayyad properties, and on the Byzantine frontier, where he was an active builder of fortifications. He and his family had a celebrated residence at Salamiyyah in central Syria. He was the same age as his nephew al-Manṣūr but died before him, in 152/769. See al-Ṭabarī, III, 48; al-Balādhurī, *Buldān*, 170, 197; Ibn al-ʿAdīm, *Zubdat*, 59–60; al-Kindī, *Governors*, 102–6. See also Kennedy, *ʿAbbasid Caliphate*, 74–75.

93. An important Muslim base on the Byzantine frontier, north of Aleppo. Yāqūt, *Muʿjam*, II, 416–17; Le Strange, *Palestine*, 426.

In this year Ja'far b. Abī Ja'far al-Manṣūr[94] led the pilgrimage, and the governors of the *amṣār*[95] in this year were the same as in the year before.

---

94. Known as Ja'far the Elder, to distinguish him from his younger brother of the same name. He was at one time considered as a possible rival to al-Mahdī for the succession but died in 150/758 (see below pp. 49, 145–46).

95. Plural of *miṣr*. The *amṣār* were orginally the towns established by the Muslims in the years immediately after the conquests at al-Kūfah, al-Baṣrah and al-Fusṭāṭ. In the early 'Abbāsid period, the term is applied generally to the major provincial capitals.

The Events of the Year

149

(February 16, 766–February 5, 767)

The events of this year:

In this year al-ʿAbbās b. Muḥammad led the summer raid on the Byzantine lands. With him were al-Ḥasan b. Qaḥṭabah[96] and Muḥammad b. al-Ashʿath, and Muḥammad b. al-Ashʿath died on the road.[97]

In this year al-Manṣūr completed the building of the walls of the city of Baghdad and finished with the ditch and all the work.

96. Brother of Ḥumayd (see note 91 above). On his father's death, he took over command of the ʿAbbāsid army. The rest of his career was spent in Armenia and on the Byzantine frontier, where he built numerous fortresses and frequently led expeditions against the Greeks. He died in 181/797, full of honor and years, at the age of eighty-four (al-Ṭabarī, III, 17, 95, 353, 493, 495, 646; al-Balādhurī, *Buldān*, 223). For the family properties in Baghdad, see Le Strange, *Baghdad*, 140–41.

97. Al-Khuzāʿī. A close colleague of Abū Muslim, he was sent to Ifrīqiyah by Abū Jaʿfar in 144/761, but he was subsequently driven out by a mutiny of his Khurāsānī troops. (al-Ṭabarī, II, 2001, III, 71, 122; Ibn Idhārī, *Bayān*, 72). In the Leiden edition of al-Ṭabarī, III, 74, his appointment to Ifrīqiyah is wrongly dated to 133. See Crone, *Slaves*, 184–85

In this year he went to Ḥadīthah[98] of Mosul and then back to the City of Peace. [354]

In this year Muḥammad b. Ibrāhīm b. Muḥammad b. ʿAlī b. ʿAbdallāh b. ʿAbbās[99] led the pilgrimage.

In this year ʿAbd al-Ṣamad b. ʿAlī was deposed from Mecca, and Muḥammad b. Ibrāhīm was appointed as governor.

The governors of the *amṣār* in this year were the same as those in the years 147 and 148, except for Mecca and al-Ṭā'if, where the governor in this year was Muḥammad b. Ibrāhīm b. Muḥammad b. ʿAlī b. ʿAbdallāh b. ʿAbbās.

---

98. On the east bank of the Tigris, about thirty miles southeast of Mosul. See Yāqūt, *Muʿjam*, II, 230; Le Strange, *Lands*, 90–91.

99. Son of Ibrāhīm al-Imām, the leader of the ʿAbbāsid family put to death by the Umayyads immediately before the ʿAbbāsid Revolution. He had an unspectacular career, mostly in the Holy Cities. He led the pilgrimage on three occasions in al-Manṣūr's reign (149/757, 151/759, 154/762) and was governor of Medina at the time of the caliph's death (see below, pp 86–87). He died in 185/801.

The Events of the Year 150

(February 6, 767–January 25, 768)

One of the events of this year was the rebellion of Ustādhsīs[100] with people from Harāt,[101] Bādhghīs,[102] Sijistān[103] and other areas of Khurāsān. They were said to have numbered about 300,000 fighting men and conquered most of Khurāsān and proceeded until they came up against the people of Marw al-Rūdh.[104] Al-

100. Ya'qūbī, *Tārīkh*, II, 457, and Gardīzī, *Zayn*, 74b, both make it clear that there was a religious aspect to the rebellion and that Ustādhsīs claimed to be a prophet. The independent account in Agapius of Manbij, *'Unwān*, 544–45, suggests that there were economic causes, notably a dispute over control of silver mines in Bādhghīs. See Sadighi, *Mouvements*, 155–62; Kennedy, *'Abbasid Caliphate*, 183–84; Daniel, *Khurasan*, 133–37.

101. Herat, in western Afghanistan.

102. Yāqūt, *Mu'jam*, I, 318; Le Strange, *Lands*, 412–15.

103. Or Sīstān, the province of eastern Iran around the delta of the Helmand river, near the modern Iran-Afghanistan frontier. On the history of the area, see Bosworth, *Sistan under the Arabs*.

104. Marw al-Rūdh lay on the Murghāb river south of Marw, near the modern Soviet-Afghan border. It was an important center of Muslim settlement in the area, and its people has played an important part in the 'Abbāsid Revolution. See Yāqūt, *Mu'jam*, V, 112; Le Strange, *Lands*, 404–5.

Ajtham al-Marwarrūdhī[105] went out to meet them with the people of Marw al-Rūdh, and they fought him fiercely until al-Ajtham was killed and many of the people of Marw al-Rūdh with him. Ustādhsīs defeated many commanders, including Muʿādh b. Muslim b. Muʿādh,[106] Jibra'īl b. Yaḥyā, Ḥammād b. ʿAmr,[107] Abū al-Najm al-Sijistānī,[108] and Dāwūd b. Kirāz[109] until al-Manṣūr, [355] who was then at al-Baradān,[110] sent Khāzim b. Khuzaymah[111] to al-Mahdī, who then put him in charge of the campaign against Ustādhsīs and assigned commanders to him.

It is said that Muʿāwiyah b. ʿUbaydallāh, al-Mahdī's vizier, was undermining Khāzim's position. At that time al-Mahdī was in Nishapur.[112] Muʿāwiyah despatched letters to Khāzim b. Khuzaymah and to other commanders giving himself unlimited powers. Khāzim, who was with his army, was ill, but he drank some medicine and rode with the postal service until he reached al-Mahdī in Nishapur. He greeted him and asked to speak with him alone because Abū ʿUbaydallāh was present, but al-Mahdī

105. Otherwise unknown.

106. He later became governor of Khurāsān, 161–63/780–83, but disappears from the record after that. His son Yaḥyā was prominent in the early years of al-Ma'mūn's reign, while another son, al-Ḥusayn, was foster brother to the future caliph al-Hādī, suggesting that Muʿādh was more important than his brief appearance in the historical record would suggest. (See below, pp 196, 215; Gardīzī, 76b; Ḥamzah, 141; Crone, *Slaves*, 183–84).

107. Otherwise unknown.

108. Otherwise unknown.

109. Otherwise unknown.

110. On the east bank of the Tigris, about ten miles north of Baghdad. See Yāqūt, *Muʿjam*, I, 375; Le Strange, *Lands*, 50.

111. Al-Tamīmī al-Marwarrūdhī, one of the most important figures in the ʿAbbāsid Revolution in Khurāsān and subsequently in the army of the early ʿAbbāsid caliphate. He led the people of Marw al-Rūdh in support of the ʿAbbāsid Revolution and was one of the leaders of the ʿAbbāsid armies in Iran and Iraq In 134/751–52 he took ʿUmān for the ʿAbbāsids, and in 141/758–59 he was sent with the young al-Mahdī to al-Rayy and played a prominent part in the defeat of the rebel governor ʿAbd al-Jabbār al-Azdī; he was governor of Khurāsān on two occasions. He disappears from the record after 151/768. His son Khuzaymah was an important military figure in Hārūn's reign and in the civil war that followed his death (al-Ṭabarī, II, 1959, III, 13, 20, 69, 76–78, 134–35; Ḥamzah 140–41; Crone, *Slaves*, 180–81; Kennedy, *ʿAbbasid Caliphate*, 81–82).

112. In northeastern Iran, some thirty miles west of Mashhad, and one of the most important cities of Khurāsān in the early Islamic period. Yāqūt, *Muʿjam*, V, 331–33; Le Strange, *Lands*, 382–88.

said, "Abū ʿUbaydallāh will not spy on you, so say what is on your mind," but Khāzim refused to tell him or talk to him until Abū ʿUbaydallāh rose and left. When he was alone with him, he complained to him about Muʿāwiyah b. ʿUbaydallāh and his hostility and his prejudice against him and what he was saying in his letters to him and the commanders under him. He explained how they were corrupted, how they acquired a domineering manner, how they tried to be independent in their opinions and became heedless and rather disobedient. Khāzim argued that the war could not be conducted properly without a sole head and that no banner[113] should fly over the head of anyone in the army except his banner or a banner he had given. He also told al-Mahdī that he would not return to fight Ustādhsīs and his men unless he was given complete control and exempted from the authority of Muʿāwiyah b. ʿUbaydallāh. He asked for permission to unfurl the banners of the commanders who were with him, and that al-Mahdī write to them ordering them to obey him.

Al-Mahdī granted him everything he requested and Khāzim departed for his army. He did what he had said and unfurled the banners of the commanders that he deemed wise to unfurl, and he
[356] entrusted banners to those he wished. He was joined by those soldiers who had fled, using them as a surplus reinforcement in the rear, just to increase the numbers of the soldiers. He did not put them in the vanguard because of the feelings of fear of defeat that were in the hearts of those who had been defeated; those in this category who joined him numbered 22,000. He then chose 6,000 of the army and joined them to 12,000 specially chosen men who were with him. Bakkār b. Muslim al-ʿUqaylī[114] was among those chosen.

Then he prepared for battle; he dug a trench and appointed al-

113. The banner (*liwā'*) was important as a symbol of command of an army or of the governorate of a province. Here it means that Khāzim should have an independent command and be able to choose his own subordinates.

114. He came from a family that had been prominent supporters of the last Umayyad caliph, Marwān, and he himself had been one of the leaders of ʿAbdallāh b. ʿAlī's rebellion against al-Manṣūr. Despite this, the caliph valued his military expertise and support; he later, in 153/770, became governor of Armenia. See also his brother Isḥāq (al-Ṭabarī, III, 96, 371; Crone, *Slaves*, 106–7).

Haytham b. Shu'bah b. Ẓuhayr[115] in charge of the right wing and Nahār b. Ḥuṣayn al-Sa'di[116] over the left wing. Bakkār b. Muslim al-'Uqaylī led the vanguard and Turārkhudā[117] was over the rear guard; he was one of the descendants (*abnā'*) of the Persian kings of Khurāsān. His banner was held by al-Zibriqān and his standard by his freedman Bassām.[118] He tricked and deceived the enemy by moving from place to place and trench to trench, so that they were totally exhausted, as most of them were on foot.

Then Khāzim went to a place and stopped there and dug a trench around it. He brought inside it all that he wanted to, including all his companions. He made four gates in it and appointed man from his chosen companions, who were 4,000 strong, in charge of every gate. He assigned to Bakkār b. Muslim, the commander of his vanguard, 2,000 men to supplement the 18,000 he had already.

The other side came, bringing with them spades, axes, and large baskets, intending to fill in the trench and enter it. They reached the trench at the gate that Bakkār b. Muslim was in charge of and attacked it so fiercely that Bakkār's companions had no choice but to flee and they were pursued into the trench by the enemy. When Bakkār saw that, he dismounted and rushed and stood at the gate of the trench and shouted to his companions, "You sons [357]
of harlots, the Muslims are attacked from the side I guard!"[119] and there dismounted about fifty of his tribe and family who were with him and they blocked the gate so that they held the enemy back from it.

Then a man from Sijistān called al-Ḥarīsh,[120] who was with

115. Al-Tamīmī, like Khāzim. He had fought under Khāzim's command before and was later to serve his son Khuzaymah (al-Ṭabarī, III, 69, 130, 856).

116. Otherwise unknown.

117. The second element of his name, *khudā*, means "lord" in Persian. The word "kings" (*mulūk*) is used loosely here to refer to the semi-independent princes and lords of Khurāsān. See Shaban, *Political Geography of Khurasan*. Turārkhudā himself had been, like Bakkār b. Muslim, a supporter of 'Abdallāh b. 'Alī but is otherwise unknown.

118. Zibriqān is a Persian word meaning either the moon or the man with the little beard. Neither he nor Bassām is recorded elsewhere.

119. Suggesting, of course, that Ustādhsīs' supporters were non-Muslims, a useful clue to the nature of the rebellion.

120. The name means "rough" or "harsh" in Arabic, but it may be either a nickname or a corruption of a Persian word; it is not recorded elsewhere.

Ustādhsīs and was the man who was managing his affairs, came to the gate where Khāzim was. When Khāzim saw him coming, he sent to al-Haytham b. Shuʿbah who was on the right wing, saying, "Go out of the gate you are in charge of and take a different route from the one that leads to Bakkār's gate while the enemy is occupied with fighting and attacking us and, when you are behind them and beyond the range of their vision, come upon them from the rear." At that time they were expecting the arrival of Abū ʿAwn[121] and ʿAmr b. Salm b. Qutaybah[122] from Ṭukhāristān[123] so Khāzim ordered Bakkār, "When you see the banners of al-Haytham b. Shuʿbah approaching you from behind, say, 'God is great!' and, 'The people of Ṭukhāristān have arrived!'" So al-Haytham's men did that while Khāzim, with the main body of the army, attacked al-Ḥarīsh al-Sijistānī and engaged in fierce and prolonged sword fighting. While they were locked in combat they saw al-Haytham's banners and shouted to each other, "The people of Ṭukhāristān have come!" and when the people of al-Ḥarīsh and those who were fighting Bakkār saw those standards, Khāzim's men attacked them fiercely and exposed them so that al-Haytham's men attacked them with spears and arrows. Nahār b. Ḥuṣayn and
[358] his men from the left and Bakkār b. Muslim and his men from their direction also attacked and they routed them and put them to the sword. The Muslims made a great slaughter and those who were killed in that battle numbered about 70,000 and 14,000 were taken prisoners.

Ustādhsīs took refuge in the mountains with a small number of his companions. Khāzim took the fourteen thousand prisoners and cut off their heads. Then he went and besieged Ustādhsīs in

121. ʿAbd al-Malik b. Yazīd al-Azdī, a Khurāsānī from Jurjān who played an important role in the ʿAbbāsid Revolution and came west with the ʿAbbāsid armies. He was later governor of Egypt, 133–36/751–35 and 137–41/755–58, and of Khurāsān, in c. 159–60/775–77, but was deposed by al-Mahdī for his failure to defeat the rebel al-Muqannaʿ. He died in 168/784–85. See al-Ṭabarī, III, 38, 48, 72, 459, 477, 536–37, for his relations with al-Mahdī and his son; Gardīzī, *Zayn*, 74b, 76b, gives him two periods as governor of Khurāsān; Kindī, *Governors*, 102–5, says he was a mawlā of Hunā'ah of Azd; see Crone, *Slaves*, 174.

122. Son of Salm b. Qutaybah; see note 27 above; not recorded elsewhere.

123. A district of Khurāsān in the Oxus valley east of Balkh; see Le Strange, *Lands*, 426–27.

his mountain refuge, and there joined him Abū 'Awn and 'Amr b. Salm b. Qutaybah with their companions at that place. Khāzim settled them in an area and told them to stay where they were until they were needed. Khāzim besieged Ustādhsīs and his companions until they agreed to accept the judgment of Abū 'Awn:[124] they would not accept any other terms and Khāzim agreed to that and ordered Abū 'Awn to allow them to accept his judgment so he did. When they came down to the judgment of Abū 'Awn, he decided that Ustādhsīs and his sons and his household[125] should be secured with irons and that the rest, 30,000 in number, should be released. Khāzim put Abū 'Awn's judgment into effect and gave each of them two garments. Khāzim wrote about the conquests God had given him and the destruction of his enemies to al-Mahdī who in turn wrote to the Commander of the Faithful al-Manṣūr about it.

Muḥammad b. 'Umar[126] mentioned that the rebellion of Ustādhsīs and al-Ḥarīsh took place in the year 150/767 and that Ustādhsīs was defeated in the year 151/768.

In this year al-Manṣūr deposed Ja'far b. Sulaymān from Medina and appointed al-Ḥasan b. Ḥasan b. Zayd b. Ḥasan b. 'Alī b. Abī Ṭālib.[127]

In it Ja'far b. Abī Ja'far al-Manṣūr the Elder died in Baghdad and his father al-Manṣūr prayed over him. He was buried by night in the cemetery of Quraysh.[128]

There was no summer expedition for the people against the Byzantines in this year: it is said that Abū Ja'far had put Usayd[129] [359]

124. Abū 'Awn was clearly known and trusted by the rebels as no other Muslim leader was, but the sources give no indication as to why this was so.

125. According to other sources (Gardīzī, *Zayn*, 74b; Mas'ūdī, *Murūj*, IV, 299), Ustādhsīs' daughter Marājil, mother of the future caliph al-Ma'mūn, was among the captives taken to Baghdad on this occasion.

126. Al-Wāqidī.

127. An important and significant move: Al-Ḥasan was an 'Alid who had proved loyal to al-Manṣūr, and there is no doubt that his appointment to Medina, a center of 'Alid support, was a conciliatory gesture He remained governor until 155/772 and died in 168/784–85.

128. Le Strange, *Baghdad*, 158, says that this was situated at Kāẓimayn, north of Baghdad, on the west bank.

129. Possibly Usayd (or Asīd) b. 'Abdallāh al-Khuzā'ī (Crone, *Slaves*, 175–76), but he is said to have been governor of Khurāsān at this time (Ḥamzah, 141). More

in charge of the expedition in this year but he did not lead the people to the land of the enemy but stayed in Marj Dābiq.[130]

ʿAbd al-Ṣamad b. ʿAlī b. ʿAbdallāh b. ʿAbbās led the pilgrimage in this year.

The governor of Mecca and al-Ṭā'if was ʿAbd al-Ṣamad b. ʿAlī b. ʿAbdallāh b. al-ʿAbbās but it is also said that the governor of Mecca and al-Ṭā'if was Muḥammad b. Ibrāhīm b. Muḥammad. The governor of Medina was al-Ḥasan b. Zayd al-ʿAlawī. The governor of al-Kūfah was Muḥammad b. Sulaymān b. ʿAlī and of al-Baṣrah ʿUqbah b. Salm, with Sawwār[131] in charge of the judiciary, and the governor of Egypt was Yazīd b. Ḥātim.

---

likely this is a mistake for Yazīd b. Usayd al-Sulamī (see note 190 below), as Brooks suggests ("Byzantines and Arabs", 734).

130. The fertile meadows and pastures around Dābiq (see note 93, above), which were frequently used as a base for Muslim raids.

131. Sawwār b. ʿAbdallāh, d. 157/773–74, was *qāḍī* of al-Baṣrah for many years.

The Events of the Year

151

(January 26, 768–January 13, 769)

Among the events of this year was the seaborne attack on Jeddah by the Kurk[132] mentioned by Muḥammad b. ʿUmar.

In this year ʿUmar b. Ḥafṣ b. ʿUthmān b. Abī Ṣufrah[133] was appointed governor of Ifrīqiyah. He was deposed from Sind and replaced by Hishām b. ʿAmr al-Taghlibī.[134]

The circumstances of the deposition of ʿUmar b. Ḥafṣ from Sind and his appointment as governor of Ifrīqiyah, and of the appointment of Hishām b. ʿAmr as governor of Sind.

According to ʿAlī b. Muḥammad b. Sulaymān b. ʿAlī al-ʿAbbāsī —his father: The reason for that was that al-Manṣūr had appointed [360]

---

132. Pirates of unknown origin. See Omar, *ʿAbbasid Caliphate*, 319.

133. A member of the Muhallabī family (see note 90 above). He had been governor of Sind since 142/759–60. He remained governor of Ifrīqiyah until he was killed by the Berbers and the Khārijites in an uprising in 153/770 (al-Ṭabarī, III, 139, 370; al-Balādhurī, *Futūḥ*, 232; Ibn Idhārī, *Bayān*, 75–76).

134. A chief of the Jazīrah tribe of Taghlib, he is said to have secured the allegiance of Mosul to the ʿAbbāsids at the time of the revolution. According to Yaʿqūbī (*Tārīkh*, II, 448), he conquered Multan and died soon after his return from Sind in 157/773–74 (al-Ṭabarī, III, 47, 380).

ʿUmar b. Ḥafṣ al-Ṣufrī, called Hazārmard[135] to Sind. He remained there until the rebellions of Muḥammad b. ʿAbdallāh in Medina and Ibrāhīm in al-Baṣrah. Muḥammad b. ʿAbdallāh sent his son ʿAbdallāh b. Muḥammad who was known as al-Ashtar,[136] with some members of the Zaydiyyah[137] to Baṣrah and ordered them to buy the foals of excellent horses and take them with them to Sind so that Muḥammad could use them as a means to reach ʿUmar b. Ḥafṣ. He did this because ʿUmar b. Ḥafṣ was one of Abū Jaʿfar commanders who had taken the oath of allegiance to Muḥammad b. ʿAbdallāh, as he was a sympathizer of the family of Abū Ṭālib.

They went to Ibrāhīm b. ʿAbdallāh in al-Baṣrah and bought foals from there. There is nothing in the land of Sind and Hind[138] more valuable than good horses. They traveled by sea until they reached Sind and then they went to ʿUmar b. Ḥafṣ and said to him, "We are horse dealers and have some excellent horses with us," and he ordered them to show their horses so they showed them to him. When they came to him one of them said to him, "Come near me and I will tell you something," so he came near and he went on, "We have brought you something that is better for you than the horses and that has in it for you all the best of his world and the next. Give us a guarantee on two points: that you accept what we bring you or that you will conceal it and refrain from making it public until we leave your country on our return journey." He gave them the guarantee and they said, "We did not come to you because of the horses but we have here the son of the Prophet of God, ʿAbdallāh b. Muḥammad b. ʿAbdallāh b. Ḥasan b. Ḥasan who has been sent to you by his father who has come out in rebellion in Medina and proclaimed himself Caliph. His brother Ibrāhīm has

---

135. The name means "thousand men" in Persian, but it is not clear why he was so called.

136. The word is applied to someone who has either an inversion of the eyelid or a split bottom lip (see Lane, s.v. *shtr*).

137. The Zaydiyyah were originally followers of Zayd b. ʿAlī, who rebelled unsuccessfully in al-Kūfah against the Umayyads in 122/740. They continued in existence as a small group of ʿAlid activists, based mostly in al-Kūfah, and they supported all the main ʿAlid rebellions of the early ʿAbbāsid period (see Kennedy, *ʿAbbasid Caliphate*, 203–9).

138. Sind was the Muslim province on the lower Indus, roughly equivalent to the modern province of Sind in Pakistan. Hind was used in a more general sense for the neighboring parts of the Indian subcontinent not under Muslim rule.

risen in al-Baṣrah and taken it over." He said, "You are most welcome," and he took the oath of allegiance to him from them and ordered him to be concealed with him. [361]

Then he called the people of his household, his commanders and the great men of the town to take the oath of allegiance and they accepted. He cut up white standards, white turbans and white *qalansūwahs* and on Thursday he prepared white garments in which to go up to the pulpit. On Wednesday there came a boat from Baṣrah with a messenger of Khulaydah bint al-Muʿārik, wife of ʿUmar b. Ḥafṣ with a letter telling him of the killing of Muḥammad b. ʿAbdallāh. He went to ʿAbdallāh, told him the news and consoled him and said to him, "I have sworn the oath of allegiance to your father and now this had happened." ʿAbdallāh said, "My activities are now notorious and my position well-known and my safety is your responsibility so look after yourself or leave." ʿUmar replied, "I have a suggestion to make: there is here one of the Kings of Sind with a great kingdom and following. He is, despite his polytheism, a great admirer of the Prophet of God and he is a trustworthy man. I will write to him and make an agreement between you and him and send you to him to stay with him, and you will be beyond reach with him." ʿAbdallāh replied, "Do as you wish." So he did that and he went to the king who was very generous to him and showed him great kindness. The Zaydiyyah escaped to join him until there were about 400 "people of perspicacity"[139] with him and he used to go out riding and hunting among them and he amused himself in the manner of kings and their families.

When Muḥammad and Ibrāhīm were killed, news of ʿAbdallāh al-Ashtar reached al-Manṣūr and he was worried about it so he wrote to ʿUmar b. Ḥafṣ, informing him what he had heard. ʿUmar b. Ḥafṣ gathered his kin and read al-Manṣūr's letter to them and told them that if he admitted the story, al-Manṣūr would not hesitate to depose him and if he went to him, he would kill him and if he refused he would make war on him. Then one of his kin said, "Put the blame on me and write to him telling him about me. Arrest me immediately, put me in chains and throw me into [362]

139. *Ahl al-baṣā'ir*, presumably the description they adopted for themselves.

prison. If he writes that I should be sent to him, send me to him. He will not dare to take action against me because of your position in Sind and the status of your family in Baṣrah." 'Umar replied, "I fear things may not turn out as you think." "If I am killed," the man said, "I will be a sacrifice for you, and I am pleased to be a sacrifice for you, and if I am spared that is God's will." So 'Umar ordered him to be chained and imprisoned and he wrote to al-Manṣūr about that. Al-Manṣūr wrote back ordering 'Umar to send the man to him and he arrived; he was brought before him and he was executed.

Al-Manṣūr continued to think whom he might appoint as governor of Sind. He would begin to talk of someone and then change his mind. One day he was going along with Hishām b. 'Amr al-Taghlibī and al-Manṣūr observed him in his retinue when he went off to his house. When he had thrown off his robe, al-Rabī' came in and announced Hishām. Al-Manṣūr said, "Has he not just been with me?" and al-Rabī' replied, "He said that he has a request that has become important." So he called for a chair and installed himself on it and then he gave Hishām permission to enter. When he appeared before him he said, "Commander of the Faithful, when I left the retinue and went to my house, my sister, so-and-so, daughter of 'Amr, met me. I saw her beauty, her intelligence and her piety which would please the Commander of the Faithful, so I came to offer her as a gift to him." Al-Manṣūr bowed his head and began to scratch the ground with a cane he had in his hand. "You may go," he said, "and my decision will reach you later." When he left he said, "Al-Rabī', if it were not for a verse of Jarīr's[140] about the Banū Taghlib, I would marry his sister. This was Jarīr's verse:

Do not seek maternal unclehood among the Taghlib;
    even the Zanj are more high-bred than they as maternal
    uncles.

I am afraid she will bear me a son who will be taunted with this verse. But go out and say to him, 'The Commander of the Faithful

140. Jarīr b. 'Aṭiyyah al-Tamīmī, d.c. 110/728–29, the celebrated poet of Umayyad times, active at the courts of al-Ḥajjāj and 'Abd al-Malik and famous for his invective against his great rival al-Farazdaq; see *EI*², s.v. "Djarīr."

says, "I would not refuse you any request except marriage, and, if I had need to marry, I would accept what you offered me, so may [363] God reward you for the good you intended to do for him. Instead of that I have given you the governorate of Sind."' He ordered him to write to the king commanding him to hand over ʿAbdallāh b. Muḥammad and, if he did not obey, to make war on him. He also wrote to ʿUmar b. Ḥafṣ appointing him governor of Ifrīqiyah.

Hishām b. ʿAmr al-Taghlibī left for Sind as governor, and ʿUmar b. Ḥafṣ began to make his way through the provinces to Ifrīqiyah. When Hishām b. ʿAmr reached Sind, he was extremely reluctant to capture ʿAbdallāh and pretended to people that he was writing to the king and treating him gently. Abū Jaʿfar heard about this and he began to write to urge him into action. While this was going on, a group of rebels rose up in a certain part of Sind, so Hishām sent his brother Safannajā against the rebels. He led his army out and his route lay along the borders of that kingdom, and while he was going there appreared a cloud of dust that arose from a troop of horsemen. Safannajā thought that it was the advance guard of the enemy he was attacking, so he sent out scouts.

When they returned, they said, "This is not the enemy you are looking for but ʿAbdallāh b. Muḥammad al-Ashtar al-ʿAlawī riding for pleasure along the banks of the Indus." Safannajā went to meet him, and his advisers said to him, "This is the son of the Prophet of God. You know that your brother is leaving him alone intentionally for fear of shedding his blood. He has not come to attack you but only for pleasure and you have come out seeking someone else; so turn away from him." Safannajā replied, "I will not leave him for any other to capture him, and I will not give up the prospect of gaining favor with al-Manṣūr by taking him and killing him."

He was with ten men, so he rushed toward him and urged on his companions and he attacked him. ʿAbdallāh fought and his companions fought in front of him until ʿAbdallāh and all his companions were killed and not a single one of them escaped to take the news and he was among the slain. His fate was not known, but it is said that his companions hurled him into the [364] Indus when he was killed so that his head would not be taken.[141]

---

141. As a trophy and sent to al-Manṣūr.

Hishām b. ʿAmr wrote a victory letter about this to al-Manṣūr, telling him that he had attacked ʿAbdallāh vigorously, so al-Manṣūr wrote back, praising his conduct and ordering him to make war on the king who had given ʿAbdallāh refuge. This was because ʿAbdallāh had taken slave girls when he was staying with that king, and one of them had given birth to a son, Muḥammad b. ʿAbdallāh, Abū al-Ḥasan Muḥammad al-ʿAlawī, who was known as Ibn al-Ashtar. So Hishām made war on the king until he had conquered his kingdom and killed him. The slave girl of al-Ashtar and her son were sent to al-Manṣūr. Al-Manṣūr wrote to his governor of Medina,[142] telling him that the boy was of true descent. He sent the boy to him and ordered that he should gather all the family of Abū Ṭālib and read them his letter about the true descent of the boy and hand him over to his relations.

In this year al-Manṣūr's son al-Mahdī came to him from Khurāsān in the month of Shawwāl (October 18–November 15, 768). There came to meet him and welcome him many members of his family from Syria, al-Kūfah, al-Baṣrah, and other places. Al-Mahdī rewarded them, gave them robes, and was generous to them, and al-Manṣūr did the same for them. He appointed some of them as courtiers (*ṣaḥābah*)[143] for al-Mahdī and assigned each of them an allowance of five hundred *dirhams*.

In this year al-Manṣūr began the building of al-Ruṣāfah[144] on the east side of the City of Peace for his son Muḥammad al-Mahdī.

The reasons for building it.

According to Aḥmad b. Muḥammad al-Sharawī—his father:
[365] When al-Mahdī came from Khurāsān, al-Manṣūr ordered him to stay on the east bank (of the Tigris) and built al-Ruṣāfah for him, making a wall, a moat, a square,[145] and a garden and he brought water to it. The water used to run from the River of al-Mahdī to al-Ruṣāfah.[146]

---

142. At this time the ʿAlid, al-Ḥasan b. Zayd.

143. *Ṣaḥābah* were advisers and friends permanently attached to an important figure and given salaries. They were often poets and scholars, as opposed to important political or military figures.

144. Al-Ruṣāfah was to form the nucleus of the developments on the east bank of the river. Le Strange, *Baghdad*, 187–98. See also note 54, above.

145. *Maydān* implies a large open space for horse racing and polo, a smaller piazza would have been called a *raḥbah*.

146. A branch of the Khāliṣ Canal; see Le Strange, *Baghdad*, 175.

According to Khālid b. Yazīd b. Wahb b. Jarīr b. Khāzim—Muḥammad b. Mūsā b. Muḥammad b. Ibrāhīm b. Muḥammad b. ʿAlī b. ʿAbdallāh b. ʿAbbās[147]—his father: When the Rāwandiyyah rioted against Abū Jaʿfar and did battle with him at the Golden Gate,[148] Qutham b. al-ʿAbbās b. ʿUbaydallāh b. al-ʿAbbās,[149] who was at that time a very old man, respected by the people, came in to him. Abū Jaʿfar said to him, "What is your opinion about the situation we are in concerning the slowness of the army to help us? I am afraid that they will agree together and this power will slip from our hands. What do you think?"

He replied, "O Commander of the Faithful, I have an idea but if I explain it to you it will not work, but if you let me I will go ahead with it, and your caliphate will be made secure for you and your soldiers will be in awe of you." The caliph asked, "Are you going ahead with a plan for my caliphate that you will not tell me about?"

He said, "If you think I am suspect in regard to your state, do not ask my opinion, but if you think I am faithful to it let me go ahead with my idea."

Al-Manṣūr said, "Go ahead."

Qutham went to his lodging and called a page of his and said to him, "When tomorrow comes, go ahead of me and sit in the palace of the Commander of the Faithful. When you see that I have entered and am in the middle of the people of rank (*aṣḥāb al-marātib*),[150] take hold of the bridle of my mule and stop me and entreat me, by the Prophet of God, by al-ʿAbbās, and by the Commander of the Faithful, to halt, to hear your request, and to fulfill it for you. I will chide you and speak harshly to you, but do not let that make you frightened of me but repeat your request, [366]
and I will curse you, but do not let that intimidate you but repeat

---

147. For Muḥammad b. Ibrāhīm, see note 99, above.

148. The Rāwandiyyah rioted in 141/758–59, three or four years before the beginning of work on Baghdad (see al-Ṭabarī, III, 129–30). The Golden Gate, or Bāb al-Dhahab, was one of the names given to al-Manṣūr's palace in the Round City in Baghdad; see also note 391 below.

149. A distant cousin of the caliph's who was governor of al-Yamāmah in eastern Arabia for many years, until his death in 159/775–76.

150. In formal audiences courtiers lined up in order of precedence or rank before the caliph

your speech and request to me, and I will hit you with my whip, but let that not be unbearable and say to me, 'Which tribe is more noble, al-Yaman or Muḍar?'[151] and when I answer you, let go of the bridle of my mule and you will be a free man."

The page left early in the morning and sat where he had ordered him in the palace of the caliph and, when the old man came, the page did as his master had ordered, and his master did as he had said he would and then he said to him, "Speak!" and he asked, "Which of the two tribes is more noble, al-Yaman or Muḍar?"

Qutham said, "Muḍar among which was the Prophet of God and in which is the Book of God and the House of God (the Kaʿbah) and among which is the caliph of God."

Al-Yaman were resentful that he had mentioned nothing of their honor and one of the commanders of al-Yaman said to him, "The matter is not absolutely like that, with no honor or merit in al-Yaman." Then the Yamanī commander said to his page, "Get up and take the bridle of the old man's mule and restrain it forcibly until he is lowered down."

The page did as his master ordered him, so that he almost brought it down on its hamstrings. Muḍar were annoyed about this and said, "Is he doing this to our old man (*shaykh*)?" and one of them ordered his page "Cut off the hand of the slave," so he came up to the Yamanī's page and cut off his hand. The two tribes began to quarrel and Qutham sent away his mule and went in to Abū Jaʿfar. The army split into groups, Muḍar being a group, al-Yaman another, the Khurāsāniyyah[152] another, and Rabīʿah another, and Qutham said to Abū Jaʿfar, "I have split your army into groups and divided them into parties, each one fearing that, if it does any evil to you, you will strike it with the other. It remains to you to organize the rest."

---

151. Muḍar, al-Yaman, and Rabīʿah were the large groupings to which Arab tribes were traditionally assigned. Under the Umayyad caliphate these divisions had become a major source of conflict, and this continued, though to a lesser extent, under the ʿAbbāsids. The word used for tribe here is *ḥayy*, while the smaller tribes that made up the group might be called *qabīlah* (pl. *qabāʾil*), but the usages are not always consistent (cf. *EI*², s.v. "Ḥayy," where it is defined as the smallest unit).

152. Interestingly, the Khurāsāniyyah are considered here as a group with a separate indentity, though many of them in fact came from Arab tribes attached in theory to one of the other groups.

Al-Manṣūr asked, "What is that?" and he replied, "Cross your son over and settle him on the other side (of the Tigris) in a palace and move him over and move over some of your army with him, and make that a town and this a town. If the people of this side turn against you, you can strike them with the people of the other side, and, if the people of the other side turn against you, you can strike them with the people of this side. If Muḍar turn against you, you can strike them with al-Yaman and Rabīʿah and the Khurāsāniyyah, and, if al-Yaman turn against you you can strike them with Muḍar and others who obey you." [367]

He accepted his idea and opinion, and his power was firmly established. This was the reason for building on the east side and in al-Ruṣāfah and the granting of property to commanders there.

Ṣāliḥ Ṣāḥib al-Muṣallā[153] was put in charge of the plots on the east side, and he did as Abū al-ʿAbbās al-Ṭūsī had done about distributing the remaining[154] plots on the west bank. He had for himself building plots at the Gate of the Bridge, the market of Yaḥyā, the mosque of Khuḍayr and in al-Ruṣāfah and the Road of the Skiffs on the Tigris,[155] which he asked for as a gift from the plots that were undistributed among owners. Ṣāliḥ came from the people of Khurāsān.

In this year al-Manṣūr caused the oath of allegiance to himself, to his son Muḥammad al-Mahdī after him, and to ʿĪsā b. Mūsā after al-Mahdī to be renewed by all the people of his family in his audience on Friday. He gave them a general permission to enter, and every one who took the oath to him kissed his hand and the hand of al-Mahdī and then pressed the hand of ʿĪsā b. Mūsā but did not kiss it.

In this year ʿAbd al-Wahhāb b. Ibrāhīm b. Muḥammad led the summer raid (against the Byzantines).

---

153. A high-ranking palace servant; from his title he would seem to have been in charge of the caliph's oratory, but he seems actually to have been employed extensively as a financial administrator, and (p. 82, below) he was a friend of Khālid b. Barmak. He served al-Mahdī, Hārūn, and al-Amīn and is last recorded in 202/817–18, among the opponents of al-Ma'mūn in Baghdad (see al-Ṭabarī, III, 1016).

154. See note 21, above.

155. Le Strange, *Baghdad*, 197–99. The word for skiffs is *zawāriq* (sing., *zawraq*).

In this year ʿUqbah b. Salm left al-Baṣrah, where he left his son Nāfiʿ b. ʿUqbah in charge, for al-Baḥrayn[156] and killed Sulaymān
[368] b. Ḥakīm al-ʿAbdī[157] and took prisoner the people of al-Baḥrayn. He sent some of those he captured and made prisoner to Abū Jaʿfar, who killed some of them and gave the rest to al-Mahdī, who was generous to them, released them, and attired each of them with two Marw cloaks. Then ʿUqbah b. Salm was deposed from al-Baṣrah.

According to Afrīk, the slave girl of Asad b. al-Marzbān: Al-Manṣūr sent Asad b. al-Marzbān to ʿUqbah b. Salm to al-Baḥrayn when he executed those he executed to investigate his affairs. Asad got on well with ʿUqbah and did not examine him in depth and did not expose him fully. Abū Jaʿfar heard about this and that Asad had taken money from him so he sent Abū Suwayd al-Khurāsānī,[158] a friend and brother of his, to him. When Asad saw him coming on the post, he was happy. He was in the neighborhood of ʿUqbah's camp and greeted him and said, "My friend." Abū Suwayd stopped by him, and he jumped up to stand by him. Abū Suwayd said (in Persian) "Sit down, sit down," so he sat down and he asked, "Are you heeding and obeying?" "Yes," replied Asad. "Stretch out your hand." So he stretched it out and Abū Suwayd struck it and cut if off. Then he stretched out his leg. then his hand, and then his leg until all four were cut off. Then he said, "Stretch out your neck," so he stretched it out, and his head was cut off. Afrīk said: I took his head and kept it, but he took it from me and brought it to Abū Jaʿfar. Afrīk never again ate meat until her death.

Al-Wāqidī claimed that Abū Jaʿfar appointed Maʿn b. Zāʾidah[159] to Sijistān in this year.

---

156. Al-Baḥrayn at this time referred not just to the island now known by that name but also to the mainland areas opposite (around modern Dhahran). The island itself was called Uwāl at this time; see Yāqūt, *Muʿjam*, I, 274, 346–49.

157. Nothing else is known of him. He came from ʿAbd al-Qays, an Arab tribe powerful in al-Baḥrayn since pre-Islamic times.

158. According to Balādhurī, he was sent by ʿUqbah b. Salm on the orders of Abū Jaʿfar. Ibn al-Athīr says that his son Suwayd was governor of al-Baḥrayn in 169/785–86.

159. Al-Shaybānī, an almost legendary figure at the court of al-Manṣūr, many picturesque anecdotes were recorded about him. He had supported the Umayyads at the time of the ʿAbbāsid Revolution and claimed to have killed Qaḥṭabah,

The leader of the pilgrims in this year was Muḥammad b. Ibrāhīm b. Muḥammad b. 'Alī b. 'Abdallāh b. 'Abbās. The governor of Mecca and al-Ṭā'if was Muḥammad b. Ibrāhīm. Al-Ḥasan b. Zayd was in charge of Medina, Muḥammad b. Sulaymān b. 'Alī of al- [369]
Kūfah, Jābir b. Tūbah al-Kilābī[160] of al-Baṣrah, with Sawwār b. 'Abdallāh over the judiciary, and Yazīd b. Ḥātim was over Egypt.

---

leader of the 'Abbāsid armies. Al-Manṣūr restored him to favor as a reward for his help against the Rāwandiyyah rebels. He was later appointed as governor of Yemen in 142/759–60 and Sīstān in 151/768 and was assassinated in the latter in the next year. He was important as a patron of poets, notably Marwān b. Abī Ḥafṣah, and as a symbol of old Arab bedouin qualities (al-Ṭabarī, II, 16, 63, 129–30, 368, 369, 394–97; *'Uyūn*, 229, 264; Ya'qūbī, *Tārīkh*, II, 448, 462, Crone, *Slaves*, 169–70; *EI*², s.v. "Ma'n b. Zā'idah."

160. According to Iṣfahānī, *Maqātil*, 322, he had sent Abū Ja'far to al-Baṣrah to oppose the 'Alid revolt of 145/762–63; he is otherwise unknown.

The Events of the Year 152

(January 14, 769–January 3, 770)

Among these was the assassination of Ma'n b. Zā'idah al-Shaybānī by the Khawārij in Bust[161] in Sijistān.

In this year Ḥumayd b. Qaḥṭabah raided Kābul.[162] Al-Manṣūr had appointed him governor of Khurāsān in 152.

It is said that 'Abd al-Wahhāb b. Ibrāhīm led the summer expedition but that he did not go through the passes. It is also said that Muḥammad b. Ibrāhīm led the summer expedition in this year.

In this year al-Manṣūr dismissed Jābir b. Tūbah from al-Baṣrah and appointed Yazīd b. Manṣūr[163] as governor.

---

161. One of the most important towns in Sīstān, on the Helmand river, some sixty miles west of Kandahar in the south of modern Afghanistan; see Yāqūt, *Mu'jam*, I, 414–19; Le Strange, *Lands*, 344–45.

162. Capital of modern Afghanistan. Although repeatedly raided by the Muslims, Kābul was never incorporated permanently into the caliphate.

163. He was al-Mahdī's maternal uncle, brother to Arwā, wife of al-Manṣūr and mother of al-Mahdī and Ja'far the elder. He came from Yemen, of which he was later governor. He was a close adviser to al-Mahdī as caliph but died in 163/779–80.

In this year Abū Ja'far killed Hāshim b. al-Ishtākhanj,[164] who had mutinied and raised a rebellion in Ifrīqiyah. He and Abū Khālid al-Marwarrūdhī[165] were brought to Abū Ja'far, and he killed Ibn al-Ishtākhanj at Qādisiyyah[166] while he was on the way to Mecca.

The leader of the pilgrims in this year was al-Manṣūr. It is said that he set out from the City of Peace in the month of Ramaḍān and that neither Muḥammad b. Sulaymān, his governor of al-Kūfah at that time, nor 'Īsā b. Mūsā nor anyone else in al-Kūfah knew that he had set out until he was nearly there.

In this year Yazīd b. Ḥātim was dismissed from Egypt, and [370] Muḥammad b. Sa'īd was appointed as governor.[167]

The governors of the main cities (*amṣār*) in this year were the same as in the previous year except al-Baṣrah, where the governor was Yazīd b. Manṣūr, and Egypt, where the governor in this year was Muḥammad b. Sa'īd.

---

164. Otherwise unknown except for a reference in Jāḥiẓ, *Manāqib al-Turk*, where the Khurāsāniyyah boast of his prowess.

165 From Marw al-Rūdh in Khurāsān, an early supporter of the 'Abbāsid Revolution, he and the Marwarrūdhiyyah had a quarter in Baghdad. He and Hāshim seem to have represented "rank and file" opinion among the Khurāsāniyyah, and neither held government office. Abū Khālid survived this incident and was one of the leaders of the Khurāsāniyyah who demanded the removal of 'Īsā b. Mūsā from the succession. He is last recorded in 171/787–88, but his son Muḥammad was to be one of the leaders of the Khurāsāniyyah in the civil wars that followed the death of Hārūn (al-Ṭabarī, II, 2004, III, 21, 455, 606; Yāq'ūbī, *Buldān*, 247)

166. About ten miles southeast of al-Kūfah on the road to Mecca (Yāqūt, *Mu'jam*, IV, 391–93; Le Strange, *Lands*, 76).

167. The governors of Egypt given by al-Ṭabarī at this period differ from those recorded by the local historian al-Kindī. It seems that al-Ṭabarī recorded the names given in the records of the financial administration in Baghdad, whereas al-Kindī gives those of the prayer leaders and military commanders; see Kennedy, "Provincial Elites," 33–34, n. 46.

The Events of the Year 153

(January 4, 770–December 23, 770)

In this year al-Manṣūr prepared a naval expedition to fight the Kurk when he reached al-Baṣrah, returning from Mecca after completing the pilgrimage. The Kurk had sacked Jeddah and when he reached al-Baṣrah in this year he prepared an army to fight them. It is said that he stayed at the Great Bridge when he was there.[168] This was his last visit to al-Baṣrah, although it is said that his last visit was in 155 (771–72); his first visit was in 145 (752–53). He stayed there for forty days and built a palace before he left for the City of Peace.

In this year al-Manṣūr was angry with Abū Ayyūb al-Mūryānī[169] and imprisoned him and his brother and his brother's sons, Saʿīd, Masʿūd, Mukhallad, and Muḥammad, and demanded restitution

168. Great Bridge at al-Baṣrah.

169. Sulaymān b. Ayyūb, from the village of Mūryān in Khūzistān. A confidant and adviser to al-Manṣūr, he had helped plan the assassination of Abū Muslim. He became vizier, and he and his family amassed vast estates and had a bad reputation for taking bribes and financial oppression (al-Ṭabarī, III, 108; al-Jahshiyārī, 97–121; Sourdel, *Vizirat*, I, 78–87).

from them. Their dwellings were at al-Manāthir. It is said that the reason for his anger against him was the intrigue of Abān b. Ṣadaqah, Abū Ayyūb's secretary, against him.

In this year 'Umar b. Ḥafṣ b. 'Uthmān b. Abī Ṣufrah was killed in Ifrīqiyah by Abū Ḥātim al-'Ibāḍi and Abū 'Ād and those Berbers [371] who were with them. It was said that they were 350,000 in number, of whom 35,000 were horsemen. Abū Qurrah al-Ṣufrī was with them with 40,000 men; forty days previously he had been acknowledged as caliph.[170]

In this year 'Abbād, freedman of al-Manṣūr, Harthamah b. A'yan, and Yūsuf b. 'Ulwān[171] were brought from Khurāsān in chains because of their support for 'Īsā b. Mūsā.

In this year al-Manṣūr urged the people to wear extremely tall *qalansūwahs*,[172] which they used to keep up, it was said, by putting canes inside. Abū Dulāmah[173] said,

We used to look to the *imām* for increase (in donations)
  but so the chosen *imām* increased *qalansūwahs*.
You will see them on the heads of men looking like
  a Jew's wine jugs covered with cloaks.

In this year 'Ubayd b. bt. Abī Laylā,[174] judge of al-Kūfah, died and was replaced by Sharīk b. 'Abdallāh al-Nakha'ī.[175]

The leader of the summer expedition this year was Ma'yūf b.

---

170. Abū Ḥātim, Abū 'Ād, and Abū Qurrah were the Khārijite leaders of this largely Berber rebellion (Ibn Idhārī, *Bayān*, 74–75; Kennedy, *'Abbasid Caliphate*, 187–91).

171. Neither 'Abbād nor Yūsuf is recorded elsewhere. Harthamah b. A'yan was to achieve great power as a trusted servant of Hārūn and played a central role in the civil war that followed Hārūn's death (Crone, *Slaves*, 177–78).

172. See above, note 52.

173. Zand b. al-Jawn, d. ca. 160/776–77; he was a sort of court jester for the first three 'Abbāsid caliphs, famous for his outrageous humor and doubtful religious views. He is also quoted in al-Ṭabarī, III, 541. See *Aghānī*, Būlāq, IX, 120; Beirut, X, 247; *EI*², s.v. "Abū Dulāma."

174. That is 'Ubayd, son of the daughter of Abū Laylā. Ibn Abī Laylā was *qāḍī* of al-Kūfah under the last Umayyads and was reappointed by 'Īsā b. Mūsā after the 'Abbāsid Revolution. For the family, see *EI*², s.v. "Ibn Abī Laylā," but nothing more seems to be known of 'Ubayd.

175. Born in Bukhārā in 75/694–95, died in Ahwāz, where he was *qāḍī*, in 177/793–94 (Ibn Khallikan, I, 622). Later, it seems, he combined the offices of *qāḍī* and governor in al-Kūfah, most unusual for this period (see below, pp. 168–69).

Yaḥyā al-Ḥajūrī.[176] He attacked a Byzantine fortress by night when its inhabitants were asleep. He captured the garrison and took them prisoner before going on to Burnt Laodiceia,[177] which he took, taking 6,000 prisoners beside mature men.

In this year al-Manṣūr appointed Bakkār b. Muslim al-ʿUqaylī governor of Armenia.

Muḥammad al-Mahdī, son of Abū Jaʿfar, led the pilgrimage this year.

At that time Muḥammad b. Ibrāhīm was in charge of Mecca and al-Ṭā'if, al-Ḥasan b. Zayd b. al-Ḥasan of Medina, Muḥammad b. Sulaymān of al-Kūfah, Yazīd b. Manṣūr of al-Baṣrah, with Sawwār
[372] in charge of the judiciary there, and Muḥammad b. Saʿīd was in charge of Egypt. Al-Wāqidī mentioned that Yazīd b. Manṣūr was governor of Yemen for Abū Jaʿfar al-Manṣūr in this year.

---

176. Brooks, "Byzantines and Arabs," 734; Maʿyūf led the summer expedition again in 158/775 and 169/785–86 and a naval raid on Cyprus in 191/807. Ḥajūr was a branch of Ḥamdān, well established in Syria (see al-Ṭabarī, III, 385, 568, 711).

177. Laodikeia Katakekaumene, northwest of Iconium, on the road to Amorion.

The Events of the Year 154

(December 24, 770–December 12, 771)

Among these was the expedition of al-Manṣūr to Syria and his visit to Jerusalem. He sent Yazīd b. Ḥātim to Ifrīqiyah with 50,000 men, it was said, to fight the Khawārij who were there and who killed his governor ʿUmar b. Ḥafṣ. It was said that he spent 63,000,000 *dirhams* on that army.

In this year, it is said, al-Manṣūr decided on the building of the city of al-Rāfiqah.[178]

According to Muḥammad b. Jābir—his father: When Abū Jaʿfar wished to build it, the people of al-Raqqah opposed him and wanted to make war on him, saying that it would ruin their markets, take away their livelihood, and reduce the size of their dwellings. He was anxious about fighting them and sent to a monk in a monastery there and asked him if he had any knowledge that a man would build a city there. He replied that he had been informed

178. On the Euphrates by al-Raqqah, it soon merged with the older city, and the whole became known as al-Raqqah; for the design of the city and outlines of the walls, which are still visible, see Creswell, *Early Muslim Architecture*, II.

that a man called Miqlāṣ would build it, so al-Manṣūr said, "I, by God, am Miqlāṣ."[179]

Muḥammad b. ʿUmar (al-Wāqidī) mentioned that a thunderbolt fell this year in the Mosque of the Ḥarām,[180] killing five people.

In this year Abū Ayyūb al-Mūryānī and his brother Khālid perished. Al-Manṣūr ordered Mūsā b. Dīnār,[181] the chamberlain of Abū al-ʿAbbās al-Ṭūsī, to cut off the hands of the nephews of Abū Ayyūb and their legs and their heads, and he wrote to that effect to al-Mahdī. Mūsā did that and carried out what he had been ordered to do to them.

[373] In this year ʿAbd al-Malik b. Ẓabyān al-Numayrī[182] was appointed governor of al-Baṣrah.

Zufar b. ʿĀsim al-Hilālī[183] led the summer expedition in this year and reached the Euphrates.

Muḥammad b. Ibrāhīm led the pilgrims this year; he was Abū Jaʿfar's governor of Mecca and al-Ṭā'if. Al-Ḥasan b. Zayd was governor of Medina, Muḥammad b. Sulaymān of al-Kūfah, ʿAbd al-Malik b. Ayyūb b. Ẓabyān was in charge of al-Baṣrah, with Sawwār b. ʿAbdallāh (in charge) of its judiciary, Hishām b. ʿAmr was in charge of Sind, Yazīd b. Ḥātim of Ifrīqiyah and Muḥammad b. Saʿīd of Eygpt.

---

179. This prophecy also appears in connection with the foundation of Baghdad and is discussed in Lassner, *ʿAbbasid Rule*, 164–65. The word *miqlāṣ* is said to mean a "fat she-camel." See Lane, s.v. *qlṣ*.

180. In Mecca.

181. Unknown elsewhere.

182. Properly ʿAbd al-Malik b. Ayyūb b. Ẓabyān. He was briefly governor of al-Baṣrah a second time in 159/775–76 but is not recorded elsewhere.

183. Brooks, "Byzantines and Arabs," 734; Zufar's father had been governor of Armenia for the Umayyad caliph Marwān b. Muḥammad. He himself joined the rebellion of ʿAbdallāh b. ʿAlī against al-Manṣūr. He led the *ṣā'ifah* several times and was governor of Medina in 160–63/776–80 and, according to Azdī, *Tārīkh*, 243–44, briefly of al-Jazīrah thereafter (see al-Ṭabarī, III, 94, 378, 482, 500; Crone, *Slaves*, 166).

The Events of the Year 155

(December 13, 771–December 1, 772)

Among these was Yazīd b. Ḥātim's conquest of Ifrīqiyah and his killing of Abū ʿĀd and Abū Ḥātim and their supporters. The lands of the Maghrib became peaceful, and Yazīd b. Ḥātim entered Qayrawān.[184]

In this year al-Manṣūr sent his son al-Mahdī to build the city of al-Rāfiqah. He went there and built it with the same gates, arcades (*fuṣūl*), squares, and streets as Baghdad. He built the walls and dug the moat and then departed for his city.[185]

In this year, according to Muḥammad b. ʿUmar, Abū Jaʿfar dug moats around al-Kūfah and al-Baṣrah and constructed walls for them.[186] He paid for the expenses of the walls and moats out of the wealth of their inhabitants.

In this year al-Manṣūr dismissed ʿAbd al-Malik b. Ayyūb b.

---

184. See Ibn Idhārī, *Bayān*, 78–82, for a fuller account.

185. I.e., al-Rusāfah. In what sense the plan of al-Rāfiqah resembled that of Baghdad is not clear; certainly the surviving walls show an irregular plan very different from the round plan of Baghdad.

186. These towns seem to have been unfortified before this date.

Ẓabyān from al-Baṣrah and appointed as governor al-Haytham b Mu'āwiyah al-'Atakī[187] and attached Sa'īd b. Da'laj to him.[188]
[374] He ordered him to build walls to surround the city and a moat outside the walls using the wealth of its people, so he did this.

It is said that, when al-Manṣūr wanted to order the building of the walls of al-Kūfah and the digging of the moat, he ordered that each of the people of al-Kūfah should be given five *dirhams* to find out how many there were of them. When he knew the number, he ordered forty *dirhams* to be collected from each person, and when this was done he directed that the money should be spent on the walls of al-Kūfah and the digging of the moat. Their poet said:

O my people, look what came to us
from the Commander of the Faithful.
He distributed five to us
and collected forty.

In this year the Byzantine emperor sought peace from al-Manṣūr on condition that he paid the poll tax.[189]

The leader of the summer expedition in this year was Yazīd b. Usayd al-Sulamī.[190]

In this year al-Manṣūr dismissed his brother al-'Abbās b. Muḥammad from al-Jazīrah, fined him heavily, was angry with him, and imprisoned him.

According to one of the Banū Hāshim: Al-Manṣūr appointed al-'Abbās b. Muḥammad as governor of al-Jazīrah after Yazīd b.

187. Al-Khurāsānī; he had been governor of Mecca in 140–43/758–61 and possessed properties in Baghdad, both inside and outside the Round City. Al-Ṭabarī (III, 129) reports that the Rāwandiyyah considered that he was the incarnation of the Angel Gabriel, but it is difficult to know quite what to make of this information.

188. Al-Tamīmī; he was later governor of al-Baḥrayn, Ṭabaristān and Rūyyān, and Sīstān for short periods and disappears from the record after 164/780–81.

189. Brooks, "Byzantines and Arabs," 734. Al-Ṭabarī uses the word *jizyah*, the name given to the poll tax paid by non-Muslim subjects of the caliph.

190. His father was a comrade in arms of Marwān, the last Umayyad caliph, his mother the daughter of the Christian patrician of Sīsajān in the Caucasus. His career was spent largely on the Byzantine and Caucasus frontiers. He was governor of Armenia in the reign of al-Saffāḥ and became a trusted adviser of Abū Ja'far; he disappears from the historical record after 162/779 (al-Ṭabarī, III, 81, 493; al-Balādhurī, *Futūḥ*, trans., 322, 328).

Usayd. Then he was angry with him and continued to be angry with him so that his anger extended to one of his paternal uncles of the children of ʿAlī b. ʿAbdallāh b. ʿAbbās, either Ismāʿīl b. ʿAlī or someone else. His family, his uncles, and their women took it in turns to speak to him on his behalf and put pressure on him so that he was restored to favor.

ʿĪsā b. Mūsā said, "O Commander of the Faithful, look at the family of ʿAlī b. ʿAbdallāh! Your generosity to them was abundant and they returned it with envy toward us, and for that reason you were angry with Ismāʿīl b. ʿAlī for some days and they put pressure on you. You have been angry with al-ʿAbbās b. Muḥammad for such-and-such a time, but I have not seen any of them [375] intercede with you on his behalf," so he called al-ʿAbbās b. Muḥammad and restored him to favor.[191]

When Yazīd b. Usayd was dismissed by al-ʿAbbās from al-Jazīrah, he complained to Abū Jaʿfar about al-ʿAbbās, saying that his brother had done evil by dismissing him and had insulted his honor. Al-Manṣūr replied, "Consider whether my goodness to you and my brother's evil to you balance each other out."

Yazīd b. Usayd said, "O Commander of the Faithful, if your goodness were only to balance with your evil, then our obedience would be given to you as a mere courtesy."

In this year al-Manṣūr put Mūsā b. Kaʿb[192] in charge of the military and fiscal administration of al-Jazīrah.[193]

---

191. ʿĪsā b. Mūsā is expressing the rivalry in the ʿAbbāsid family between the descendants of Muḥammad b. ʿAlī, who included al-Saffāḥ, al-Manṣūr, and their brothers, and the families of the other sons of ʿAlī b. ʿAbdallāh. For the political background, see Lassner, *ʿAbbasid Rule*, 19–38.

192. This presents problems. Al-Ṭabarī, III, 138, states clearly that Mūsā b Kaʿb died in 141/758–59, and he is not recorded after this date, except III, 383, where his deposition from al-Jazīrah is noted. Al-Azdī, *Tārīkh*, has Mūsā b. Kaʿb appointed to al-Jazīrah in 154 and deposed in 155 (771–72) but Muṣʿab as governor at the death of Abū Jaʿfar (Azdī, 222–26). Michael the Syrian records the appointment of Mūsā b. Muṣʿab sub anno 1083 (trans. Chabot, III, 526), which is the equivalent of 155/772. His exactions in al-Jazīrah provoked the long diatribe in the history of Pseudo Dionysius of Tell Mahré (*Chronique*, trans. Chabot, see the discussion in Cahen, "Fiscalité"). Mūsā b. Muṣʿab later became governor of Egypt, where his oppressions were equally severe and led to his death in 168/785 (al-Kindī, 124). It seems most likely that Mūsā b. Muṣʿab should be read for Mūsā b. Kaʿb in both al-Ṭabarī and al-Azdī. See Crone, *Slaves*, 186.

193. He was in charge of *ḥarb* and *kharāj*. This unusual formula may mean that

In this year, according to some sources, al-Manṣūr dismissed Muḥammad b. Sulaymān b. 'Alī from al-Kūfah and appointed 'Amr b. Zuhayr, brother of al-Musayyab b. Zuhayr, in his place. 'Umar b. Shabbah,[194] on the other hand, holds that he dismissed Muḥammad b. Sulaymān from al-Kūfah in 153 (770) and appointed 'Amr b. Zuhayr al-Ḍabbī, brother of al-Musayyab b. Zuhayr, as governor in that year and that it was he who dug the moat round al-Kūfah.

The reasons for the dismissal of Muḥammad b. Sulaymān b. 'Alī:

It is said that 'Abd al-Karīm b. Abī al-'Awjā',[195] the maternal uncle of Ma'n b. Zā'idah, was brought before Muḥammad b. Sulaymān when he was governor of al-Kūfah and he ordered his imprisonment.

According to Abū Zayd[196]—Qutham b. Ja'far and al-Ḥusayn b. Ayyūb and others: Many people interceded for him in the City of Peace and importuned Abū Ja'far, and, since everyone who interceded on his behalf was suspect, he wrote to Muḥammad ordering him to leave him alone so that he might come to an opinion about him.

[376] Ibn Abī al-'Awjā' spoke to Abū al-Jabbār,[197] who was an intimate of Abū Ja'far and Muḥammad and then of their sons after them, and said, "If the Amīr delays (punishing me) for three days there will be 100,000 *dirhams* for him and you yourself will get such and such." Abū al-Jabbār told Muḥammad about this and he said, "You have reminded me about him, by God, for I had forgotten him. When I leave Friday prayers, remind me about him." When he left he reminded him and he summoned Ibn Abī al-'Awjā' and ordered him to be beheaded. When he was certain that he would be killed, he said, "But if you kill me, by God I have invented four thousand traditions of the Prophet in which I forbid which is

he was not in charge of the prayers (*ṣalāt*) as well and that he was a military fiscal agent, rather than full governor.

194. The important historian and compiler 'Umar b. Shabbah, d. 262/876, who wrote on the 'Alid rebellions of 145/762 and the early 'Abbāsid caliphs; see *Fihrist*, 246–47.

195. Crone, *Slaves*, 169; Vajda, *Les Zindiqs*, 169.

196. I.e., 'Umar b. Shabbah.

197. Not known elsewhere.

lawful and make lawful what is forbidden. By God I have made you break fast when you should be fasting and fast when you should be breaking your fast!" So he was beheaded.

Then Abū Ja'far's messenger arrived with his letter to Muḥammad, "Be careful what you do in the case of Ibn Abī al-'Awjā'! If you have taken action (against him) I will do this and that," threatening him. Muḥammad said to the messenger, "This is the head of Ibn Abī al-'Awjā' and his body is crucified in al-Kunāsah,[198] so inform the Commander of the Faithful what I have told you."

When the messenger reached Abū Ja'far he was furious and ordered that a letter be written dismissing him and he said, "By God, I considered killing him for Ibn Abī al-'Awjā'." Then he sent for 'Īsā b. 'Alī and when he came to him he said, "This is your doing. You advised me to appoint this youth as governor so I appointed him, an ignorant young man with no knowledge of what he perpetrates in daring to kill a man without asking my opinion about him and waiting for my orders. I have written ordering his dismissal and, by God, I will do this and that," threatening him.

'Īsā remained silent until his anger had subsided and then he said, "O Commander of the Faithful, Muḥammad only killed this man on account of his *Zandaqah*.[199] If his killing was right then the credit goes to you and if it was wrong the responsibility is Muḥammad's. By God, O Commander of the Faithful, if you depose him for acting as he did, he will go with praise and reputation [377] and the common people will criticize you." So he ordered that the letters be torn up and that he be confirmed in his post.

One source said that al-Manṣūr only deposed Muḥammad b. Sulaymān from al-Kūfah because of some evil matters that he heard he was accused of. The man who informed him of that was al-Musāwir b. Sawwār al-Jarmī,[200] his chief of police, about whom Ḥammād said:

198. An open place, a traditional site for executions in al-Kūfah.

199. That is to say, his alleged Manichaean tendencies. It seems that the term *zandaqah* was used fairly generally at this time for different sorts of atheism or attacks on Islam, and it often carried the death penalty.

200. Not known elsewhere.

Do you not consider it one of the wonders of the age
that I am afraid and on my guard against the authority of Jarm?[201]

In this year also al-Manṣūr dismissed al-Ḥasan b. Zayd from Medina and appointed 'Abd al-Ṣamad b. 'Alī as its governor, and he appointed Fulayḥ b. Sulaymān with him to supervise him.[202] Muḥammad b. Ibrāhīm b. Muḥammad was in charge of Mecca and al-Ṭā'if, 'Amr b. Zuhayr of al-Kūfah, al-Haytham b. Mu'āwiyah of al-Baṣrah, Yazīd b. Ḥātim of Ifrīqiyah and Muḥammad b. Sa'īd of Egypt.

---

201. A branch of Quḍā'ah. Ḥammād was Ḥammād b. Yaḥyā b. 'Amr, known as Ḥammād 'Ajrad (or "naked Ḥammād"). He was known for his poems of invective against his greater rival Bashshār b. Burd and was patronized by al-Manṣūr but particularly attached to Muḥammad b. Abī al-'Abbās. See *Aghānī*, Būlāq, XIII, 73; Beirut, XIV, 304; *EI*², s.v. "Ḥammād."

202. 'Abd al-Ṣamad's relations with al-Manṣūr and al-Mahdī were often stormy (cf. p. 214, below), which is why the caliph took the unusual step of appointing Fulayḥ (otherwise unknown) as a *mushrif*, or supervisor, for him.

The Events of the Year 156

(December 1, 772–November 20, 773)

Among these was the capture by al-Haytham b. Muʿāwiyah, Abū Jaʿfar's governor of al-Baṣrah, of ʿAmr b. Shaddād,[203] Ibrāhīm b. ʿAbdallāh's governor of Fārs, and he was executed in al-Baṣrah and crucified.

The reason for this:

According to ʿUmar—Muḥammad b. Maʿrūf—his father: ʿAmr b. Shaddād struck one of his servants who came to the governor, either Ibn Daʿlaj or al-Haytham b. Muʿāwiyah and led him to [378] him. The governor arrested him and executed him and crucified him in the Mirbad,[204] on the site of the house of Isḥāq b. Sulaymān. ʿAmr was a mawlā of the Banū Jumaḥ.

One source says that al-Haytham b. Muʿāwiyah arrested him and left for the City of Peace and stayed in a palace of his on the

203. In the rebellion of 145/762–63, he had taken over Fārs with thirty men in the name of the ʿAlid rebel Ibrāhīm b. ʿAbdallāh. On the death of Ibrāhīm he fled to Kirmān and then went into hiding in al-Baṣrah (al-Ṭabarī, III, 287, al-Iṣfahānī, *Maqātil*, 330–31).

204. The principal open space and meeting place in al-Baṣrah.

banks of the river known as the Nahr Ma'qil.[205] The post(man) came from Abū Ja'far with a letter to al-Haytham b. Mu'āwiyah ordering him to hand over 'Amr b. Shaddād to him, which al-Haytham did. He took him to al-Baṣrah and then to the district of al-Raḥbah, where he was kept in solitary confinement for interrogation, but no useful information was obtained from him, so he cut off his hands and his legs and he was beheaded and crucified in the Mirbad of al-Baṣrah.

In this year al-Manṣūr dismissed al-Haytham b. Mu'āwiyah from al-Baṣrah and its offices and appointed Sawwār b. 'Abdallāh al-Qāḍī in charge of the prayers, so that he was responsible for the prayers and the judiciary, and al-Manṣūr appointed Sa'īd b. Da'laj in charge of the police and the *aḥdāth* there.[206]

In this year, after being dismissed from al-Baṣrah, al-Haytham b. Mu'āwiyah died suddenly in the City of Peace, while he was having sexual intercourse with a slave girl of his. Al-Manṣūr prayed over his body, and he was buried in the cemetery of the Banū Hāshim.[207]

In this year the summer expedition was led by Zufar b. 'Āṣim al-Hilālī.

The leader of the pilgrims in this year was al-'Abbās b. Muḥammad b. 'Alī. The governor of Mecca was Muḥammad b. Ibrāhīm,[208] but he stayed in the City of Peace and his son Ibrāhīm b. Muḥammad was his deputy in Mecca with al-Ṭā'if. 'Amr b. Zuhayr was

205. One of the main canals of al-Baṣrah, connecting the city with the Tigris; see Le Strange, *Lands*, 44, 46.

206. It is not clear what the reason was for the division of the functions of the governorship of al-Baṣrah at this time. There seem to have been four or more elements, the leading of the prayers with the giving of the *khuṭbah*, or Friday sermon; the *qaḍā'*, or judiciary; the *shuraṭ* (pl. of *shurṭah*), meaning police but cf. note 17 above; and the *aḥdāth*. *Aḥdāth* at this stage means "incidents," presumably any matter that required the governor to take action. In later centuries the word came to mean "young men." I am indebted to Professor I. Abbas for putting me right on this matter.

207. The cemetery of the Banū Hāshim is probably to be identified with the Cemetery of the Quraysh (at Kāẓimayn, on the west bank, north of the Round City). It is not clear why he was so honored; he was an 'Atakī, that is, he came from a branch of Azd; see note 187, above.

208. According to Ya'qūbī, (*Tārīkh*, II, 498), he was an early governor of Yemen in Hārūn's name, but he is otherwise unknown.

in charge of al-Kūfah, Sa'īd b. Da'laj of the incidents (*aḥdāth*), poll tax[209] (*jawālī*), police, and the tithes[210] of the land of the Arabs in al-Baṣrah, while Sawwār b. 'Abdallāh was in charge of [379] the prayers and the judiciary there. 'Umārah b. Ḥamzah[211] was in charge of the districts of the Tigris, Ahwāz, and Fārs; Hishām b. 'Amr of Kirmān and Sind; Yazīd b. Ḥātim of Ifrīqiyah, and Muḥammad b. Sa'īd of Egypt.

209. The word for poll tax here is *jawālī*. See Lane, s.v. *jlw*.

210. *Ṣadaqāt*, another sign of the way in which al-Baṣrah retained its early Islamic administrative institutions; elsewhere in the Muslim world land was usually subject to the *kharāj*, or basic land tax.

211. A mawlā, or freedman, appointed to office by al-Manṣūr. He became governor of al-Baṣrah briefly at the beginning of al-Mahdī's reign but seems to have been most important as a financial administrator. He was a friend of Khālid b. Barmak (see below, p. 82), but others, like the people al-Baṣrah, found him overbearing and corrupt. His period in high office seems to have been short, and he disappears after 160/777 (see Crone, *Slaves*, 195).

The Events of the Year 157

(November 21, 773–November 10, 774)

Among these was that al-Manṣūr began building his palace on the banks of the Tigris, which is called al-Khuld.[212] He divided reponsibility for construction between his freedman al-Rabīʿ and Abān b. Ṣadaqah.

In this year Yaḥyā Abū Zakariyyā' the *muḥtasib* was executed. We have already mentioned the reasons for his execution.[213]

In this year al-Manṣūr moved the markets from the City of Peace to the Karkh Gate and other areas. We have also mentioned the reasons for this previously.[214]

In this year al-Manṣūr appointed Jaʿfar b. Sulaymān as governor of al-Baḥrayn but he never took up office, and Saʿīd b. Daʿlaj was appointed governor in his place and sent his son Tamīm[215] there.

---

212. The name means eternity. It lay to the east of the Round City, between it and the Tigris. See Le Strange, *Baghdad*, 101–5.

213. See above, p. 9.

214. See above, pp. 7–10.

215. In 166/782–83 he appears as governor of Sijistān but is not recorded elsewhere.

In this year al-Manṣūr inspected his army with their weapons and horses at a meeting he held on the banks of the Tigris below Qaṭrabbul.[216] He ordered his family, his relatives, and his courtiers to don their arms that day, and he appeared dressed in a coat of mail and a low Egyptian *qalansūwah* under the helmet.

In this year ʿĀmir b. Ismāʿīl al-Muslī[217] died in the City of Peace. Al-Manṣūr prayed over his body, and he was buried in the cemetery of the Banū Hāshim. [380]

In this year Sawwār b. ʿAbdallāh died and Ibn Daʿlaj prayed over his body. Al-Manṣūr appointed ʿUbaydallāh b. al-Ḥasan b. al-Ḥuṣayn al-ʿAnbarī in his place.[218]

In this year al-Manṣūr constructed the bridge at the Barley Gate.[219] This was achieved by Ḥumayd b. al-Qāsim al-Ṣayrafī[220] on the orders of al-Rabīʿ the chamberlain.

In this year Muḥammad b. Saʿīd the Secretary was dismissed from Egypt and Maṭar, the freedman of Abū Jaʿfar al-Manṣūr,[221] was appointed as governor.

In this year Maʿbad b. al-Khalīl[222] was appointed to Sind, and Hishām b. ʿAmr was dismissed. At this time Maʿbad was in Khurāsān, and his appointment was made by letter.

The summer expedition this year was led by Yazīd b. Usayd al-Sulamī. He sent Sinān, freedman of al-Baṭṭāl to one of the

---

216. The district that included the northwestern quarters of Baghdad, see Le Strange, *Baghdad*, 50–51. "Below" (*dūna*) Qaṭrabbul must mean on the west bank of the Tigris, just north of the Round City.

217. A soldier of no great distinction He served in Egypt and Ifrīqiyah at the beginning of al-Manṣūr's reign and was sent to police al-Kūfah at the time of the ʿAlid revolt of 145/762–63 He had a property near the Kūfah Gate of Baghdad (al-Ṭabarī, III, 302; al-Kindī, *Governors*, 103, 110).

218. That is, over the prayers and the judiciary there. He remained *qāḍī* until 166/782–83 but seems to have been removed from the prayers in 159/775–76, at the beginning of al-Mahdi's reign.

219. This was the lower of the bridges of boats across the Tigris (Le Strange, *Baghdad*, 95).

220. Unknown elsewhere.

221. Al-Kindī does not report his appointment at all He had been a slave bought by Abū Ayyūb al-Mūryānī, who gave him to al-Manṣūr, who employed him in the post before appointing him to Egypt (Crone, *Slaves*, 193)

222. Al-Muzanī. He remained governor for two years until his death in 159/775–76. He did not take the banner of appointment from the caliph in person, as was usual

fortresses, and he took prisoners and booty.[223] Muḥammad b. ʿUmar[224] said that the summer expedition in this year was led by Zufar b. ʿĀṣim.

The leader of the pilgrims this year was Ibrāhīm b. Yaḥyā b. Muḥammad b. ʿAlī b. ʿAbdallāh b. ʿAbbās. Muḥammad b. ʿUmar said that he, meaning this Ibrāhīm, was in charge of Medina, but other sources say that ʿAbd al-Ṣamad b. ʿAlī was in charge there this year. Muḥammad b. Ibrāhīm was in charge of Mecca and al-Ṭā'if, ʿUmārah b. Ḥamzah of Ahwāz and Fārs, Maʿbad b. al-Khalīl of Kirmān and Sind, and Maṭar, freedman of al-Manṣūr, of Egypt.

---

223. Brooks, "Byzantines and Arabs," 734. Al-Baṭṭāl was a semilegendary Muslim hero of the early wars against the Byzantines.

224. Al-Wāqidī.

The Events of the Year 158 [381]

(November 11, 774–October 30, 775)

Among these was al-Manṣūr's sending his son al-Mahdī to al-Raqqah and ordering him to dismiss Mūsā b. Kaʿb[225] from Mosul and appoint Yaḥyā b. Khālid b. Barmak as governor.

According to al-Ḥasan b. Wahb b. Saʿīd[226]—Ṣāliḥ b. ʿAṭiyyah: The circumstances of that were that al-Manṣūr imposed a fine of 3,000,000 (*dirhams*) on Khālid b. Barmak on pain of his life and gave him three days to pay. Khālid said to his son Yaḥyā, "O my little son, I have been mulcted and required to pay what I do not have and he had only done this to take my life. Go to your women and your family and do to them what you would do to them after my death." Then he continued, "Do not let that pre-

225. See note 193, above.

226. Brother of the third-century vizier Sulaymān b. Wahb. This is the only time al-Ṭabarī uses him or the otherwise unknown Ṣāliḥ b. ʿAtiyyah as a source. An abbreviated version of this story appears in Jāḥiẓ, 99–100, where al-Manṣūr's anger is instigated by the vizier Abū Ayyūb al-Mūryānī. In keeping with the author's more romantic presentation, al-Khayzurān, wife of al-Mahdī and mother of al-Hādī and Hārūn, lends Khālid an extremely valuable jewel because of the milk brotherhood between his son al-Faḍl and the young Hārūn.

vent you from going to our brothers and visiting ʿUmārah b. Ḥamzah, Ṣāliḥ, Ṣāḥib al-Muṣallā, and Mubārak al-Turkī[227] to tell them of my position."

According to Ṣāliḥ b. ʿAṭiyyah—Yaḥyā: I came to them and some of them frowned at me but sent money secretly and others would not receive me but sent money after I had gone. I asked permission to see ʿUmārah b. Ḥamzah and I went in and found him in the courtyard of his house facing the wall, and he did not turn his head to me. I greeted him and he replied without warmth. Then he said, "O my son, how is your father?" "Well," I replied; "he sends you greetings and informs you of the fine that has been demanded and asks to borrow 100,000 *dirhams* from you." He made no reply of any sort to me, and my position became awkward and the earth swayed under me.

Then I spoke to him on the matter I had come about, and he
[382] said, "If I can manage anything, I will send it to you." So I went on my way saying to myself, "God curse everything that comes from your haughtiness, your pride, and your arrogance," and I came to my father and told him the news and then said, "I think you relied on ʿUmārah b. Ḥamzah for what he could not be relied on for." By God, I was just saying that when ʿUmārah b. Ḥamzah's messenger arrived with 100,000 *dirhams*. So we collected 2,700,000 *dirhams* in two days, leaving only 300,000 to find to reach our target, and if not we would fail.

By God I was on the bridge of Baghdad, preoccupied and gloomy, when a fortune-teller (relying on the flight of birds) accosted me and said, "The young bird has told you," but I left him behind with heavy heart, so he followed me and seized my bridle and said to me, "You are, by God, much concerned and, by God, God will free you from your anxieties and you will pass this way tomorrow with a banner[228] in your hands." I began to wonder at his words

227. All important figures in the palace and fiscal administration at the end of al-Manṣūr's reign. Mubārak al-Turkī appears again as a leader of the ʿAbbāsid forces against the uprising of al-Ḥusayn b. ʿAlī the ʿAlid in Medina in 169/785–86. He had property on the east bank in Baghdad. The geographer al-Hamadhānī says that he built a stronghold in Qazvīn in central Iran; al-Hamadhānī, 282).

228. That is the *liwāʾ*, which is the symbol of the governorate of a province. See note 113, above.

and he went on, "If that happens, will you give me five thousand *dirhams*?" and I replied "Yes" and if he had said fifty thousand, I would still have agreed because it was so unlikely.

I went on my way and news came to al-Manṣūr of the rebellion in Mosul and the spread of the Kurds in the area, and he asked who should be appointed to deal with it. Al-Musayyab b. Zuhayr, who was a friend of Khālid b. Barmak, said, "I have a suggestion, O Commander of the Faithful, which I do not think you will consider good advice and which I think you will refuse but I will still offer and counsel it." He said, "Speak! I do not think you are being dishonest." I[229] said, "Why do you not despatch someone like Khālid?"

The caliph replied, "Woe to you! Will he be loyal to us after what we have done to him?"

"Yes, O Commander of the Faithful. If you appoint him to that, I will be his guarantor."

"He has it! Let him be brought to me tomorrow." So he was brought and excused the 300,000 still outstanding and appointed. [383]

Yaḥyā said: Then I passed by the fortune-teller who had accosted me and, when he saw me, he said, "I have been waiting for you since this morning." I told him to come with me and he came and I gave him 5,000 *dirhams*.

My father said to me, "O my little son, ʿUmārah is a man of great responsibilities, and he is exposed to many difficulties. Go to him and give him greeting and say to him, 'God has given us the good will of the Commander of the Faithful and he has excused us what remained due from us and has appointed me governor of Mosul and ordered the return of the money I borrowed from you.'"

I came to him and found him in the same position as I had met him in before and I greeted him, but he did not return my greeting and said nothing except "How is your father?" and I replied that he was well and that he said such-and-such and he sat up and said, "Was I only a treasurer for your father from whom he takes when he wants to and returns when he wants to? Go away, won't you?"

---

229. Meaning al-Musayyab; the narrative slips into the first person.

I returned to my father and told him and he said to me, "O my little son, he is ʿUmārah and one does not argue with him."

Khālid remained in charge of Mosul until al-Manṣūr died and Yaḥyā was in charge of Azerbaijān.

According to Aḥmad b. Muḥammad b. Sawwār al-Mawṣilī:[230] We were never in awe of a governor as we were of Khālid b. Barmak, not because of the severity of his judgments or because we experienced tyranny at his hands, but awe was in our breasts.

According to Aḥmad b. Muʿāwiyah b. Bakr al-Bāhilī[231]—his father: Abū Jaʿfar was angry with Mūsā b. Kaʿb, who was his governor of al-Jazīrah and Mosul, so he sent al-Mahdī to al-Raqqah to build al-Rāfiqah and said publicly that he was going to Jerusalem, but he ordered him to pass on and proceed to Mosul. When he reached the town (or al-Balad)[232] he arrested Mūsā b. Kaʿb and put him in chains and appointed Khālid b. Barmak to Mosul in his
[384] place. Al-Mahdī did that and left Khālid in charge of Mosul. Two of Khālid's brothers, al-Ḥasan and Sulaymān, sons of Barmak,[233] set out with him.

Before this, al-Manṣūr had summoned Yaḥyā b. Khālid and said to him, "I have an important command in mind for you and I have chosen you for one of the frontier provinces, so be prepared and do not tell anyone about this until I summon you." He kept the news secret from his father and, when he was waiting at the door with those who were waiting, al-Rabīʿ came out and said, "Yaḥyā b. Khālid!" So he stood up and al-Rabīʿ took him by the hand and brought him in to al-Manṣūr. When he came out before the people, his father being present, he had the banner of Azerbaijān in front of him, and he ordered the people to go with him and they went with him in his retinue and they congratulated him and con-

230. Presumably a local Mosul source, not otherwise used by al-Ṭabarī.

231. Also quoted in al-Ṭabarī, III, 567. His father, Muʿāwiyah, appears as a source (below, p. 146) for an anecdote that can be dated to 145–48/762–66, when Jaʿfar the elder was governor of Mosul. There he quotes from an eyewitness directly; we can probably extrapolate from that that Muʿāwiyah lived before the end of the second century and his son Aḥmad early in the third.

232. Al-Balad can either mean "the town," i.e. Moṣul, or be the name of a small town on the Tigris north of Mosul; see Yāqūt, *Muʿjam*, I, 481; Le Strange, *Lands*, 99.

233. Al-Ḥasan and Sulaymān also accompanied Yaḥyā on the summer expedition of 163/780, when he went with Hārūn (see al-Ṭabarī, III, 497).

gratulated his father Khālid on his appointment and their two offices were joined together. Aḥmad b. Mu'āwiyah said that al-Manṣūr admired Khālid and he used to say, "Khālid gave birth to a son and Yaḥyā gave birth to a father."

In this year al-Manṣūr settled in his palace known as al-Khuld.

In this year al-Manṣūr was angry with al-Musayyab b. Zuhayr and dismissed him from command of the police and ordered that he be imprisoned and chained up. The reason for this was that he had flogged Abān b. Bashīr[234] the Secretary to death because of a grudge he bore him concerning his partnership with his brother 'Amr b. Zuhayr in the governorate of al-Kūfah and the collection of its taxes. In place of al-Musayyab, he appinted al-Ḥakam b. Yūsuf, Commander of the Lances,[235] but then al-Mahdī spoke to his father on behalf of al-Musayyab, and he was restored to favor after he had been in prison for some days and he was given back his command of the police.

In this year al-Manṣūr sent Naṣr b. Ḥarb al-Tamīmī as governor of the frontier regions of Fārs.[236]

In this year al-Manṣūr fell off his mount at Jarjarāyā[237] and fractured his skull between his eyebrows. This was when he had gone out, when he sent his son al-Mahdī to al-Raqqah, to say farewell to him. When he reached a place called Jubb Summāqā[238] he turned aside to Ḥawlāyā[239] and then went on to the Nahrawāns. [385]
He reached, it is said, the sluice gates and the point[240] where the Nahrawān flows into the Diyālā river, and he stayed by the dam there for eighteen days and it wearied him so he went on to

234. Not known elsewhere.

235. Ya'qūbī, *Buldān*, 248, records that he had a property in the Ḥarbiyyah quarter in Baghdad. *Ḥirāb* were small, throwing spears (see Lane, s.v. *ḥrb*), but the title *ṣāḥib al-ḥirāb* is not, to my knowledge, recorded elsewhere. From the context, it must be presumed that he was second-in-command of the *shurṭah*.

236. *Thughūr Fārs*, a curious usage, *thughūr* usually being applied to the Byzantine frontier area. Perhaps it refers to the wild, eastern part of the province, on the Kirmān border.

237. Small town on the Tigris, southeast of Baghdad. See Yāqūt, *Mu'jam*, II, 123; Le Strange, *Lands*, 37.

238. Not noted by Yāqūt or Le Strange. *Jubb* means a well.

239. A village near Nahrawān. See Yāqūt, *Mu'jam*, II, 322.

240. The hydrology of the Nahrawān area is explained in Adams, *Land behind Baghdad*.

Jarjarāyā and went out from it to inspect an estate belonging to ʿĪsā b. ʿAlī there. That day he was thrown from his gray horse and fractured his skull. When he was in Jarjarāyā, Indian prisoners came to him from ʿUmān. They had been sent by Tasnīm b. al-Ḥawārī[241] with his son Muḥammad. He contemplated having them executed, so he interrogated them and what they told him about their affairs confused him and he refrained from killing them and divided them among his commanders and agents (*nuwwāb*).[242]

In this year al-Mahdī came to the City of Peace from al-Raqqah and entered in the month of Ramaḍān (July 5–August 3, 775).

In this year al-Manṣūr ordered the repair of the White Palace, which Chosroes had built, and the fining of all those in whose houses Sasanian brickwork, taken from the buildings of the Chosroes, was found. He said, "This is the booty of the Muslims,"[243] but this was never completed, nor were the repairs to the Palace.

In this year the summer raid was led by Maʿyūf b. Yaḥyā along the Darb al-Ḥadath,[244] and they met the enemy and fought and then broke off the engagement.

In this year Muḥammad b. Ibrāhīm b. Muḥammad b. ʿAlī, the governor of Mecca, was imprisoned because, it is said, al-Manṣūr ordered him to imprison Ibn Jurayj,[245] ʿAbbād b. Kathīr,[246] and al-

---

241. He appears once as a source for the ʿAlid rebellion of 145/762–63 (al-Ṭabarī, III, 206, 293), and his son al-Ḥasan was governor of ʿUmān in 169/785–86. For his family, see Crone, *Slaves*, 121.

242. *Nuwwāb*, not a usual administrative term at this period; its significance is unclear.

243. In Ctesiphon/al-Madāʾin. The building was still used by the Muslims for official purposes in early Umayyad times (Morony, *Iraq*, 76). Al-Manṣūr was claiming that it formed part of the *fay'* (booty) of the Muslims and hence should not be divided up but used for the common good.

244. Brooks, "Byzantines and Arabs," 734. The Darb al-Ḥadath was the pass that led from the Muslim base at al-Ḥadath across the mountains into Byzantine territory.

245. Probably to be identified with the Ibn Jurayj whom al-Ṭabarī cites extensively as a source in the early part of the *History*, notably on Old Testament material. He had been in Mecca at the time of the ʿAlid rebellion of 145/762 but does not seem to have played a very active part.

246. He had been in Medina in the immediate aftermath of the ʿAlid rebellion and interceded for one of the participants, but, like Ibn Jurayj, he does not seem to have played a major part.

Thawrī,[247] and then he released them without Abū Jaʿfar's permission and Abū Jaʿfar was angry with him. [386]

According to ʿUmar b. Shabbah—Muḥammad b. ʿImrān, freedman of Muḥammad b. Ibrāhīm b. Muḥammad b. ʿAlī b. ʿAbdallāh b. ʿAbbās—his father: Al-Manṣūr wrote to Muḥammad b. Ibrāhīm, governor of Mecca, ordering him to imprison a man of the family of ʿAlī b. Abī Ṭālib who was in Mecca along with Ibn Jurayj, ʿAbbād b. Kathīr, and al-Thawrī, so he imprisoned them. He had companions with whom he used to talk at night[248] and, when it was time for his nighttime conversation, he sat down looking intently at the ground and not uttering a syllable until they dispersed. I approached him and said, "I saw what you did; what is the matter?" He replied, "I came upon the possessor of kinship[249] and imprisoned him and some of the most worthy people[250] and imprisoned them. The Commander of the Faithful might come, and I do not know what will happen. Maybe he will order that they be killed and his authority will be strengthened, but my religion will be destroyed."

I asked him what he would do and he replied, "I will placate God and release the people. Go to my camels and take a female riding camel and take fifty *dīnār*s and give them to the Ṭālibī,[251] give him greeting and say to him, 'Your cousin[252] asks you to release him from his guilt about you. Ride this camel and take this money.'"

When he saw me he had begun to ask God's protection from my evil, but when I told him he said, "He is released.[253] I have no

247. This is the celebrated traditionist Sufyān b. Saʿīd al-Thawrī, d. 161/778, like Ibn Jurayj an important source for the early sections of al-Ṭabarī's history. He spent much of his life in hiding in the Ḥijāz and Yemen to escape appointment as a *qāḍī*. See *EI*[1], s.v. "Sufyān."

248. The *sāmir* or *samīr* was a friend or courtier with whom one had relaxed conversations at night. These nighttime gatherings were an important social and cultural institution of the period.

249. With the Prophet, by which he means the (anonymous) ʿAlid referred to above.

250. The three learned men mentioned above.

251. That is, the ʿAlid. The term Ṭālibī was used for desecendants of ʿAlī's father, Abū Ṭālib, either through ʿAlī himself or through his brother Jaʿfar.

252. Muḥammad b. Ibrāhīm, being an ʿAbbāsid, speaks as a cousin, albeit a very distant one, of the ʿAlid.

253. The ʿAlid releases Muhammad b. Ibrāhīm from his guilt for imprisoning him.

need of the camel and no need of the money," but I said, "It would be better for his soul if you took them," so he did.

Then I came to Ibn Jurayj, Sufyān b. Saʿīd, and ʿAbbād b. Kathīr and told them what he had said and they said, "He is released." I said to them that Muḥammad b. Ibrāhīm had said that none of
[387] them should appear as long as al-Manṣūr was staying.

When al-Manṣūr approached, Muḥammad b. Ibrāhīm sent me with gifts but, when al-Manṣūr was told that the messenger of Muḥammad b. Ibrāhīm had arrived, he ordered that the faces of his camels be struck. When he reached Bi'r Maymūn,[254] Muḥammad b. Ibrāhīm came to meet him but, when he was told of that, he ordered that the faces of his mounts should be struck. So Muḥammad was traveling on one side of the road while Abū Jaʿfar was diverted from the road to the left-hand side and the camel was made to kneel for him (to relieve nature). Muḥammad was waiting facing him, and his doctor was with him. When Abū Jaʿfar mounted and he and his companion al-Rabīʿ went on, Muḥammad ordered his doctor to go over to Abū Jaʿfar's camel-kneeling place, and he saw his excrement and he said to Muḥammad, "I saw the excrement of a man who does not have long to live." When he entered Mecca he remained there only a short time before he died and Muḥammad was saved.

In Shawwāl of this year (August 4–September 1, 775) Abū Jaʿfar set out from the City of Peace heading for Mecca. It is said that he stayed at Qaṣr ʿAbdawayh[255] and while he was there a meteorite fell on 26 Shawwāl (August 29) after the beginning of dawn and remained visible until sunrise; then he went on to al-Kūfah and stayed at al-Ruṣāfah[256] and then set out from there on the pilgrimage and the lesser pilgrimage.[257] With him he drove the camels to be slaughtered in Mecca, branded them, and put signs on their necks for some days into Dhū al-Qaʿdah (September 2–

254. On the borders of the sacred area of Mecca, where al-Manṣūr died. See Yāqūt, *Muʿjam*, I, 302.

255. Not noted by Yāqūt or Le Strange.

256. That is al-Ruṣāfah of al-Kūfah; see note 54, above.

257. For the differing rituals of the pilgrimage (*ḥajj*) and lesser pilgrimage (*ʿumrah*), see *EI*², s.v., "Ḥadjdj;" *EI*¹ s.v. "ʿUmra."

October 1, 775). When he had gone some stages from al-Kūfah the disease of which he died became apparent.

Opinions differ as to the nature of the disease that he died from.

According to 'Alī b. Muḥammad b. Sulaymān al-Nawfalī,[258] his father used to say: Al-Manṣūr was unable to digest his food and he complained of that to the doctors and asked them to bring [388] him digestives, but they did not want to do that so they told him to eat less food and that the digestives would be digested immediately but that the illness would recur and intensify, until an Indian doctor came to him and said the same thing to him as the others had but prepared a drug for him, a digestive powder with hot spices and medicaments, and he took it and his food was digested and he praised the doctor highly.

He continued: My father said that many doctors from Iraq said that Abū Ja'far would die only of a stomach complaint. I asked him what the symptoms were of this and he said, "He takes a digestive and it digests his food, but every day some of the lining of his stomach and the fat of his bowels is eroded, and he will die because of his stomach. I will give you an analogy: What would you think if you put a jar on a high place and put a new brick under it and it drips? Is it not the case that its dripping will pierce the brick in the course of time and do you not then know that every drip makes an impression?" Abū Ja'far died, as he said, because of his stomach.

One source said: The illness of which he died began when he suffered heatstroke from riding in the midday sun. He was a hot-blooded person in his eating and the red bile afflicted him and he got dysentery in his stomach. He continued in that condition until he reached the Garden of Ibn 'Āmir, where it became more severe. He moved on from there but could not reach Mecca and stopped at Bi'r Ibn al-Murtafi',[259] where he stayed for a day and a night before going on to Bi'r Maymūn. He asked whether he had entered the Ḥaram and bequeathed what he wished to al-Rabī', and then he died at dawn or sunrise of Saturday 6 Dhū al-Ḥijjah [389]

258. See note 23, above.

259. Bustān Abū 'Āmir and Bi'r Ibn al-Murtafi' were, like Bi'r Maymūn, stages on the route from Iraq to Mecca and Medina.

(October 7, 775). Only his servants and al-Rabīʿ, his freedman, were with him at his death.

Al-Rabīʿ kept his death hidden and prevented the women and others from weeping and wailing. In the morning the members of his household came as they were accustomed to and sat in their places. ʿĪsā b. ʿAlī was the first to be summoned and he remained a little while and then permission was given to ʿĪsā b. Mūsā, although in time past he used to be given permission before ʿĪsā b. ʿAlī and that was the rank in which he was established. Then the senior and older members of the family[260] were given permission and then the main body of them. Al-Rabīʿ took their oath of allegiance to the Commander of the Faithful al-Mahdī and to ʿĪsā b. Mūsā after him at the hand of Mūsā,[261] son of al-Mahdī.

When the Banū Hāshim[262] had all taken the oath, he summoned the commanders and they took the oath and none of them showed any reluctance except ʿAlī b. ʿĪsā b. Māhān[263] and he refused, at the mention of ʿĪsā b. Mūsā, to take the oath to him. Muḥammad b. Sulaymān slapped him and said, "Who is this lout?"[264] and taunted him with being a sucker[265] and considered beheading him, so he took the oath. The people took the oath in

260. Probably meaning the ʿAbbāsid family but possibly the family of the Prophet, including the ʿAlids, at least one of whom, al-Ḥasan b. Zayd, is known to have been present.

261. The future caliph al-Hādī, at this time a young boy.

262. Hāshim was the ancestor of both ʿAbbāsids and ʿAlids (and, of course, the Prophet himself) but not of the Umayyads.

263. A soldier of Khurasānī origin, probably the son of ʿĪsā b. Māhān, who had been one of the original supporters of the ʿAbbāsid movement in Khurāsān. In al-Mahdī's reign ʿAlī became a partisan of Mūsā al-Hādī, the heir apparent, and an opponent of the Barmakids. Between 180/796 and 192/807 he was governor of Khurāsān, making himself very unpopular with the local notables. After Hārūn's death, he became the leading champion of al-Amīn and the Khurāsāniyyah of Baghdad but was killed in battle by the forces of al-Maʾmūn led by Ṭāhir at al-Rayy in 195/811 (see below, pp. 455, 494; al-Ṭabarī, III, 666, 675, 714, 799–801, 822–85; al-Jahshiyārī, 167, 228; Ḥamzah, 143; Crone, *Slaves*, 178–79).

264. *ʿIlj*; originally referring to a strong or sturdy man, the word acquired a perjorative sense. Here it can mean either "Persian" (which is probably appropriate for ʿAlī) or other unbeliever or, more simply, "lout."

265. *Amaṣṣahu*. The root *maṣṣa* means "to suck." In this context "sucker" is used as an obscene term of abuse, being short for "sucker of your mother's clitoris." The full form is used below p. 146. The American "mother fucker" is probably the most effective colloquial translation. See Lane s.v., *maṣṣa*.

turn and the first one who said "If God wills" was al-Musayyab b. Zuhayr, and ʿĪsā b. Mūsā said, "It will be thus," and they called him a sucker. Mūsā b. al-Mahdī went out to the public audience and took the oath from the rest of the commanders and leading men. Al-ʿAbbās b. Muḥammad and Muḥammad b. Sulaymān proceeded to Mecca to take the oath from the people there, and al-ʿAbbās acted as spokesman at that time. The people took the oath to al-Mahdī between the *rukn* and the *maqām*.[266] A number of members of the household of al-Mahdī were sent out in the neighborhood of Mecca and the camp, and they had the people take the oath to him.

Al-Manṣūr was prepared for burial and he was washed and covered in a shroud. Those of his household who were in charge [390] of this were al-ʿAbbās b. Muḥammad, al-Rabīʿ, al-Rayyān,[267] and a number of his servants and freedmen. The preparations for burial were completed by the afternoon prayer and his face and all his body were covered with his shroud up to the beginning of the hair, and his head remained uncovered because he was in a state of *iḥrām*.[268] The people of his household and the most intimate of his freedmen went out with him and, as al-Wāqidi claimed, ʿIsa b. Mūsā prayed over him in Shiʿb al-Khūz.

It is said that Ibrāhīm b. Yaḥyā b. Muḥammad b. ʿAlī[269] prayed over him, and it is said that al-Manṣūr had stipulated that in his will because he was his deputy in charge of the prayers in the City of Peace.

According to ʿAlī b. Muḥammad al-Nawfalī—his father: Ibrāhīm b. Yaḥyā prayed over him in the tents before he was carried out because al-Rabīʿ said, "No one should pray over him who is aspiring to the caliphate," so they fetched Ibrāhīm b. Yaḥyā,

---

266. The *rukn* is the corner of the Kaʿbah in which is the Black Stone, the *maqām*, short for "*maqām* Ibrāhīm," is a small building, containing the mark of Abraham's footprint, near the Kaʿbah; both of these are in the mosque in Mecca.

267. Mawlā al-Manṣūr; in an anecdote dated 145–48/762–66 he was sent to Mosul to execute a political suspect (see below, p. 145) but is otherwise unknown.

268. That is, he was in the ritual dress for pilgrimage, having entered the *ḥarām* (sacred area) at Bi'r Maymūn. The *iḥrām* involves being bareheaded.

269. B. ʿAbdallāh b. al-ʿAbbās and therefore a member of the ʿAbbāsid family. He was later governor of Medina from 166 until 167 (782–84), when he died. For Shiʿb al-Khūz, see Yāqūt, *Muʿjam*, III, 347.

who was at that time a young man. He was buried in a grave at Thaniyyat al-Madaniyyīn, which is called that and Thaniyyat al-Ma'lāt,[270] because it is above Mecca. 'Īsā b. 'Alī, al-'Abbās b. Muḥammad, 'Īsā b. Mūsā, al-Rabī' and al-Rayyān, his freedmen, and Yaqṭīn b. Mūsā[271] lowered him into his grave.

Opinions differ about his age when he died; some say he was sixty-four years old, some that he was sixty-five, and some that he was sixty-three on the day he died. Hishām b. al-Kalbī[272] said that al-Manṣūr died when he was sixty-eight and that he held power for twenty-two years less twenty-four days. Different *riwāyas* are
[391] related to Abu Ma'shar[273]: Aḥmad b. Thābit al-Rāzī told me on the authority of those who were told by Isḥāq b. 'Īsā on his (Abū Ma'shar's) authority that he said:[274] Abū Ja'far died one day before the day for providing oneself with water (Yawm al-Tarwiyyah: 8 Dhū'l-Ḥijjah/October 9, 775), which was a Saturday. His caliphate lasted twenty-two years less three days. It is related on the authority of Ibn Bakkār that he (Abū Ma'shar)[275] said: Less seven nights. Al-Wāqidī said that the reign of Abū Ja'far was twenty-two years less six days. 'Umar b. Shabbah said that his caliphate was two days short of twenty-two years.

The leader of the pilgrims in this year was Ibrāhīm b. Yaḥyā b. Muḥammad b. 'Alī.

In this year the Byzantine emperor died.[276]

Information about the appearance of Abū Ja'far al-Manṣūr:

---

270. Pass of the Medinans, or High Pass.

271. He had a background in the 'Abbāsid movement in Khurāsān and was chiefly employed as a civil servant, dividing up booty and supervising construction work on the road to Mecca and in the *ḥarām* itself. He died in 185/801 (see al-Ṭabarī, III, 486, 520; Yāqūt, *Mu'jam*, II, 439).

272. Celebrated early Islamic historian, ca. 120–204/737–819, and author of surviving *Jamharat al-Nasab*, the definitive work on early Arab genealogy; see *EI*², s.v. "Ibn al-Kalbī."

273. Najīh al-Sindī. An important source for the earlier sections of al-Ṭabarī's history, he contributes only occasional details of appointments and dates, the last being the date of the death of al-Hādī (see al-Ṭabarī, III, 579).

274. He being Abū Ma'shar; Aḥmad b. Thābit and Isḥāq b. Ibrāhīm, both otherwise unknown, are al-Ṭabarī's usual *isnād* for Abū Ma'shar's information.

275. Presumably Abū Ma'shar again, by a different *isnād*. Ibn Bakkār is al-Zubayr b. Bakkār, who is occasionally used elsewhere by al-Ṭabarī.

276. Constantine V, A.D 741–75.

It is said that he was brown-skinned, tall, thin, with a sparse beard. He was born in al-Ḥumaymah.[277]

Some Stories about al-Manṣūr and His Conduct[278]

According to Ṣāliḥ b. al-Wajīh[279]—his father: Al-Manṣūr heard that ʿĪsā b. Mūsā had killed one of the descendants of Naṣr b. Sayyār[280] who was hiding in al-Kūfah. ʿĪsā was directed to him and cut off his head. Al-Manṣūr disapproved of that and was appalled. He was planning something that would be the destruction of ʿĪsā, but ʿĪsā's ignorance of the significance of what he had done stopped him. So he wrote to him:

> Were it not for the discernment and restraint of the Commander of the Faithful, your punishment for the killing of the son of Naṣr b. Sayyar and your high-handedness in going beyond the aspirations of governors would not be delayed. Stop such actions against those whom the Commander of the Faithful appointed you to, whether [392] Arab or non-Arab, white[281] or black. Do not act arbitrarily contrary to the Commander of the Faithful in inflicting punishment on anyone who has a case to answer. He does not think that anyone should be arrested for an evil thought for which God will accept penance as reparation, or for any act of his in war that God has brought him safely

277. The estate in southern Jordan that was the main base of the ʿAbbāsid family in late Umayyad times (Yāqūt, *Muʿjam*, II, 307, Le Strange, *Palestine*, 455–56).

278. Al-Ṭabarī usually follows the account of the death of a caliph with some undated anecdotes. In general these are arranged at random, but some are loosely arranged according to themes; Abū Jaʿfar's meanness, the contrast between him and his son al-Mahdī, the activities of Maʿn b. Zāʾidah are some of these. The sources of this material are usually named, in contrast with the main body of the text, but are often individuals who contribute only single narratives and about whom nothing else is known.

279. This is the only time al-Ṭabarī uses this source, and nothing more is known of him or his father. The story should probably be dated 145–47/762–65 when ʿĪsā was still governor of al-Kūfah, but al-Manṣūr was attempting to remove him from the succession.

280. Naṣr b. Sayyār was the last Umayyad governor of Khurāsān and an ancient enemy of the ʿAbbāsids.

281. The Arabic uses *aḥmar* (red) to mean "white."

through, thereby concealing him from the rancorous and preventing investigation of what is in men's hearts. The Commander of the Faithful will not despair of anyone, nor of himself, of God's causing the retreater to advance just as the retreating of one who advances is not sure, if God wills, and peace.

According to ʿAbbās b. al-Faḍl[282]—Yaḥyā b. Sulaym,[283] secretary to al-Faḍl b. al-Rabīʿ: Entertainment was never seen in the house of al-Manṣūr, nor anything like entertainment games or amusements, except one day, when we saw a son of his called ʿAbd al-ʿAzīz, the brother of Sulaymān and ʿĪsā,[284] sons of Abū Jaʿfar by the Ṭalḥī woman, who died when he was a youth. He came out to the people with a bow on his shoulder, wearing a turban and a striped outer garment and looking like a bedouin boy. He was riding on a young camel between two saddlebags in which there were *muql*,[285] sandals, and sticks for cleaning the teeth[286] and the things that the bedouin gave as gifts. The people were amazed at this and disapproved of it. The young man went on until he crossed the bridge and came to al-Mahdī in al-Ruṣāfah and gave them to him. Al-Mahdī took what was in the saddlebags and filled them with *dirham*s, and he set off with the saddlebags. It was made known that this was a sort of royal joke.

According to Ḥammād al-Turkī: I was standing by al-Manṣūr's head when he heard a clamor in the house and he said, "What is that, Ḥammād? Have a look." I went and found one of his servants sitting among the slave girls and playing a *ṭunbūr*[287] for them,
[393] and they were laughing. I came to him and told him and he said, "What sort of thing is a *ṭunbūr*?" and I replied that it was made of wood and I described it to him. He said, "You have given me a

282. That is, al-ʿAbbās b. al-Faḍl b. al-Rabīʿ, later *ḥājib* to al-Amīn as his grandfather had been to al-Manṣūr and al-Mahdī (ʿ*Uyūn*, 342; Jahshiyārī, 289).

283. Yaḥyā took over some of al-Rabīʿ's administrative functions on his death and later worked for al-Amīn (see below 598, Jāḥiẓ, 266, 289, 292.)

284. Both Sulaymān and ʿĪsā reached maturity and played a part in political life in Hārūn's reign and after.

285. *Bdellium*. See Groom, *Frankincense and Myrrh*, 124–26.

286. Sticks for cleaning teeth, used by the bedouin; see *EI*[1], s.v. *miswāk*.

287. A kind of lute or guitar with a long neck.

good description of it. How do you know what a *ṭunbūr* is?" and I replied that I had seen one in Khurāsān. He said, "Yes, there," and then asked me to bring him his sandals, so I brought them and he got up and walked slowly until he looked down on them and saw them. When they caught sight of him, they scattered. He said, "Seize him!" so he was taken and he went on, "Beat him over the head with it!" and I went on striking him on the head with it until I broke it. Then he said, "Take him out of my palace and go to Ḥamrān in al-Karkh[288] and tell him to sell him."

According to al-ʿAbbās b. al-Faḍl—Sallām al-Abrash:[289] When I was a young servant, I and another page used to wait on al-Manṣūr inside in his residence. There he had an enclosure with a tent and pavilion with bedding and covers for him to be alone in. He was the best-natured of people whenever he did not appear in public, and the most tolerant of boys' games, but when he put on his official robes his complexion changed and his face became gloomy, his eyes reddened, and he went out and did as he was used to doing. When he got up from his audience, he returned in that state. When we received him in the hallway, he sometimes used to face us with blame. He said to me one day, "O my son, when you see me dressed in my official robes or returning from my audience, do not any of you approach me for fear that I should abuse him for something."

According to Abū al-Haytham Khālid b. Yazīd b. Wahb b. Jarīr b. Ḥāzim[290]—ʿAbdallāh b. Muḥammad, called Minqār, of the people of Khurāsān, who was one of al-Rashīd's agents[291]—Maʿn b. Zā'idah: We were seven hundred men in the *ṣaḥābah* who used to [394]
go in to al-Manṣūr every day. I asked al-Rabīʿ to put me among the last of those who were going in but he said to me, "You are not one of the most noble of them to be put first of them nor the

---

288. A slave dealer. Al-Karkh was the commercial quarter of Baghdad, south of the Round City.

289. A palace servant, who was later in charge of the *maẓālim* (complaints) for al-Mahdī. *Abrash* means speckled or marked with various colors.

290. Great-grandson of Jarīr b. Ḥāzim, an important source for the earlier sections of al-Ṭabarī's work; he himself contributes only two short narratives.

291. He may be identified with ʿAbdallāh b. Muḥammad al-Munaqqirī, who appears as a source in al-Ṭabarī, III, 565, neither name is recorded elsewhere. *Minqār* means "the beak of a bird."

most humble in descent to be put among the last of them. Your rank corresponds to your genealogy."[292] I went into al-Manṣūr that day wearing a loose, flowing outer garment, a Ḥanafī sword[293] the point of whose scabbard touched the ground, and a turban that I let hang down behind and in front of me. I greeted him and went out and, when I reached the curtain, he shouted to me, "O Maʿn" with a shout I did not like. I said, "Your servant, O Commander of the Faithful," and he ordered me to come to him. When I came near him, he had gotten down from his throne to the ground and he was kneeling and pulling out a rod from between the two cushions. His color changed, and his neck veins swelled out. He said to me, "You were my parallel combatant on the day of Wāsiṭ?[294] May I not escape death if you escape from me," and I said, "O Commander of the Faithful, that was my support for their false one; what about my support for your truth?" He said, "What are you saying?" I repeated my words to him and he went on asking me to repeat until he returned the rod to its resting place and sat down on his throne. His complexion turned pale and he said to me, "O Maʿn, I have some trifles in Yemen," and I replied, "A man who is denied secrets cannot have an opinion about them," and he said, "You are the man I need, so sit down," so I sat down and he ordered al-Rabīʿ to send out all those who were in the palace, and they were sent out. Then al-Manṣūr said, "The lord of Yemen[295] is considering rebelling against me and I want to take him prisoner and not to let any of his wealth escape me. What is your opinion?" and I replied, "O Commander of the Faithful, appoint me governor of Yemen but say in public that you have attached me to him. Order al-Rabīʿ to prepare whatever equipment I need and to send me off this very day so that the news does not get out." He took out a diploma of appointment
[395] from between the two cushions, inscribed my name on it, and

---

292. That is, the order of precedence was established by descent, but Maʿn, wanting to attract attention to himself, asked for a more conspicuous position.

293. It is not clear what a Ḥanafī sword was. The point was to wear unconventional garb to attract the caliph's attention.

294. Maʿn b. Zāʾidah had been one of the leading defenders of the Umayyad base at Wāsiṭ when it was besieged by Abū Jaʿfar at the beginning of al-Saffāḥ's caliphate.

295. *Ṣāḥib al-Yaman* means the governor.

handed it over to me. Then he called al-Rabīʿ and said, "We have attached Maʿn to the lord of Yemen so prepare the equipment he needs, horses and arms, and do not delay for he is going now." Then he said, "Take your leave of me," so I took my leave of him and went out into the vestibule, where the father of the governor met me and said, "O Maʿn, I am not very pleased that you have been attached to your brother's son," and I replied to him, "It is no disgrace for a man that his Sulṭān attaches him to his brother's son."[296] I left for the Yemen and I came to the man and took him prisoner, read the diploma of appointment to him, and sat in his place.

According to Ḥammād b. Aḥmad al-Yamānī—Muḥammad b. ʿUmar al-Yamānī—Abū al-Rudaynī:[297] Maʿn b. Zā'idah wanted to send a delegation to al-Manṣūr to assuage his ill will and soften his heart toward him, and he said, "I have consumed my life in his service, worn myself out and exhausted my men in war in Yemen, and then he is angry with me because I have spent money in his service." He chose a group of his tribe of the small lineages of Rabīʿah,[298] and among those he selected was Mujjāʿah b. al-Azhar,[299] and he began to call the men one after the other and asked them what they would say to the Commander of the Faithful if he sent them to him, and they replied that they would say this and that until Mujjāʿah b. al-Azhar came to him and said, "May God glorify the Amīr. You are asking me what I would say in Iraq when I am in Yemen. I shall pursue your business until I complete it as is possible and appropriate." Maʿn said, "You are the man for me." Then he turned to ʿAbd al-Raḥmān b. ʿAtīq al-Muzanī[300] and said to him, "Be strong in support of your paternal

296. It is unusual for *sulṭān* to be used of a person at this date, it is more commonly an abstract word meaning "authority." As the governor is not named, it is not clear what the relationship between him and Maʿn was. The story relates to Maʿn's appointment as governor of Yemen in 142/759–60.

297. This is the only time al-Ṭabarī uses this *isnād*, and the transmitters cannot be identified. The anecdote dates from Maʿn's governorate of Yemen, 142–51/759–69.

298. Maʿn's tribe, Shaybān, was part of Bakr b. Wā'il, which was a section of the larger Rabīʿah tribal group.

299. Not known elsewhere.

300. Not known elsewhere.

uncle's son,[301] give him precedence over you, and, if he overlooks anything, put him right." He chose eight people from his companions with them so that the total number was ten, and then he said farewell to them.

[396] They traveled until they reached Abū Ja'far and, when they were in his presence, they came forward and Mujjā'ah b. al-Azhar began by praising God and extolling him and thanking him so that the people thought that he intended to do no more than that. Then he turned to mention the Prophet and how God had chosen him from the midst of the Arabs and expanded on his virtue, so that people were surprised. Next he turned to the description of the Commander of the Faithful al-Manṣūr and how God had exalted him and to what he had appointed him. Finally, he turned to the business of mentioning his lord. When he had finished his speech, al-Manṣūr said, "As for the praise you gave God, God is more glorious and greater than description can say, and, as for your mention of the Prophet, God has given him more virtue than you said, and, as for your description of the Commander of the Faithful, God has favored him with that and He will support him in obeying Him, if God wills. As for your description of your lord, you lied and behaved disgracefully. Get out! What you said is not acceptable."

Mujjā'ah replied, "The Commander of the Faithful has spoken the truth but, by God, I did not lie about my master." They were sent out and, when they reached the end of the *īwān*,[302] al-Manṣūr ordered that he return with his companions and he asked, "What did you say?" and he repeated his speech as if it were on a page and he were reading it, and al-Manṣūr replied as he had done the first time, and they were sent out until they had all emerged and he ordered them to stop. Then he turned to those of Muḍar[303] who were present and asked, "Do you know among you anyone like this man? By God he spoke until I was envious (of his eloquence) and nothing prevented me from completely agreeing to his request except that it might be said that I was prejudiced for him because he was a Raba'ī. I have never seen a man more self-

301. That is, Mujjā'ah.
302. The arched structure in which the audience was held.
303. Rivals of Rabī'ah.

possessed or clearer in eloquence than he was today. Bring him back, page." When he came before him, he returned his greeting and that of his companions and al-Manṣūr said to him, "Mention your request and the request of your lord."

He replied, "O Commander of the Faithful, Ma'n b. Zā'idah is your slave, your sword and your arrow that you shot at your [397] enemy, and he struck and thrusted and shot so that what was rough became smooth and what was difficult became easy and what was stirred up in Yemen was settled and they became the chattels of the Commander of the Faithful, may God prolong his life. If the Commander of the Faithful did have in his mind a criticism from a slanderer, or a calumniator, or an envious person, the Commander of the Faithful has now shown his favor to his slave, the man who has spent his life in his service."

He accepted their representations and accepted the excuses of Ma'n and ordered them to return to him. when they reached Ma'n and he read the letter restoring him to favor, he kissed him (Mujjā'ah) between the eyes and thanked his companions, gave them robes of honor, and rewarded them according to their rank and the part they had played in the journey to al-Manṣūr. Mujjā'ah said,

I swore in the assembly of Wā'il[304] an oath
 that I would not sell you, O Ma'n, for greed.
O Ma'n, you have brought me prosperity.
 It has become general for Lujaym and special for the family of Mujjā'ah.[305]
I shall remain attached to you
 until the time when the voice of the herald of death announces my passing.

The prosperity that Ma'n gave to Mujjā'ah was that he asked him for three wishes. One of these was that he was courting a noble woman from his household called Zahrā', whom nobody had yet married. This was told to her and she said, "With what

304. See note 298, above.

305. That is, Mujjā'ah's tribe. For the relationships of Bakr b. Wā'il, Shaybān, and Lujaym, see Caskel, table 141.

will he marry me? With his woollen *jubbah* and garments?" When he returned to Maʿn, the first thing he asked him was that he should marry him to her. Her father was in Maʿn's army. He said, "I want Zahrāʾ and her father is in your army, O Amīr." He married him to her for ten thousand *dirhams*, which he gave her as a dowry. Then Maʿn said, "What is your second wish?" and he replied, "The palm grove in which my house is in Ḥajar.[306] Its owner is in the army of the Amīr." Maʿn bought it from him and
[398] handed it over to Mujjāʿah and said, "What is your third wish?" "Give me money," he replied. Maʿn ordered that he be given thirty thousand, one hundred thousand *dirhams* in total, and he sent him away to his house.

According to Muḥammad b. Sālim al-Khwārazmī, whose father was one of the commanders of Khurāsān,—Abū al-Faraj, the maternal uncle of ʿAbdallāh b. Jabalah al-Ṭāliqānī:[307] I heard Abū Jaʿfar saying, "How much I need four people at my door and they should be the most decent people there." He was asked, "O Commander of the Faithful, who are they?" and he replied, "They are the pillars of the state and the state would not be safe without them as a couch would not be safe without four legs and, if one of them is missing, it is weakened. The first of these is a judge whom no reproach can deviate from what pleases God. The second is a chief of police who defends the rights of the weak from the strong. The third is a chief of taxation who investigates and does not oppress the peasants because I can dispense with their oppression. The fourth. . . ." Then he bit on his index finger three times, saying each time "Ah, ah," and he was asked, "Who is that, O Commander of the Faithful?" and he replied, "A head of the post who writes reliable information about these men."

It is said: Al-Manṣūr summoned one of his agents who had defaulted on his taxes and said to him, "Pay what you owe," and he replied, "By God, I do not owe a single thing." The muezzin called, "I bear witness that there is no god but God," and he said, "O Commander of the Faithful, give what I owe to God and to the call that there is no god but God," and he let him go.

---

306. The capital of al-Yamāmah province of east central Arabia; see Yāqūt, *Muʿjam*, II, 221.

307. None of these individuals is known elsewhere.

He said: Al-Manṣūr appointed a Syrian to an office in the tax administration, and he approached him with his advice and said, "How well do I know what is in your mind at the moment, O brother of the people of Syria. You will go out from my presence now and you will say, 'Keep upright in your work and your work sticks to you.'" He also appointed an Iraqi to something in the taxation of the Sawād and approached him with his advice and [399] said, "How well do I know what is in your mind. You will go out now and say, 'If you become poor after that may you not thrive again.' Leave me and go to your work and, by God, If you become open to that, I will surely inflict on you the punishment you deserve!" They were both appointed to it and put things right and were sincere in their intentions.[308]

According to al-Ṣabbāḥ b. ʿAbd al-Malik al-Shaybānī—Isḥāq b. Mūsā b. ʿĪsā:[309] Al-Manṣūr appointed a man of the Arabs as governor of Ḥaḍramawt and the chief of the post wrote to al-Manṣūr that the governor often went out in pursuit of game with falcons and dogs that he had prepared. He dismissed him and wrote to him, "May your mother lose you, and may your tribe miss you. What is this equipment you prepared to slaughter wild animals? We put you in charge only of the affairs of the Muslims, not the affairs of the wild animals. Hand over the office you have been entrusted with by us to so-and-so, son of so-and-so, and go to your family, censured and banished."

According to al-Rabīʿ:[310] Suhayl b. Sālim al-Baṣrī[311] was brought in to al-Manṣūr after he had been appointed to an office and dismissed. He ordered that he be put in prison and that money be demanded of him. Suhayl said, "Your slave, O Commander of the Faithful." "What an evil slave you are," he said, "But you are a kind master, O Commander of the Faithful," he replied. "Not to you, I'm not," said the caliph.

According to al-Faḍl b. al-Rabīʿ—his father: When I was standing

308. Freytag, *Proverbia*, II, 576, 584, and II, 687, 329.

309. Neither of these can be securely identified. Isḥāq b. Mūsā b. ʿĪsā may have been the grandson of ʿĪsā b. Mūsā, who was briefly governor of Yemen in al-Ma'mūn's reign (*ʿUyūn*, 348).

310. B. Yūnus, *ḥājib* to al-Manṣūr; see note 16, above.

311. He is not mentioned elsewhere, nor is it known what office he held.

before al-Manṣūr, or by his head, a Khārijī who had defeated his armies was brought to him. He was preparing him for execution when his eye lighted on him in disdain, and he said, "You son of a whore! Does someone like you put armies to flight?" and the Khārijī replied to him, "Woe to you and evil to you! Between me and you yesterday there was the sword and killing and today there
[400] is abuse and insult. What makes you so sure that I will respond, for I have despaired of life and you will never rescind my punishment even if asked?" Al-Manṣūr spared his life and released him and he never saw his face again.

According to ʿAbdallāh b. ʿAmr al-Mulaḥī—Hārūn b. Muḥammad b. Ismāʿīl b. Mūsā al-Hādī[312]—ʿAbdallāh b. Muḥammad b. Abī Ayyūb al-Makkī—his father[313]—ʿUmārah b. Ḥamzah: I was with al-Manṣūr and I left him at midday after the people had taken the oath of allegiance to al-Mahdī. Al-Mahdī came to me at the time when I left and said to me, "I have heard that my father intends that the oath of allegiance should be given to my brother Jaʿfar,[314] and I swear by God that, if he does, I will kill him." I went immediately to the Commander of the Faithful and I said, "This matter will not wait," and the chamberlain said, "You have only just left," but I replied, "The matter is new." He gave me permission and I went in to al-Manṣūr and he said, "Hey, ʿUmārah, what has brought you?" and I replied, "A new matter, O Commander of the Faithful, that I wish to tell you about." He said, "I will tell you about it before you tell me: Al-Mahdī came to you and said such-and-such," and I said, "By God, O Commander of the Faithful, it is as if you were present as the third of us." He continued, "Tell him that we are too solicitous of him (Jaʿfar) to expose him to you."

According to Aḥmad b. Yūsuf b. al-Qāsim—Ibrāhīm b. Ṣāliḥ:[315] We were in the audience waiting for permission to go in to al-Manṣūr and we were reminiscing about al-Ḥajjāj.[316] There were

312. A great-grandson of the caliph.

313. Muḥammad b. Abī Ayyūb, along with other notables, was arrested on a charge of *zandaqah* (see note 199 above) in 166/782–83 (see p. 234, below).

314. That is, Jaʿfar the Elder (see above, note 94).

315. B. ʿAlī al-ʿAbbāsī, son of Ṣāliḥ b. ʿAlī (see note 92, above) and himself governor of Palestine and Egypt in al-Mahdī's reign.

316. B. Yūsuf al-Thaqafī, the famous governor of Iraq and the east for the Umayyad caliphs.

those among us who praised him and those who condemned him; among those who praised him was Ma'n b. Zā'idah and among those who condemned him was al-Ḥasan b. Zayd. Then we were given permission to go in to al-Manṣūr, and al-Ḥasan b. Zayd let fly and said, "O Commander of the Faithful, I did not think that I would live to see the day when al-Ḥajjāj would be discussed in your house and on your carpet and given praise." Abū Ja'far replied [401] to him, "Why do you disapprove of that? He was a man whom a people (i.e., the Umayyads) entrusted with power, and he served them well. I would be happy, by God, if I could find a man like al-Ḥajjāj so that I could hand over my reponsibilities to him and settle him in one of the two Ḥarams (Mecca or Medina)." Then Ma'n said to him, "O Commander of the Faithful, you have a number of men who would serve you well if you entrusted them with power," and he asked, "Who are they? It is as if you were referring to yourself." He said, "If I wanted to, I would be close to that." "You are not at all like that," the caliph replied, "A people (the Umayyads) had trust in al-Ḥajjāj, and he repaid them with trustworthiness. We had trust in you, and you betrayed us."

According to al-Haytham b. 'Adī[317]—Abū Bakr al-Hudhalī:[318] I went with the Commander of the Faithful al-Manṣūr to Mecca. I was traveling with him one day when there appeared a man on a red-colored camel riding in the open country, wearing a silk *jubbah*[319] and an Adenī turban. He had a whip in his hand that almost touched the ground and a notable appearance. When al-Manṣūr saw him, he ordered me to call him. He came, and the caliph asked him about his genealogy, his country, the desert his people lived in, and about the officials in charge of the *ṣadaqah*.[320]

---

317. Al-Ṭā'ī, ca. 120–206/738–821, a historian who attended the court of Hārūn and a source intermittently used by al-Ṭabarī throughout his history. In the 'Abbāsid period, he mostly contributes anecdotal material in the sections following the deaths of al-Manṣūr and al-Mahdī, from court sources including al-Rabī'. The traditionists accused him of falsehood, but al-Mas'ūdī had a good opinion of his material on the history of the Arabs; see EI^2, s.v., "al-Haytham b. 'Adī."

318. Salama b. 'Abdallāh, another occasional source of anecdote.

319. Long outer garment with open front and wide sleeves (Ahsan, *Social Life*, p 40).

320. The alms Muslims are enjoined to pay. At this time it was a compulsory tax, rather than a voluntary contribution, and probably the only tax a bedouin would pay.

He gave the best of answers and al-Manṣūr was amazed at what he saw in him. Then he said, "Recite to me." He recited to him a poem of Aws b. Ḥajar[321] and of other poets of the Banū 'Amr b. Tamīm. He continued to recite until he came to the poem of Ṭarīf b. Tamīm al-'Anbarī[322] which goes:

My lance is a strong wood (*nab'*), which neither the pinching and pressing
of the straightening instrument nor grease nor fire can soften.
When I take a fearful man under my protection, his grazing places are safe,
and, when I make a safe man fearful for his safety, the house looks not spacious enough for him.
When I initiate matters, they are brought to fruition;
matters have a beginning and a completion.

Al-Manṣūr said, "Woe to you! What was Ṭarīf's reputation among you when he spoke this poem?" He replied, "He was the most severe of the Arabs in trampling on his enemies and the most
[402] determined in retaliation, the most fortunate in character, the hardest of them with spears on those who tried his patience, the most hospitable to his guests, and the most protective to those who were in his charge. When the Arabs gathered at 'Ukāẓ,[323] all of them acknowledged that he had these qualities except one man who wanted to belittle him and he said, 'By God, you do not search far for food and do not pursue game.' He called upon him to take it upon himself not to eat anything except the meat of game he had hunted and not to avoid going every year on a raid to distant parts." Al-Manṣūr said, "O brother of the Banū Tamīm, you have done very well in describing your friend, but I myself am more truthfully described in his two verses, not he."

According to Aḥmad b. Khālid al-Fuqaymī:[324] A number of the

---

321. A well-known Tamīmī poet of the pre-Islamic period; *Aghānī*, Būlāq, X, 6; Beirut, XI, 64.

322. This poet is not quoted elsewhere by al-Ṭabarī, nor does he appear in the *Aghānī*.

323. The site of the famous fairs outside Mecca, where poets are said to have gathered in pre-Islamic times.

324. A source used several times in this section of the *History* but otherwise unknown.

Banū Hāshim related that al-Manṣūr worked at daybreak, ordering and forbidding, appointing and dismissing, policing the frontiers and borders, safeguarding the roads and supervising the taxes and the expenses and protecting the livelihood of the subjects, to drive away their poverty and to find the best means to keep them quiet and comfortable. When he had prayed the afternoon prayer, he sat down with the people of his household except those he wished to be his nighttime companions. When he had prayed the last evening prayer, he looked at the letters that had arrived from the frontiers, the borders, and outlying districts and sought the advice of his nighttime companions about whatever he needed. When a third of the night had passed, he went to his bed and his companions left. When the second third of the night had passed, he got up from his bed, performed his ablutions, and prayed before his mihrab until dawn broke, when he went out and prayed with the people. Then he went in and sat down in his audience hall (*īwān*).

According to Isḥāq[325]—'Abdallāh b. al-Rabī':[326] Abū Ja'far said to Ismā'īl b. 'Abdallāh,[327] "Describe the people to me," and he replied, "The people of the Ḥijāz are the beginning of Islam and the most excellent of the Arabs; the people of Iraq are the pillar of [403] Islam and the militia of the Faith; the people of Syria are the fortress of the Muslim community and the spearheads of the Imāms; the people of Khurāsān are the the horsemen of battle and the bridles of the men; the Turks are the people of the rocks and the sons of raids. The people of India are wise men who are satisfied with their country and content with it and do not aspire to what lies beyond it. The Byzantines are people of the book and of piety and whom God had removed from near to far, and the Nabaṭ[328] had an ancient kingdom but now are slaves to every nation."

---

325. Presumably Isḥāq b. Mūsā b. 'Īsā, mentioned above (see note 309).

326. Probably 'Abdallāh b. al-Rabī' al-Ḥārithī (see note 34), who is described as one of the night companions (*summār*) of al-Manṣūr (Ya'qūbī, *Tārīkh*, II, 468).

327. Al-Qasrī, a firm supporter of Marwān, the last Umayyad caliph, who was reconciled to Abū Ja'far and was briefly appointed governor of Mosul. Thus this story belongs to a genre in which Abū Ja'far looks for advice and example to the Umayyads and their supporters.

328. A term cognate with Nabataeans but generally used of the indigenous

The caliph asked, "Which governors are the best?" and he replied, "The one who gives freely and avoids evil." He asked, "Which of them is the most evil?" and he replied, "The one who is hardest on the subjects and who inflicts most violations and punishments on them." He asked, "Is obedience through fear more useful to the interests of the state or obedience through love?" and he replied, "O Commander of the Faithful, obedience through fear engulfs treachery, and it is exaggerated when it is exposed, while obedience through love engulfs diligence and goes to exaggeration when it is not examined." He asked, "Which man is most worthy of obedience?" and he replied, "The most capable in need and useful service." He asked, "What is the sign of that?" and he replied, "Quickness to answer and self-sacrifice." He asked, "Who must be appointed as *wazīr* to the king?" and he replied, "The soundest of heart and the farthest from passion."

According to Abū ʿUbaydallāh the secretary, I heard al-Manṣūr saying to al-Mahdī when he made him heir apparent, "O Abū ʿAbdallāh, make prosperity last by giving thanks, power by forgiveness, obedience by affection, and victory by humility. Do not forget, because of your fortune in this world, your fortune from the mercy of God."

According to al-Zubayr b. Bakkār—Mubārak al-Ṭabarī[329]—Abū ʿUbaydallāh: I heard al-Manṣūr say to al-Mahdī, "Do not settle a matter without thinking about it, for the thought of the intelligent man is his mirror in which he sees his good and his evil."

According to al-Zubayr again—Muṣʿab b. ʿAbdallāh[330]—his father: I heard Abū Jaʿfar al-Manṣūr say to al-Mahdī, "O Abū
[404] ʿAbdallāh, the Sulṭān is not safe except with piety, and its subjects are not safe except with obedience. The country will not thrive without justice, the prosperity of the Sulṭān and obedience to him will not last without money. You will not achieve security with-

inhabitants of Iraq.

329. Probably to be identified with Mubārak al-Turkī (see note 227, above). Al-Ṭabarī means that he came from Ṭabaristān in northern Iran on the Caspian coast, as, of course, did the great historian himself.

330. B. Muṣʿab al-Zubayrī, d. 233/847–84, a descendant of the Prophet's companion al-Zubayr b. al-ʿAwwām and a source used occasionally throughout the *History*.

out the movement of information. The most powerful of men in forgiveness is the most powerful in punishment, and the weakest of men is he who oppresses those beneath him. Consider the work of your friend and his knowledge by putting him to the test."

According to Mubārak al-Ṭabarī—Abū 'Ubaydallāh: I heard al-Manṣūr say to al-Mahdī, "O Abū 'Abdallāh, do not hold an audience without people of knowledge to talk to you, for Muḥammad b. Shihāb al-Zuhrī[331] said, 'Conversation is male; only masculine men like it, and only effeminate men hate it.' The brother of Zuhra spoke the truth."

According to 'Alī b. Mujāhid b. Muḥammad b. 'Alī:[332] Al-Manṣūr said to al-Mahdī, "O Abū 'Abdallāh, he who loves praise has the best conduct, and he who hates praise has the worst. No one hates praise except he who seeks to be derogated, and nobody is derogated without being hated."

According to Mubārak al-Ṭabarī—Abū 'Ubaydallāh: Al-Manṣūr said to al-Mahdī, "O Abū 'Abdallāh, the intelligent man is not the one who makes efforts when disaster befalls him until he escapes from it but he who makes efforts when disaster threatens so that it does not befall him."

According to al-Fuqaymī—'Utbah b. Hārūn:[333] Abū Ja'far said to al-Mahdī one day, "How many banners do you have?"[334] and he replied, "I do not know," and Abū Ja'far said, "This, by God, is utter heedlessness, which denotes that in the caliphate you will be more heedless. But I have gathered for you what will not be affected by loss, no matter how negligent you are. Fear God in what He has bestowed on you."

According to 'Alī b. Muḥammad[335]—Ḥafṣ b. 'Umar b. Ḥammād[336]—Khāliṣah:[337] I went in to al-Manṣūr and he was com- [405]

331. Al-Zuhrī, d. 119/737, was one of the great early authorities on the Traditions of the Prophet; see *EI*[1], s.v. "al-Zuhrī."

332. A source used fairly commonly in sections I and II of his history but only twice for the 'Abbāsid period (see al-Ṭabarī, III, 51 above).

333. Unknown elsewhere.

334. Meaning "How many offices are at your disposal?"

335. Probably al-Nawfalī; see note 23, above.

336. Not known elsewhere.

337. One of only three examples of a female narrator in this volume. For the others, see Afrīk, above, p. 60, and Jamrah al-'Aṭṭārah, below, p. 152.

plaining of a toothache and, when he heard my noise, he said, "Come in," so I went in and there he was resting his hand on his temples. He was silent for a while and then he said to me, "O Khāliṣah, how much money do you have?" and I replied that I had a thousand *dirhams*. He said, "Put your hand on my head and swear," so I said that I had ten thousand *dīnārs*. He then said, "Bring them to me," so I returned and went in to al-Mahdī and al-Khayzurān[338] and told them. Al-Mahdī kicked me with his foot and said to me, "Why did you go to him? He has no illness, but I asked him yesterday for money and he pretended to be ill. Take him the sum you mentioned." I did that and when al-Mahdī came to him he said, "O Abū ʿAbdallāh, you were complaining of need, while Khāliṣah had all this!!"

According to ʿAlī b. Muḥammad—Wāḍiḥ, freedman of Abū Jaʿfar: Abū Jaʿfar said one day, "See what worn-out clothes you have and collect them together and, when you know of the approach of Abū ʿAbdallāh, bring them to me before he enters and bring rags with them." I did this and, when al-Mahdī came to him, he was assessing the value of the rags and al-Mahdī laughed and said, "O Commander of the Faithful, people say about this, 'They look after the *dīnār* and the *dirham* and what is less than that,'" but he did not say the *dāniq*.[339] Al-Manṣūr replied, "There are not new clothes for him who does not mend his worn garment. This winter has arrived, and we need clothes for the family and children." Al-Mahdī said, "I will pay for the clothing of the Commander of the Faithful and his family and children." He said, "Fine, get on with it."

According to ʿAlī b. Marthad[340] Abū Diʿāmah the poet—
[406] Ashjaʿ b. ʿAmr al-Sulamī[341]—al-Muʾammil b. Umayl:[342] This

338. Mother of al-Hādī and Hārūn al-Rashīd. Al-Mahdī married her in 159/775–76, and she died in 173/789–90.

339. Small copper coin of very little value. This refers to the nickname al-Manṣūr was given by the people because of stinginess, i.e., Abū al-Dawānīq.

340. The addendum suggests this name should read Yazīd. He is also recorded as a transmitter of poetry. See Ṭabarī, III, 593.

341. See *Aghānī*, Būlāq, XVII, 30; Beirut, XVIII, 143.

342. B. Usayd al-Muḥāribī. For this poet, see *Aghānī*, Būlāq, XIX, 147; Beirut, XXII, 255, where the narrative and the poem are given with minor variations. He had been a poet in Umayyad times but was attached to al-Mahdī, and it was for him that his best-known work was done.

is also according to ʿAbdallāh b. al-Ḥasan al-Khwārazmī[343]—Abū Qudāmah[344]—al-Mu'ammil b. Umayl: I came to al-Mahdī, says Ibn Marthad in his narrative, when he was heir apparent (al-Khwārazmī says: I came to him in al-Rayy when he was heir apparent), and he ordered that I be given twenty thousand *dirhams* for some verses in which I praised him. The head of the post wrote about this to al-Manṣūr, who was in the City of Peace, telling him that al-Mahdī had ordered that twenty thousand *dirhams* be paid to a poet. Al-Manṣūr wrote to him reproving and criticizing him, saying that he needed to give the poet, after he had remained at his gate for a year, only four thousand *dirhams*.

According to Abū Qudāmah: Al-Mahdī's secretary wrote to me asking me to send him the poet; he was sought but could not be found, so he wrote saying that he had set out for the City of Peace. Al-Manṣūr sent one of his commanders to wait at the bridge of Nahrawān and ordered him to scrutinize the people who were crossing one by one until he came across al-Mu'ammil. When he saw him he said, "Who are you?" and he replied, "I am al-Mu'ammil b. Umayl, one of the guests of the Prince al-Mahdī." He said, "You are the one I am looking for," and al-Mu'ammil said that his heart almost burst for fear of Abū Jaʿfar. "He seized me and brought me to the gate of al-Maqṣūrah and handed me over to al-Rabīʿ. Al-Rabīʿ went in to al-Manṣūr and said, 'This is the poet whom we have arrested,' and he said, 'Bring him in to me,' so I was brought in to him. I greeted him and he returned the greeting, and I said to myself, 'There is nothing but good in this.' He said, 'You are al-Mu'ammil b. Umayl?' and I said, 'Yes, may God preserve the Commander of the Faithful.' He said, 'You came to an inexperienced youth and cheated him,' and I replied, 'Yes, may God preserve the Commander of the Faithful, I came to an [407]
inexperienced and generous young man and cheated him and he allowed himself to be cheated.' That seemed to please him, and he asked me to recite to him what I said about al-Mahdī. I recited:

He is al-Mahdī, except that in him
    is the similarity to the appearance of the shining moon.

---

343. Called al-Ḥarrānī in the *Aghānī* narrative.

344. Possibly ʿUthmān b. Muḥammad, who is recorded twice before in al-Ṭabarī's *History*.

The one and the other are similar when they both shine;
    they are confusing to the discerning.
One in the dark is the lamp of night;
    the other in the day is the lamp of light.
But the Merciful One has preferred one to the other
    by giving him pulpits and the throne
And a glorious kingdom. For that one is the Prince;
    but the other is neither a prince nor a *wazīr*.
The decline of the month darkens one,
    but the other shines at the decline of months.
O pure son of the caliph of God!
    In him the boasting of the boastful overtops.
If you have outstripped the kings, and they come to you
    from flat lands and rugged places,
Your father (before you) preceded the kings also, so that
    they are left one stumbling and one lagging behind.
You come after him, running swiftly.
    There is no weariness in you when you run.
The people say, 'What are these two if not
    perfectly suited and competent for the rank?
If the elder comes first he is worthy of his precedence;
    he has the virtue of the elder over the younger.
If the younger covers the same distance as the elder had,
    the younger was created from the elder.'

Al-Manṣūr said, 'You have done well, but this is not worth twenty thousand *dirhams*,' and he continued, 'Where is the money?' and I said, 'Here it is.' He said, 'Rabīʿ, go down with him and and give him four thousand *dirhams* and take the rest.' Al-Rabīʿ went out and he put down my load, weighed out four thousand *dirhams* for me and took the rest. When the caliphate passed
[408] to al-Mahdī he appointed Ibn Thawbān[345] to the *maẓālim*. He used to hold audience for the people in al-Ruṣāfah and, when his robe was full of notes, he would take them up to al-Mahdī. One day I took him in a note in which I told my story. When Ibn Thawbān brought them in, al-Mahdī began to look through the

345. Not known elsewhere.

notes until, when he saw mine, he laughed and Ibn Thawbān said to him, 'God preserve the Commander of the Faithful, I did not see you laugh at any of these notes except this one.' He replied, 'I know the reason behind it; give him back the twenty thousand *dirhams*,' so they were returned to me and I left."

According to Wāḍiḥ, freedman of al-Manṣūr: One day I was standing at the head of Abū Ja'far when al-Mahdī came in to him, wearing a new, black cloak. He gave a greeting, sat down and then got up to go. Abū Ja'far followed him with his eyes because of his love for and delight in him. When he was in the middle of the portico, he stumbled on his sword and tore his black cloak. He got up and continued on his way unperturbed and unconcerned with what had happened. Abū Ja'far said, "Bring back Abū 'Abdallāh," so we brought him back to him and he said, "O Abū 'Abdallāh, is it disparaging of gifts or arrogance in prosperity or lack of knowledge of the occasion of misfortune, as if you were ignorant of what you have and of your responsibilities?! The position you are in is a gift from God; if you give thanks to Him for it, He will increase it for you, and, if you acknowledge that the time of misfortune in it is from Him, He will forgive you." Al-Mahdī replied, "May God not shorten your life, O Commander of the Faithful, or your guidance. Praise be to God for His beneficence and I give God thanks for His gifts and the glorious compensation by His mercy." Then he left.

According to al-'Abbās b. al-Walīd b. Mazyad[346]—Nā'im b. Mazyad—al-Waḍīn b. 'Aṭā': Abū Ja'far wanted me to visit him, as there had been friendship between him and me before the ('Abbāsid) caliphate. I went to the City of Peace, and one day when we were alone together he said to me, "O Abū 'Abdallāh, [409]
what is your wealth?" and I replied, "The wealth the Commander of the Faithful knows of," and then he asked, "What is your household?" and I replied, "Three daughters, my wife, and a maidservant for them." He said, "That is four in your house?" and I said, "Yes," and, by God, he repeated that to me, so that I thought that he was going to make me rich. Then he raised his head and

346. Al-Āmulī al-Bayrūtī contributes a number of narratives to the first section of the *History* but nothing else in the Umayyad or 'Abbāsid period. The other two names in the *isnād* are unknown.

said, "You are the most prosperous of the Arabs with the four spindles they are turning in your house."

According to Bishr al-Munajjim:[347] Abū Ja'far called me one day at sunset and sent me off on some errand, and when I returned he lifted the corner of his prayer mat and there was a *dīnār*, and he said to me, "Take this and keep it," and I have it to this hour.

According to Abū al-Jahm b. 'Aṭiyyah[348]—Abū Muqātil al-Khurāsānī: One of his pages let Abū Ja'far know that he had ten thousand *dirhams*, and Abū Ja'far took it from him, saying, "This is my money." The man asked, "How can it be your money? By God, I was never appointed in any office by you, and there is no kinship or relationship between you and me." Abū Ja'far said, "Yes, you were married to a freedwoman of 'Uyaynah b. Mūsā b. Ka'b,[349] and she bequeathed you some wealth. That man was disobedient, and he took my money when he was governor of Sind, and this is part of that money."

According to Muṣ'ab—Sallām—Abū Ḥārithah al-Nahdī, the master of the treasury:[350] Abū Ja'far appointed a man to Bārūsamā,[351] and when his governorship was over the caliph wanted an excuse for not giving him anything, so he said, "I took you into my confidence and appointed you to part of the *fay'*[352] of the Muslims and you have betrayed it," and he replied, "I ask God's protection against you, O Commander of the Faithful; I kept nothing from that office except a little bit of a *dirham* which I slipped into my sleeve so as to use it when I go out from you, to hire a mule to go to my family, and I shall enter my house without any of the wealth of God or of your wealth," and al-Manṣūr said,

---

347. Al-Munajjim means "the astrologer." Not known elsewhere.

348. This *isnād* poses problems. Abū al-Jahm b. 'Aṭiyyah played an important role in the proclamation of al-Saffāḥ as caliph and is described as his *wazīr*. He disappears from the record after 137/755, but the narrative must date from after 'Uyaynah's rebellion in 142/759–60.

349. He was governor of Sind and rebelled in 142/759–60 but was captured and executed (see al-Ṭabarī, III, 138–39; Ya'qūbī, *Tārīkh*, II, 448).

350. *Ṣāḥib Bayt al-Māl*. Nothing seems to be known of this individual or of the office he held. Nahd were a Yemeni clan, many of whom settled in al-Kūfah.

351. In the *sawād* of Baghdad. See Yāqūt, *Mu'jam*, I, 320; Le Strange, *Lands*, 70, 81.

352. The booty taken in the Islamic conquests, which, it was argued, should be treated as the common propoerty of the Muslim community as a whole.

"I do not doubt that you are telling the truth. Give us our *dirham*!" [410]
and he took it from him and put it under his skullcap and said, "You and I are like the protector of Umm 'Āmir," to which the man said, "What is the protector of Umm 'Āmir?" and he told him the story of the hyena and its protector.[353] Al-Manṣūr only treated him harshly in order not to give him anything.

According to Muṣ'ab—Hishām b. Muḥammad:[354] Qutham b. al-'Abbās went in to Abū Ja'far and made a request and Abū Ja'far said to him, "Do not bother me with this request of yours. Tell me why you are called Qutham," and he replied, "By God, O Commander of the Faithful, I do not know," and he said, "Qutham is someone who eats and carries away food. Have you not heard the words of the poet?

The great ones eat how they wish.
The eating of the little ones is gulping down and carrying away."

According to Muṣ'ab—Ibrāhīm b. 'Īsā: Al-Manṣūr gave twenty thousand *dirhams* to Muḥammad b. Sulaymān and ten thousand to his brother Ja'far. Ja'far said, "O Commander of the Faithful, you preferred him to me, and I am older than he." He replied, "Do you think you are similar to him? Wherever we turn we find some trace of Muḥammad in it and some part of his gifts in our house, whereas you do not do any of this."

According to Muṣ'ab—Sawādah b. 'Amr al-Sulamī—'Abd al-Malik b. 'Aṭā', one of the courtiers[355] of al-Manṣūr: I heard Ibn Hubayrah[356] saying, when he was giving audience, "I never saw in battle or heard of in peace a man more crafty, more amazing, or more alert than al-Manṣūr. He besieged me in my city for nine months. I had with me the horsemen of the Arabs,[357] and we

353. Freytag, *Proverbia*, II, 333, explains the reference. The hunted hyena (Umm 'Āmir) had been protected and fed by an Arab, whom he had subsequently killed.

354. See above, note 272.

355. *Ṣaḥābah*; see above, note 143. Neither Sawādah nor 'Abd al-Malik is recorded elsewhere.

356. Yazīd b. 'Umar b. Hubayrah, the last Umayyad governor of Iraq, was besieged in Wāsiṭ by Abū Ja'far and executed after his surrender.

357. *Fursān al-'Arab*, in contrast to the 'Abbāsid troops, many of whom were Persians.

strove with all our might to take advantage of his army and defeat
[411] it, but there was no opportunity. When he began the siege there was not a white hair on my head; when I surrendered to him there was not a black one. As the poet al-Aʿshā says:[358]

He stands out in spite of his people.
He forgives, if he wishes, or takes revenge,
The brother of war, with no enfeebling weakness,
who does not wear worn-out sandals."

According to Ibrāhīm b. ʿAbd al-Raḥmān:[359] Abū Jaʿfar was staying with a man called Azhar al-Sammān, not the traditionist.[360] This was before his caliphate, and, when he succeeded to the caliphate, Azhar went to him in the City of Peace, and, when he was admitted, the caliph asked him what he wanted. He replied, "O Commander of the Faithful, I have a debt of 4,000 *dirhams* and my house is falling down, and my son Muḥammad wants to marry." He ordered that he be given 12,000 *dirhams* and said, "O Azhar, do not come to us making requests," and he agreed. After a little he returned, and the caliph asked him what had brought him. He replied, "I came to greet you, O Commander of the Faithful" and he said, "It occurs to me that you have come to us for the things for which you came to us the first time," and he ordered him to be given twelve thousand *dirhams* and said, "O Azhar, do not come to us making requests or greeting us," and he agreed. He did not wait long before he returned, and the caliph asked him what had brought him and he said, "A prayer I heard from you that I wanted to learn." The caliph replied, "You should not want it, for it has not been granted because I called on God in it to spare me from your foolishness, and he has not done so." He sent him away and did not give him anything.

According to al-Haytham b. ʿAdī—Ibn ʿAyyāsh: Ibn Hubayrah sent to al-Manṣūr when he was besieged in Wāsiṭ, and al-Manṣūr

358. Maymūn b. Qays, ca. 570–625, a well-known blind poet of the pre-Islamic period from central Arabia; see *Aghānī*, Būlāq, VIII, 77; Beirut, IX, 104; *EI*², s.v. "al-Aʿshā."

359. Not recorded elsewhere.

360. Probably to distinguish him from Azhar b. Saʿīd b. Nāfiʿ, used by al-Ṭabarī as a source earlier in section III. Sammān means "butter merchant."

was confronting him saying, "I will be coming out on such-and-such a day and meet you in single combat, for I have heard that you call me coward." Al-Manṣūr wrote to him:

> O Ibn Hubayrah, you are a man without self-control and running in the reins of your sin. God threatens you with [412] what He tells the truth about, and Satan raises your hopes with what he lies about and allows the approach of what God keeps away and gradually things will run their course. I have found a fable for you and me. I have heard that a lion met a pig, and the pig said to him, "Fight me," and the lion replied, "But you are only a pig and you are not a match or equal for me. When I do what you are asking me to and I kill you, it will be said to me, 'You killed a pig,' and I will not gain any reputation or mention from that, and if I obtain something from you it will be a disgrace to me," and the pig replied, "If you do not do this, I shall go back to the other lions and tell them that you have flinched from me and were too cowardly to fight me," and the lion said, "Bearing the dishonor of your lies is easier for me than the shame of staining my mustache with your blood."

According to Muḥammad b. Riyāḥ al-Jawharī:[361] Abū Ja'far was told about the planning of Hishām b. 'Abd al-Malik[362] in one of his wars, so he sent for a man who was with him and settled in Ruṣāfah Hishām[363] to ask him about that war. When he arrived he said to him, "You were a companion of Hishām?" and he replied, "Yes, O Commander of the Faithful." Al-Manṣūr went on, "Tell me about his war, which he handled in the year so-and-so." The man said, "He, may God have mercy on him, did such-and-such," and then he went on "he did such-and-such, may God be pleased with him." Abū Ja'far became annoyed at this and said, "May God's wrath come upon you. You tread on my carpet

361. Not recorded elsewhere. Jawharī means "a jeweler."

362. Umayyad caliph, 105–25/724–43.

363. Ancient Sergiopolis, the ruins now called al-Ruṣāfah, south of al-Raqqah in the Syrian desert, a favorite residence of Hishām. See Yāqūt, *Mu'jam*, III, 47; Le Strange, *Lands*, 106.

and ask blessings for my enemy," and the old man stood up and said, "Your enemy put a necklace on my neck and favor on my head that no one will remove except the man who washes my body when I am dead." Al-Manṣūr ordered him to return and said, "Stay. Look, what did you say?" "I said that he saved me from begging people and protected my face from asking favors. Since I saw him, I have not stopped at the gate of an Arab or a non-Arab. Should I not feel obliged to mention him favorably and bestow
[413] my praise on him?" He said, "Yes, what a mother that gave birth to you and what a night that was disclosed on you! I bear witness that you are the son of a freeborn mother and of a noble father." Then he listened to him and ordered that he be given gifts. He said, "O Commander of the Faithful, I do not take it out of need but only so that I may be honored by your generosity and boast of your gift." Then he took his gift and went out, and al-Manṣūr said, "Where in our army is there a man like that? To such a man favor is recommended, kindness finds its proper place, and the protected valuables can be given."

According to Ḥafṣ b. Ghiyāth[364]—Ibn 'Ayyāsh: A number of the people of al-Kūfah continued to speak evil of their administrator (*'āmil*) and complain about their governor (*amīr*)[365] and verbally attack their Sulṭān. This was told to al-Manṣūr in a report, and he said to al-Rabī', "Go out to those of the people of al-Kūfah who are at the gate and tell them that the Commander of the Faithful says to them, 'If two of you gather together in a place, I will shave their heads and their beards and strike their backs so go to your houses and take care of yourselves.'" Al-Rabī' went out to them with this message, and Ibn 'Ayyāsh[366] said to him, "O you who look like 'Īsā b. Maryam,[367] tell the Commander of

364. Al-Nakha'ī: *qāḍī* of the Sharqiyyah of Baghdad and later of al-Kūfah and an important traditionist of Hārūn's reign. He is also an occasional source for section I of the *History*; see al-Khaṭīb, VIII, 188.

365. It is not clear whether the *'āmil* and the *amīr* are two different officials or whether this duplication is simply for rhetorical effect. For the language of appointments, see above, note 28.

366. 'Abdallāh b. 'Ayyāsh al-Ḥamdānī, d. 158/774–75. He was a member of the *saḥābah* of al-Manṣūr and famous for his wit: see al-Khaṭīb, X, 14–16. He also appears as a source for both Umayyad and 'Abbāsid material and was used by al-Haytham b. 'Adī.

367. Possibly a reference to *Qur'ān*, XLIII: 61: "And ('Īsā) shall be a Sign for the

the Faithful from us what you told us from him and say to him, 'By God, O Commander of the Faithful, we cannot tolerate beating, but if you want beards shaved....'" Ibn 'Ayyāsh was clean-shaven. When al-Manṣūr was informed, he laughed and said, "What a really crafty and wicked man!"

According to Mūsā b. Ṣāliḥ[368]—Muḥammad b. 'Uqbah al-Ṣaydāwī[369]—Naṣr b. Ḥarb, who was in the guard of al-Manṣūr: There was brought to me a man from a distant part who had plotted to undermine the state, so I brought him in to Abū Ja'far and when he saw him he said, "Are you Aṣbagh?"[370] and he said, "Yes, O Commander of the Faithful," so the caliph continued, "Woe to you. Did I not free you and do good to you?" and he said, "Yes." "And you have striven to destroy my state and undermine [414]
my rule," and he said, "I have done wrong, and forgiveness is more becoming for the Commander of the Faithful." Abū Ja'far called 'Umārah,[371] who was present, and said to him, "O 'Umārah, this is Aṣbagh." 'Umarah started to gaze intently into my face because he had evil in his eyes and said, "Yes, O Commander of the Faithful," and al-Manṣūr said, "Bring me the purse that contains my (*'aṭā'*)," and so the purse was brought and there were five hundred *dirhams* in it, and he said, "Take it. It is pure silver, woe to you! Go to your work," and he pointed with his hand and moved it. 'Umārah said, "I asked Aṣbagh what the Commander of the Faithful meant and he replied, 'When I was a young man, I made ropes and he used to eat from my earnings.'"[372]

Naṣr said: Then he was brought again, and I took him in as I had before and, when he stood before him, he stared at him and said, "Aṣbagh!" and he replied, "Yes, O Commander of the Faithful," and he told him what he did to him and reminded him of it,

---

coming of the Hour of Judgment; therefore have no doubt about the Hour but follow ye Me; this is a Straight Way," but it may be that Ibn 'Ayyāsh is insinuating that al-Rabī'—like 'Īsā—had no father.

368. Probably the traditionist Mūsā b. Ṣāliḥ b. Shaykh, d. 257/871 (al-Khaṭīb, XIII, 42–43). He appears again as a narrator; see al-Ṭabarī, III, 589

369. Ṣaydāwī means from Sidon (Saydā) in Lebanon Not known elsewhere.

370. No further information seems to be known about him.

371. B. Ḥamzah; see note 214, above.

372. That is, during Abū Ja'far's wanderings before the 'Abbāsids came to power.

and he admitted it and said, "Stupidity, O Commander of the Faithful," so he brought him forward and cut off his head.

According to 'Alī b. Muḥammad b. Sulaymān al-Nawfalī—his father: The dye used by al-Manṣūr was saffron, and that was because his hair was soft and would not take dye. His beard was thin and I saw him in the pulpit, preaching and weeping, and the tears hastened down his beard and dripped because of its softness and thinness.

Ibrāhīm b. 'Abd al-Salām, son of the brother of al-Sindī b. Shāhik—al-Sindī:[373] Al-Manṣūr captured one of the great men of the Banū Umayyah and said, "I will ask you something and, if you tell me the truth, you will be safe." The man agreed and al-Manṣūr asked, "What happened to the Banū Umayyah that their affairs fell into disorder?" He said, "Neglecting information." Then he asked, "What sort of wealth did they find most useful?" and he said, "Jewels." He asked, "Among what people did they find most loyalty?" and he replied, "Their freedmen." Al-Manṣūr wanted to ask for help from members of his family in gathering information, but then he said, "I would diminish their status," and he sought help from his freedmen.

[415] According to 'Alī b. Muḥammad al-Hāshimī—his father, Muḥammad b. Sulaymān: I was told that al-Manṣūr took medicine on a very cold winter day and I went to him to ask him about the effect of the medicine on him. I was admitted by an entrance to the palace I had never been in before. Then I went into a little enclosure with one room in it and a portico in front of it, at the edge of the house and the courtyard, supported on teak columns. Over the front of the portico, curtains (*bawārī*) were hanging, as they do in mosques.[374] I went in and in the room was a coarse carpet and nothing else except his mattress, his pillows, and his blankets, and I said, "O Commander of the Faithful, this room is not worthy of you," and he replied, "O my uncle, this is the room

---

373. A mawlā (freedman) of al-Manṣūr, who became a powerful figure in the reigns of Hārūn and al-Amīn. He died in 204/819 (Crone, *Slaves*, 194–95). Ibrāhīm b. 'Abd al-Salām is recorded (see al-Ṭabarī, III, 580) as transmitter of another story from al-Sindī, this time about the caliph al-Hādī.

374. The architectural vocabulary is interesting here. *Hujayrah* is the word I have translated as "little enclosure," *bayt* as "room," *riwāq* as "portico."

I sleep in," and I asked if there was anything more than what I saw, and he said, "There is only what you see."

According to ʿAlī b. Muḥammad al-Hāshimī: I heard him say on the authority of someone who spoke on the authority of Jaʿfar b. Muḥammad who said that it was said that Abū Jaʿfar was accustomed to wear a ragged Harawī *jubbah*[375] and that he patched his shirt, and Jaʿfar said, "Thanks be to God, Who favored him by afflicting him with poverty on his person," or he said, "With poverty in his power."

He said that his father told him: Al-Manṣūr never appointed someone to an official post and then dismissed him without throwing him in the house of Khālid al-Baṭīn (the fat), which was on the bank of the Tigris adjoining the house of Ṣāliḥ al-Miskīn,[376] to extract money from the dismissed man. He ordered that everything that was taken should be inscribed with the name of the man from whom it had been taken and deposited in a treasury that he called the treasury of the *maẓālim*.[377] The quantity of money and goods in that treasury became enormous. Then he said to al-Mahdī, "I have given you something with which you can please the people and not spend any of your own money. When I am dead, summon those from whom I have taken this [416]
wealth that I have called the *maẓālim* and return it to them just as it was taken from them, and you will earn their praise and that of the people," and al-Mahdī did that when he succeeded.

According to ʿAlī b. Muḥammad: Al-Manṣūr appointed ʿAbdallāh b. Sulaymān b. Muḥammad b. ʿAbd al-Muṭṭalib b. Rabīʿah b. al-Ḥārith as governor of Balqāʾ[378] and then dismissed him and

375. For *jubbah*, see note 319, above. Harawī means that it was made in Herat, Afghanistan.

376. Khālid is otherwise unknown. Ṣāliḥ al-Miskīn ("the poor," apparently because of his ascetic life style) was a son of al-Manṣūr. For this palace, see Le Strange, *Baghdad*, 108.

377. *Maẓālim* means "complaints" and was the name given to the court where people could complain about government injustice.

378. I have accepted the reading of this name proposed by Houtsma, editor of the Leiden edition. The two manuscripts on which this portion of the text is based—Koprulü 1040 and Berlin—give different versions, but the editor has retrieved the correct form from Yaʿqūbī and Ibn al-Athīr; see p. 416 n. a. This may be another version of the incidents related below, pp 207 and 218, where ʿAbdallāh is appointed to Yemen and dismissed and arrested by al-Mahdī. Balqāʾ is in modern Jordan near ʿAmmān. See Yāqūt, *Muʿjam*, 489; Le Strange, *Palestine*, 34–35.

ordered that he should be brought to him with the wealth that was found on him. He was taken by the postal service along with two thousand *dīnārs*, which were carried by the post with his luggage, which consisted of a Sūsanjird prayer rug,[379] a quilt, bedding, two cushions, a bowl and an ewer, and an alkali holder[380] made of copper. He found it all together with his equipment, but the baggage was worn out, so he took the two thousand *dīnārs* but was ashamed to take the baggage and said, "I do not recognize it," and left it. Later al-Mahdī appointed him governor of the Yemen and al-Rashīd appointed his son, called Rabrā,[381] to Medina.

According to Aḥmad b. al-Haytham b. Jaʿfar b. Sulaymān b. ʿAlī[382]—Ṣabbāḥ b. Khāqān: I was with Abū Jaʿfar when the head of Ibrāhīm b. ʿAbdallāh b. Ḥasan was brought.[383] It was put in front of him on a shield. One of the executioners leaned over it and spat in its face, and Abū Jaʿfar stared at him hard and said to
[417] me, "Strike his nose." I struck his nose with a staff such a blow that you could not find his nose for a thousand *dīnārs*. Then the staffs of the guard began on him, and he was pounded by them until he became unconscious and he was dragged out by the feet.

According to al-Aṣmaʿī[384]—Jaʿfar b. Sulaymān: Ashʿab[385] came to Baghdad in the days of Abū Jaʿfar and he was surrounded by the young men of Banū Hāshim and he sang to them and, when his songs were moving and his voice was (as good) as ever, Jaʿfar said to him, "Who composed this poem?

---

379. Sūsanjird textiles were produced at Qurqub in Khūzistān. See Le Strange, *Lands*, 241.

380. *Ushnāndānah*, for holding the ashes of glasswort used for cleaning the hands.

381. Houtsma, citing ibn al-Athīr, VI, 147, establishes that his true name was Muḥammad. The reading of Rabrā is uncertain, and the editor (*Addendum*, DCLIV) suggests Zirā as a possible alternative. The significance of the name, which is described as a *laqab*, or title, is quite unclear to me.

382. A grandson of al-Manṣūr's cousin Jaʿfar b. Sulaymān (see note 35, above). He contributes one other anecdote, below, p. ooo.

383. The ʿAlid rebel killed in 145/763.

384. ʿAbd al-Malik b. Qarīb al-Nahwī, d. 210/825–86, a well-known grammarian and historian who was originally from al-Baṣrah but came to Baghdad in Hārūn's reign. He contributes occasional information on the Umayyads and ʿAbbāsids to al-Ṭabarī's *History*; see EI^2, s.v. "al-Aṣmaʿī."

385. Ashʿab b. Jubayr, d. after 154/771, a famous singer of the early ʿAbbāsid court. See *Aghānī*, Būlāq, XVII, 83; Beirut, XIX, 69.

Whose are the traces of the camp at Dhāt al-Jaysh, which became
obliterated and worn out?
They (the women on the riding camels) were out in the open
desert, and the grief-stricken passed a sleepless night."

He replied, "I took the song from Ma'bad.[386] I used to take melodies from him and if he was asked for it he would say, 'Go to Ash'ab, for he has a better rendering of it than I.'"

According to al-Aṣma'ī—Ja'far b. Sulaymān: Ash'ab said to his son 'Ubaydah "I think that I will expel you from my house and banish you," and he asked, "Why, O Father?" and his father replied, "I am the best of God's creatures in earning a loaf of bread, and you are my son and you have reached this age of maturity and you are still in my household and have not earned anything." His son said, "I do earn, but I am like the banana tree that does not bear fruit until its mother dies."

According to 'Alī b. Muḥammad b. Sulaymān al-Hāshimī—his father Muḥammad: The Sasanians used to cover the roofs of their houses with clay in the summer every day and the king had his [418] siesta there. Stems of canes and willows, long and thick, were brought and put together closely around the house. Large pieces of ice were brought and put in the spaces between them. The Umayyads did the same, and al-Manṣūr was the first to use sackcloth.

Some people say that at the beginning of his caliphate al-Manṣūr made a clay house for himself in which to take his siesta in the summer. Abū Ayyūb al-Khūzī brought heavy cloths for him, which were dampened and placed on a wooden framework, and he enjoyed its cold and said, "I reckon that if you took thicker cloths than these, they would hold more water and would be colder." So he took sackcloth, and it was made into a dome for him. Then the caliphs after him took woven palm leaves, and the people did likewise.[387]

386. Two famous singers of this name are known: Ma'bad b. Wahb, who was well known in the Umayyad court of Damascus in the reign of al-Walīd b. Yazīd, d. 126/744, and Ma'bad al-Yaqṭīnī, who appeared at court in Hārūn's reign and was attached to the Barmakids; it is difficult to link either of these chronologically to Ash'ab. See *Aghānī*, Būlāq, I, 19 XII, 168; Beirut, I, 47, XIV, 110.

387. For a discussion of these methods of cooling, see Ahsan, *Social Life*, 182–83.

According to 'Alī b. Muḥammad—his father: There was a man of the Rāwandiyyah called al-Ablaq (piebald), who was a leper, and he preached extremism[388] and called men to the Rāwandiyyah, alleging that the spirit that was in Jesus, son of Mary, passed to 'Alī b. Abī Ṭālib and then to the Imāms, one after the other, to Ibrāhīm b. Muḥammad,[389] and that they were gods. These Rāwandiyyah made the forbidden lawful to the extent that a man of them summoned a group of them to his house, fed them, gave them drink, and offered them his wife. News of this reached Asad b. 'Abdallāh,[390] and he killed them and crucified them, but this still continues among them to the present day. They worshiped Abū Ja'far al-Manṣūr, and they climbed up to the Khaḍrā'[391] and threw themselves off as if they could fly. A group of them attacked
[419] the people with arms and began shouting for Abū Ja'far, "You, you!" He went out against them in person to fight them, and they continued to say, "You, you!" while they were fighting.

He said: It was told to us on the authority of one of our shaykhs that he watched the group of the Rāwandiyyah throwing themselves off the Khaḍrā' as if they were flying, and none of them reached the ground without being broken in pieces and his soul going out.

According to Aḥmad b. Thābit,[392] the freedman of Muḥammad b. Sulaymān b. 'Alī—his father: When 'Abdallāh b. 'Alī was hiding from al-Manṣūr in al-Baṣrah with Sulaymān b. 'Alī,[393] he looked out one day, and there were with him a number of his freedmen and a freedman of Sulaymān b. 'Alī, and he saw a man of beauty and perfection walking haughtily[394] and dragging his

388. *Ghuluww*, meaning extremely heterodox ideas that often included, as here, ideas of the transmigration of souls.

389. Brother of al-Saffāḥ and al-Manṣūr, killed by the Umayyads immediately before the 'Abbāsid Revolution and often referred to as Ibrāhīm al-Imām.

390. Al-Qasrī, Umayyad governor of Khurāsān, 116–19/734–37. See Crone, *Slaves*, 102; and *EI*², s.v. "Asad b. 'Abdallāh."

391. The name given to al-Manṣūr's palace in the Round City in Baghdad because of its green dome. Le Strange, *Baghdad*, 31–33.

392. Not known elsewhere.

393. After his abortive rebellion against al-Manṣūr, 'Abdallāh b. 'Alī took refuge with his brother Sulaymān, who was at that time governor of al-Baṣrah.

394. *Khaja'a* is a kind of walk in which a man pushes his buttocks backward and goes on slowly and haughtily.

long clothes as a sign of pride. He turned to the freedman of Sulaymān b. ʿAlī and asked him who it was, and he replied that it was so-and-so, son of so-and-so the Umayyad. ʿAbdallāh flew into a rage and clapped his hands in amazement and said, "There is still a hillock in our road," and he ordered one of his freedmen to go down and bring him his head. He found a simile in the words of Sudayf:[395]

Why and wherefore do we neglect ʿAbd Shams,[396]
having a bleat in every flock?
It would not redeem the tomb in Ḥarrān,[397]
even if it were killed in its entirety.

According to ʿAlī b. Muḥammad al-Madāʾinī: After the defeat of ʿAbdallāh b. ʿAlī and his capture by al-Manṣūr and his imprisonment in Baghdad, a delegation of the people of Syria[398] came to Abū Jaʿfar al-Manṣūr, among them al-Ḥārith b. ʿAbd al-Raḥmān. A number of them stood up and made their speeches, and then al-Ḥārith b. ʿAbd al-Raḥmān[399] stood up and said, "May God protect the Commander of the Faithful. We are not a delegation of boasting but a delegation of repentance. We were put to the test in the revolt that stirred up our noble and carried away our prudent. We confess what we have done and seek pardon for our previous deeds. If you punish us, it is for the crimes we have committed, and, if you forgive us, it is because of your generosity to us. [420]
Forgive us since you have the power; give us an amnesty since you are able. Do good when you have been victorious and you have always been doing good." Abū Jaʿfar said, "It is done."

---

395. Sudayf b. Maymūn; see *Aghānī*, Būlāq, XIV, 162; Beirut, XVI, 86. A Ḥijāzī poet of Umayyad times who was a partisan of the Banū Hāshim and forced into hiding. He survived into the ʿAbbāsid period. This is the only citation of this poet in al-Ṭabarī's *History*.

396. The ancestor of the Umayyads and brother to Hāshim, ancestor of the ʿAbbāsids and ʿAlids.

397. Near Edessa (modern Urfa) just north of the Turkish-Syrian frontier. Marwān, the last Umayyad caliph, had made it his capital. Yāqūt, *Muʿjam*, II, 235, quotes a parallel verse that makes it clear that the tomb referred to is that of the ʿAbbāsid Ibrāhīm al-Imām.

398. ʿAbdallāh b. ʿAlī had received most of his support from the people of Syria; see Kennedy, *ʿAbbasid Caliphate*, 58–61.

399. Al-Ḥarashī, nothing more is known of him.

According to al-Haytham b. ʿAdī—Zayd, freedman of ʿĪsā b. Nahīk:[400] Al-Manṣūr called me after the death of my master and said, "O Zayd," and I said, "Your servant, O Commander of the Faithful," and he continued, "How much money did Abū Zayd leave?" and I replied that it was about a thousand *dīnār*s, and then he asked, "Where is it?" and I said that his widow had spent it on his funeral, and he was surprised at that and said, "The widow spent a thousand *dīnār*s on his funeral. I am amazed at this." Then he asked, "How many daughters did he leave?" and I said that there were six, and he bowed his head in silence for a long time. Then he looked up and said, "Go in the morning to al-Mahdī's gate." I went and I was asked if I had a mule with me and I replied that I had not been provided with that or with anything else and that I did not know why I had been summoned. I was given one hundred and eighty thousand *dīnār*s and ordered to give each of ʿĪsa's daughters thirty thousand *dīnār*s. Al-Manṣūr summoned me and asked me, "Have you collected what we ordered for the daughters of Abū Zayd?" and I replied, "Yes, O Commander of the Faithful," and he said, "In the morning bring to me those who are of suitable rank so that I can marry them to those men." I brought him three of the children of al-ʿAkkī and three of the family of Nahīk, their paternal cousins, and he married each of them off with a dowry of thirty thousand *dirham*s and ordered that their dowries should be brought to them from his own money. He told me to use the money he had ordered to buy estates for them to provide an income for them, so I did that.

According to al-Haytham: In one day Abū Jaʿfar distributed to a group of his family ten million *dirham*s, and he ordered that a single one of his paternal uncles be given one million. We do not know of any caliph before him or any caliph after him who con-
[421] ferred that on a single person.

According to al-ʿAbbās b. al-Faḍl: Al-Manṣūr ordered that his

400. Al-ʿAkkī. His brother ʿUthmān had been an early supporter of the ʿAbbāsids in Khurāsān and was one of Abū Muslim's assassins. He had become head of al-Manṣūr's guard, but the Rāwandiyyah, who held him to be the spirit of Adam incarnate, had killed him in their revolt. ʿĪsā succeeded him in command of the guard until his death, probably in the 140s. The point of the story is to show Abū Jaʿfar's concern for a family that had served him well (see Crone, *Slaves*, 189).

paternal uncles Sulaymān, ʿĪsā, Ṣāliḥ, and Ismāʿīl, sons of ʿAlī b. ʿAbdallāh b. ʿAbbās, should each be given a million as their salary from the treasury. He was the first caliph to give a million from the treasury and it was put into effect in the *dīwāns*.[401]

According to Isḥāq b. Ibrāhīm al-Mawṣilī[402]—al-Faḍl b. al-Rabīʿ—his father: Abū Jaʿfar al-Manṣūr held a public audience for the people of Medina in Baghdad, a number of whom had come on a delegation to him. He said, "Let every one of you who come into me give his genealogy." One of those who came in was a young man of the descendants of ʿAmr b. Ḥazm, who gave his genealogy[403] and then said, "O Commander of the Faithful, al-Aḥwaṣ recited a poem about us and we were deprived of our wealth sixty years ago because of it." Abū Jaʿfar told him to recite it so he recited:

Do not be moved with pity for a Ḥazmī if you see
 poverty in him or even if the Ḥazmī has been thrown into the fire,
Those who pricked the mule of Marwān, at Dhū Khushub[404]
 the invaders of ʿUthmān's house.[405]

He continued, "The poem is in praise of al-Walīd b. ʿAbd al-Malik,[406] and he had him recite the *qaṣīdah* and, when he reached this point, al-Walīd said, 'You have reminded me of the sin of the family of Ḥazm,' and he ordered the confiscation of their wealth." Abū Jaʿfar asked him to recite the poem to him again, and he repeated it three times, and Abū Jaʿfar said, "Certainly you will

401. That is to say that it was registered in the *dīwāns*, where official salaries were listed; the implication is that these were regular payments, not one-time gifts.

402. Perhaps the most famous of the singers of the early ʿAbbāsid court. He succeeded his father, who died in 188/804, at the cultural center of the ʿAbbāsid court. See *Aghānī*, Būlāq, V, 52; Beirut, V, 242; *EI*², s.v. "Isḥāḳ b. Ibrāhīm al-Mawṣilī."

403. He was a descendant of ʿAmr b. Ḥazm al-Anṣārī, a companion of the Prophet. The family supported ʿAlī's claim to the caliphate, hence its members' attacks on the Umayyads Marwān and ʿUthmān, their punishment by the Umayyad caliph al-Walīd, and the restoration of their properties by Abū Jaʿfar.

404. A valley one night's journey from Medina (Yāqūt, *Muʿjam*, II, 372).

405. The assailants who attacked the caliph ʿUthmān in his house in Medina and killed him in 35/656.

406. Umayyad caliph, 86–96/705–15.

be made fortunate by this poem as you were deprived by it." Then he said to Abū Ayyūb,[407] "Bring ten thousand *dirhams* and give them to him because of his singing it to us." Then he ordered him to write to his officials instructing them to return the estates of the family of Ḥazm to them and to give them their rents every year from the estates of the Umayyad family and that their wealth be divided up between them according to the Book of God in succession and, whenever any of them died, his heirs would be
[422] safeguarded. The young man left with what no one had left with before.

According to Ja'far b. Aḥmad b. Yaḥyā—Aḥmad b. Asad:[408] Al-Manṣūr delayed going out to the people and riding, and people said that he was ill and they made much of that. Al-Rabī' went in to him and said, "O Commander of the Faithful, may the Commander of the Faithful live long, the people are talking," and he asked what they were saying and al-Rabī' replied that they were saying that he was ill. He bowed his head in silence for a bit and then he said, "O al-Rabī', what do the common people want with me? The common people only need three things. If they are done for them, what more do they need? If I appoint someone for them to supervise their administration, do justice among them, make their roads safe so that they have no fear by night or day, and defend their frontiers and borders so that their enemies do not attack them, I have done that for them." He stayed for some days and then he said, "O Rabī', beat the drum," and he rode out so that the people saw him.

According to 'Alī b. Muḥammad—his father: Abū Ja'far sent Muḥammad b. Abī al-'Abbās with the Manichaeans and the dissolutes,[409] among them Ḥammād 'Ajrad.[410] They stayed with him in al-Baṣrah, and the dissolutes' profligacy became obvious. He wished to do that only to make him hateful to the people. Muḥammad revealed that he loved Zaynab, the daughter of Sulaymān b. 'Alī, and he used to ride each day to the Mirbad, preoccupied

407. Al-Mūryānī, his *wazīr*; see above, note 169. This story can be dated before Abū Ayyūb's fall in 153/770.

408. Neither of these is recorded elsewhere.

409. *Al-zanādiqah wa-al-mujjān* (plural of *mājin*). Ḥammād 'Ajrad was of the second group.

410. *Aghānī*, Būlāq, XIII, 73; Beirut, XIV, 304.

with her and hoping that she would be in some vantage point looking at him. He asked Ḥammād to compose a poem about her, and he made some verses in which he said about her:

O dweller in the Mirbad, you have stirred up in me
a longing so that I am not separated from the Mirbad.

According to ʿAlī b. Muḥammad—his father: Al-Manṣūr was staying with my father for two years, and I knew al-Khaṣīb the doctor because of the number of times he came to him. Al-Khaṣīb pretended to be a Christian, but he was an atheist Manichaean[411] who had no scruples about killing. Al-Manṣūr sent a messenger to him ordering him to put his mind to the killing of Muḥammad b. [423] Abī al-ʿAbbās.[412] He prepared a deadly poison and waited for an illness to afflict Muḥammad. He discovered a fever, and al-Khaṣīb said to him, "Take this drink of medicine," and he replied, "Prepare it for me," so he prepared it for him and put the poison in it and gave it to him to drink and he died from it. Muḥammad b. Abī al-ʿAbbās' mother wrote to al-Manṣūr about it and informed him that al-Khaṣīb had killed her son. Al-Manṣūr wrote ordering that he should be brought to him and, when he arrived, he gave him thirty light strokes of the whip and imprisoned him for some days. Then he gave him three hundred *dirhams* and released him.

According to ʿAlī b. Muḥammad—his father: Al-Manṣūr promised to Umm Mūsā al-Ḥimyariyyah[413] that he would not marry anyone in addition to her or take a concubine, and she obtained that in writing from him and had him confirm it and had it witnessed. He remained faithful to her alone for ten years of his rule, and he wrote to *faqīh*[414] after *faqīh* of the people of al-Ḥijāz seeking a legal opinion on it. A *faqīh* from the people of al-Ḥijāz and from the people of Iraq was brought to him, and he showed him the document so that he could give a legal opinion on annulling it. When Umm Mūsā knew about his position, she hastened

411. *Zindiq muʿaṭṭil.* Al-Khaṣīb is not mentioned elsewhere.

412. He died in 147/764–5 (see above, p. 39). It is not clear why al-Manṣūr should have sought his death, but he may have feared him because Muḥammad was the son of al-Saffāḥ, the previous caliph and al-Manṣūr's brother.

413. Arwā bt. Manṣūr. He married her before becoming caliph. It is not known when she died.

414. Authority on religious law.

to him and sent him a large sum of money. When Abū Ja'far showed the document to him, he gave the opinion that it could not be annulled until she died after ten years of his rule in Baghdad. He heard of her death in Ḥulwān,[415] and that night he was given a hundred virgins. Umm Mūsā bore him Ja'far and al-Mahdī.

It was said on the authority of 'Alī b. Ja'd:[416] When Bukhtīshū' the Elder[417] came to al-Manṣūr from Sūs,[418] he came in to his palace by the Golden Gate in Baghdad. He ordered food for him to have lunch and, when the table was put in front of him, he asked for wine and he was told that wine was not drunk at the table of
[424] the Commander of the Faithful, and he replied that he would not eat food without wine. Al-Manṣūr was told about this and ordered that it be called for. When it was dinner time he did the same thing and asked for wine, and he was told that wine was not drunk at the table of the Commander of the Faithful. He ate dinner and drank the water of Tigris. The next morning he looked at his water and said, "I did not think that anything would compensate for wine, but this Tigris water does compensate for wine."

He mentioned on the authority of Yaḥyā b. al-Ḥasan[419]—his father: Al-Manṣūr wrote to his governor in Medina, "Sell the fruits of the estates and do not sell them to anyone except those whom we can get the better of and not to those who get the better of us. Only the bankrupt with no money, who does not fear our punishment, gets the better of us and takes what we have for himself. Even if he offers you a good price, perhaps you should sell it below that to he who is able to deal justly with you and pay you in full."

According to Abū Bakr al-Hudhalī: Abū Ja'far used to say, "It is not man who is done a favor and who forgets it before death."

According to al-Faḍl b. al-Rabī': I heard al-Manṣūr say that the

415. On the road from Baghdad to the Iranian plateau, at the foot of the Zagros mountains. See Yāqūt, *Mu'jam*, II, 290–91; Le Strange, *Lands*, 191.

416. Al-Jawharī, d. 230/845, a traditionist who contributed just three reports to the 'Abbāsid section of al-Ṭabarī's *History*. See al-Khaṭīb, XI, 360–66.

417. Famous physician, father of Jibra'īl b. Bukhtīshū' and grandfather of Bukhtīshū' the Younger.

418. Ancient Susa, in Khūzistān, southwestern Iran. See Yāqūt, *Mu'jam*, III, 280–81; Le Strange, *Lands*, 240.

419. Yaḥyā b. al-Ḥasan b. 'Abd al-Khāliq, maternal uncle of al-Faḍl b. al-Rabī'.

Arabs say, "Oppressive thirst is better than shameful quenching of thirst."

He mentioned on the authority of Abān b. Yazīd al-'Anbarī—al-Haytham al-Qārī' al-Baṣrī:[420] He read in the presence of al-Manṣūr, "Squander not in the manner of a spendthrift,"[421] to the end of the verse, and al-Manṣūr said to him and started praying, "God preserve me and my son from squandering the gifts that You have bestowed on us!" Al-Haytham read to him, "Those who are niggardly or enjoin niggardliness on others."[422] He said to the people, "If it were not that wealth is the fortress of authority and the pillar of the Faith and of this world and the glory and ornament [425] of them, I would not pass a night retaining a *dīnār* of it nor a *dirham* because of the pleasure I find in expending wealth and because of the reward I know lies in giving it away."

A learned man entered to al-Manṣūr, and he thought little of him and he fixed him with his eyes disdainfully, but he did not ask him any questions he did not know the answer to. He said to him, "Where did you get all this knowledge?" and he replied, "I am not stingy with the knowledge I have learned, and I am not ashamed to learn," and he said, "From there." He said: Al-Manṣūr often used to say, "Whoever acts without organization," or he said, "Whoever acts from lack of organization will not lack mockery or scorn from the people."

According to Qaḥṭabah:[423] I heard al-Manṣūr say that kings will put up with anything from their intimates except three things, giving away of secrets, interfering in what is inviolate, and slandering the king.

According to 'Alī b. Muḥammad: Al-Manṣūr used to say, "Your secret is of your life blood, so take care whom you entrust it to."[424]

According to al-Zubayr b. Bakkār—'Umar: When 'Abd al-

420. Neither of these sources is known elsewhere. Al-Qārī means "the (*Qur'ān*) reader."

421. *Qur'ān*, XVII: 26.

422. *Qur'ān*, IV: 37.

423. B. Ghadānah al-Jushamī. These are the only two occasions al-Ṭabarī uses him as a source.

424. Or "Do not pour it out"; Freytag, *Proverbia*, III, 222.

Jabbār b. ʿAbd al-Raḥmān al-Azdī[425] was brought before al-Manṣūr after his rebellion against him he said, "O Commander of the Faithful, a generous execution," and he replied, "You are too late for that, O son of fornication."

According to ʿUmar b. Shabbah—Qaḥṭabah b. Ghudānah al-Jushamī, who was one of the caliph's courtiers (*ṣaḥābah*): I heard Abū Jaʿfar al-Manṣūr give the sermon in the City of Peace in the year 152/769, and he said, "O servants of God, do not do each other wrong, for that will be counted as a sin on the day of Resurrection. By God, were it not for the sinning hand and the wrongdoing injustice of the criminal, I would walk among you in your markets and, if I knew where there was a man more worthy of this authority than I, I would bring him so that I could hand it over to him."

According to Isḥāq al-Mawṣilī—al-Naḍr b. Ḥadīd:[426] One of the
[426] courtiers told me that al-Manṣūr used to say, "The punishment of the intelligent man is a hint, and the punishment of the fool is a declaration."

According to Aḥmad b. Khālid—Yaḥyā b. Abī Naṣr al-Qurashī:[427] Abān al-Qārī' (the Qur'ān reader) read in the presence of al-Manṣūr the verse, "Make not thy hand tied (like a niggard's) to thy neck, nor stretch it forth to its utmost reach (so that thou become blameworthy and destitute),"[428] and al-Manṣūr said, "What is better than the teachings of our Lord?"

He said: Al-Manṣūr said, "He who does a favor the like of which has been done to him has paid his due, and he who does double has thanked and he who thanks is noble. He who knew that he did something only for himself does not consider the people slow in gratitude and does not ask for an increase in their friendship toward him. So do not ask from others thanks for that which you have done for yourself and by which you protected your honor. Know that the man who asks you to fulfill a need for him does not

---

425. Governor of Khurāsān, who rebelled in 140/757–85. Kennedy, *'Abbasid Caliphate*, 180; Daniel, *Khurāsān*, 159–62; Crone, *Slaves*, 173–74.

426. Not recorded elsewhere.

427. Not recorded elsewhere.

428. *Qur'ān*, XVII: 29.

honor his own face to the exclusion of your face, so honor your own face rather than rejecting him."

According to 'Umar b. Shabbah—Muḥammad b. 'Abd al-Wahhāb al-Muhallabī:[429] I heard Isḥāq b. 'Īsā saying, "There was none of the Banū al-'Abbās who could speak and be spontaneously eloquent except Abū Ja'far, Dāwūd b. 'Alī,[430] and al-'Abbās b. Muḥammad."

According to Aḥmad b. Khālid—Ismā'īl b. Ibrāhīm al-Fihrī:[431] Al-Manṣūr preached in Baghdad on the Day of 'Arafat, though some said he preached on the Day of Minā,[432] and said in his sermon, "I am only the authority of God in His earth, and I govern you through His guidance and His direction to what is right. I am His treasurer in charge of the *fay'*,[433] and I work according to His will and divide it according to His wish and give it with His permission. God has appointed me over it as a lock; if He wants to open me for your salaries and divide your *fay'* and allowances, He will do so and if He wants to close me up, He will close me up. So make your requests to God, O people, and ask Him on this noble day on which He has given you His favor as He has made known to you in His book when He, Blessed and Exalted, says, 'This day [427] have I perfected your religion for you, completed My favor upon you, and have chosen for you Islam as your religion,'[434] so that He can make me successful in good conduct and direct me to the right way and inspire me with mercy and goodness toward you and open me up to giving your salaries and distributing your allowances with justice to you, for He is all-hearing and near."

According to Dāwūd b. Rashīd[435]—his father: Al-Manṣūr preached and he said, "Praise be to God. I praise Him and ask His

429. Not known elsewhere.

430. Eldest of the surviving Banū 'Alī, paternal uncles of al-Manṣūr, at the time of the 'Abbāsid revolution. He delivered the main speech at the inauguration of al-Saffāḥ as caliph and was the first 'Abbāsid governor of al-Kūfah. He died in 133/751 as governor of Mecca (see al-Ṭabarī, III, 30–33, 37, 72).

431. Not recorded elsewhere.

432. During the *Ḥajj*, or pilgrimage month.

433. For *fay'*, see above, note 352.

434. *Qur'ān*, V: 3.

435. Not recorded elsewhere, this is the first of a small group of stories in which Abū Ja'far confronts hecklers in the mosque.

help; I have faith in Him and put my trust in Him. I bear witness that there is no God but Him alone without any partner." Then a man on his right hand interrupted and said, "O man, let me remind you Whom you are reminding us about." Al-Manṣūr stopped the sermon and said, "All listening, all listening to the one who keeps God's instructions and reminds of Him. God save me from being a stubborn tyrant or getting proud by sins. In that case I have gone astray, and I am not one of the rightly guided. And you, O speaker, by God, you do not seek the way of God but rather you want it to be said, 'He stood up and spoke and was punished and he bore it bravely.' How easy it would have been, woe to you! if I wanted to. Take his opportunity for forgiveness. Beware both you and you all, O gathering of the people, of a similar attempt. Indeed wisdom has descended on us and goes out from us, so return authority to its people, sent it back to its place of origin, and despatch it to its sources." Then he returned to his sermon as if he were reading it from the palm of his hand and said, "I bear witness that Muḥammad is His servant and His Prophet."

It was reported on the authority of Abū Tawbah al-Rabīʿ b. Nāfiʿ—Ibn Abī al-Jawzā':[436] I stood up before Abū Jaʿfar when he was preaching in Baghdad in the city mosque on the pulpit, and I recited, "O ye who believe! Why say ye that which ye do not?"[437] I was brought in to him, and he said, "Who are you, woe to you? You wanted only that I should kill you. Go away from me so that
[428] I do not see you." So I went out from his presence safely.

According to ʿĪsā b. ʿAbdallāh b. Ḥumayd—Ibrāhīm b. ʿĪsā:[438] Abū Jaʿfar al-Manṣūr was preaching in this mosque, referring to the city mosque in Baghdad, and, when he reached "Fear God as he should be feared,"[439] a man stood up before him and said, "And you, ʿAbdallāh, fear God as he should be feared." Abū Jaʿfar broke off his sermon and said, "All listening, all listening to one who calls attention to God. Come on, O ʿAbdallāh (Slave of God), what is the fear of God?" The man was silenced and did not say a

436. Neither of these two is recorded elsewhere.

437. *Qur'ān*, LXI: 2.

438. Ibrāhīm b. ʿĪsā b. al-Manṣūr, who is used by al-Ṭabarī on several occasions. ʿĪsā b. ʿAbdallāh is not known elsewhere.

439. *Qur'ān*, III: 102.

thing, and Abū Jaʿfar went on, "God, God! Oh people, do not impose on us those of your affairs that you are unable to undertake. A man does not stand up in this way without my injuring his back and giving him a long term of imprisonment." Then he ordered Rabīʿ to arrest him. We were confident that he would escape, for it was a sign that he intended to harm a man if he said, "Arrest him, Musayyab."[440]

Then he resumed his sermon at the place he had stopped it, and the people approved of what he had done. When he had finished the prayers, he entered the palace, and ʿĪsā b. Mūsā began to walk behind him as was his custom. Abū Jaʿfar heard him and said, "Abū Mūsā," and he said, "Yes O Commander of the Faithful?" and the caliph continued, "I think you are afraid what I will do to this man," and he replied, "Something like that was in my mind, but the the Commander of the Faithful is too learned and has too lofty an opinion to do anything unjust about his case," and he said, "Do not be afraid for him." When the caliph had sat down, he ordered that the man should be brought to him and when he arrived he said, "O you, when you saw me on the pulpit you said, 'This is the tyrant. I cannot refrain from arguing with him.' It would be better for you if you occupied yourself with something else, so occupy yourself with the thirst of the heat of the day, with staying up all night, and with getting your feet dusty in the path of God. Give him, O Rabīʿ, four hundred *dirhams*. Go away and do not come back."

According to ʿAbdallāh b. Ṣāʿid,[441] freedman of the Commander of the Faithful: Al-Manṣūr went on the pilgrimage after [429]
he had built Baghdad,[442] and he stood up to preach in Mecca and among his words that were preserved were, "'Before this We wrote in the Psalms after the message (given to Moses): "My servants, the righteous shall inherit the earth."'[443] This is a firmly established matter, a just word, and a decisive judgment. Praise be to God who makes His authority effective and away with the op-

440. Referring to al-Musayyab b. Zuhayr, chief of police; see above, note 24.
441. Freedman of al-Manṣūr, see al-Khaṭīb, IX, 482
442. In the year 147/764–65.
443. *Qur'ān*, XXI: 105.

pressors[444] who treated the Ka'bah with contempt and took the *fay'* as an inheritance[445] and who have made the Qur'ān into shreds.[446] He has afflicted them with what they scorned. How many blocked-up wells and lofty castles do you see? God has cast them into oblivion because they changed the Sunna and oppressed the Family (of the Prophet). They turned aside and acted outrageously and became overbearing. He has frustated the hopes of every obdurate tyrant. Then He took them and said, 'Canst thou find a single one of them or hear a whisper of them?'"[447]

According to al-Haytham b. 'Adī—Ibn 'Ayyāsh: When the incidents[448] followed one another before Abū Ja'far, he quoted the verse,[449]

The gazelles were too many for Khidāsh,
    and Khidāsh did not know what he was hunting.

Then he ordered that the commanders, the freedmen, his companions, and the people of his house be summoned to his presence, and he ordered Ḥammād al-Turkī to saddle up the horses, Sulaymān b. Mujālid to take the lead, and al-Musayyab b. Zubayr to guard the gates. Then he went out one day and climbed the pulpit.
[430] He was silent for a long time, saying nothing, and a man said to Shabīb b. Shabbah,[450] "What is the matter with the Commander of the Faithful that he does not speak? For he is one of those for whom the most difficult speech is easy. What is the matter with him?" Then he began the sermon:

"Why am I repelling others from Sa'd[451] when he abuses me?
    If I were to abuse the Banū Sa'd, they would be silent
Out of rashness against us and cowardice toward their enemy.
    How evil are the two characteristics: rashness and cowardice."

---

444. That is, the Umayyads.
445. The Umayyads are accused here of taking the *fay'*, which should belong to all the Muslims communally, as their personal property.
446. *Qur'ān*, XV: 91.
447. *Qur'ān*, XIX: 98.
448. See above, note 206.
449. *Aghānī*, XI, 74.
450. Possibly a brother of 'Umar b. Shabbah, the historian; nothing else is known of him.
451. He is using this poem for an oblique attack on the 'Alids.

Then he sat down and said,

"I threw the covering from my head, and I am not the sort of man to
uncover it except because of a great calamity.

By God, they[452] were incapable of the matter we have undertaken, and they were not grateful to the one who did it. It was made smooth for them and they sought to make it rough and they refused to recognize the truth and held it in contempt. What have they sought? That I would drink muddy water that chokes or accept injustice and agony? By God, I do not honor anyone by insulting myself. By God, if they do not accept the truth, they will seek it, but they will not find it with me. The happy man is he who is warned by others. Lead on, page!" Then he rode off.

According to al-Fuqaymī—ʿAbdallāh b. Muḥammad b. ʿAbd al-Raḥmān,[453] freedman of Muḥammad b. ʿAlī:[454] When al-Manṣūr had arrested ʿAbdallāh b. Ḥasan[455] and his brothers and those of his family who were with him, he went up on the pulpit and gave thanks to God and praised Him and prayed for the Prophet. Then he said, "O people of Khurāsān, you are our party (*shīʿah*) and our helpers (*anṣār*) and the people of our state and, if you give the oath of allegiance to someone else, you will not take a better oath to him than to us. As for these members of my family from the children of ʿAlī b. Abī Ṭālib, we have left them, by the one and only God, with the caliphate. We did not oppose them in the caliphate in any way.[456] ʿAlī b. Abī Ṭālib undertook it and he was [431]
stained, and the two judges passed judgment on him and the Community split from him and opinions were divided about him. Then his own party, helpers, companions, retinue, and trusted

452. The ʿAlids.

453. Not recorded elsewhere.

454. The father of al-Saffāḥ and al-Manṣūr.

455. The father of Muḥammad the Pure Soul and Ibrāhīm, the ʿAlid rebels of 145/762. Al-Manṣūr had taken him into custody before the rebellion, as a way of putting pressure on his sons.

456. To rally the support of the Khurāsānīs, al-Manṣūr gives an account of ʿAlid attempts to secure the caliphate and explains how they failed because they were unworthy.

men rose against him and killed him.[457] Then al-Ḥasan b. ʿAlī rose up after him and, by God, he was a man who, when he was offered money for it (the caliphate), took it, and Muʿāwiyah intrigued with him, saying that he would make him his heir apparent after him and then misled him so that he abandoned and surrendered it to him. He took to women, marrying one every day and divorcing her the next, and he continued that way until he died in his bed.[458] After him al-Ḥusayn b. ʿAlī rose up. He was betrayed by the people of Iraq and the people of al-Kūfah, the people of divisions and hypocrisy and plunging into continuous civil wars, the people of this black town," indicating al-Kūfah, "By God, I would not make war with them or make peace with them but may God keep me away from it. They forsook him and handed him over so that he was killed.[459] Then Zayd b. ʿAlī rose up and the people of al-Kūfah betrayed him and deceived him and when they made him rebel they exposed him and handed him over.[460] Muḥammad b. ʿAlī[461] had come to him and implored him not to rebel and asked him not to believe the words of the people of al-Kūfah and said to him, "We have found out that one of our family will be crucified in al-Kūfah, and I am afraid that the crucified one will be you." My paternal uncle Dāwūd b. ʿAlī implored him and warned him of the treachery of the people of al-Kūfah, but he did not believe this and went on with his rebellion and was killed and crucified in al-Kunāsah. Then the Umayyads pounced on us and destroyed our honor and banished our glory, and they had no grudge to pursue against us at all, except on account of them (the ʿAlids) and their rebellion. We were driven out of the country and went sometimes to al-Ṭāʾif, sometimes to

457. ʿAlī was caliph in 35–40/656–61. After the Battle of Ṣiffīn he agreed to accept the verdict of the two judges ʿAmr b. al-ʿĀṣ and Abū Mūsā al-Ashʿarī as to whether he was worthy of the caliphate. This in turn led to the defection of many of his supporters, notably the first Khārijites.

458. ʿAlī's son al-Ḥasan surrendered his rights to the caliphate to Muʿāwiyah in exchange for a large sum of money and went to live a life of luxury in Medina.

459. At Karbalāʾ, near al-Kūfah, in 61/680.

460. He rebelled in al-Kūfah in 122/740 but was captured and executed.

461. Al-Manṣūr's father.

Syria, and sometimes to al-Sharāt[462] until God sent you[463] to us [432]
as a party and as helpers. The revival of our honor and glory is because of you people of Khurāsān. Your truth refutes the people of falsehood. It makes our right clear and gives us the inheritance of our Prophet. It establishes the right in its place and makes its light clear. It gives glory to its helpers and cuts off the roots of the people of oppression. Praise be to God, Lord of the two worlds. When authority was established with us by the grace of God and His just judgment for us, they rose up against us in evil and envy toward us, coveting what God has bestowed on us in preference to them and given us generously of His caliphate and the inheritance of His Prophet.

(They act) out of rashness against us and cowardice toward their enemy.
How evil are the two characteristics, rashness and cowardice.

I did not act the way I did in this affair, by God, O people of Khurāsān, due to rashness. I was informed of some disaffection and disturbance among them, and I had secretly sent men to them and I said, 'Off you go, so-and-so, off you go, so-and-so, and take so much money with you.' I proposed an example for them to follow. They set out until they came to them in Medina and secretly passed on this money to them. By God there was not a single old man or young, big or small, who did not take the oath of allegiance to them; because of that, I regard their blood and their wealth as lawful. It became lawful to me because of their breach of the oath of allegiance to me and their seeking of civil war and their intention to rebel against me. Do not think that I reached this point without being certain."[464]

Then he went down and he recited this verse of the Qur'ān on

462. Ancient Edom, the southern part of modern Jordan. Al-Ḥumaymah, where the 'Abbāsids lived before they came to power, is situated there. Al-Manṣūr claims that the 'Abbāsids suffered greatly because of their association with the 'Alids, but he is certainly being economical with the truth here.

463. I.e., the Khurāsānīs, who are repeatedly described as the *anṣār* (helpers) of the 'Abbāsids, just as the people of Media were the *anṣār* of the Prophet.

464. He justifies making war on the 'Alids and their supporters in Medina by claiming that his agents provocateurs had persuaded them to break their oaths of allegiance.

the steps of the pulpit, "And between them and their desires is placed a barrier as was done in the past with their partisans, for they were indeed in suspicious doubt."[465]

[433] He said: Al-Manṣūr preached in Madā'in when Abū Muslim[466] was killed and he said, "O people, do not leave the intimacy of obedience for the loneliness of rebellion. Do not conceal deceit for the Imāms. No one ever concealed a forbidden thing without its becoming visible in the works of his hand or the slips of his tongue. God will manifest it to His Imām[467] by the glory of His faith and the exaltation of His justice. We will not diminish your rights and we will not diminish the faith He has imposed on you. He who disputes with us so much as the unbuttoning of this shirt, we will consider him a sacrifice for the contents of this scabbard. Abū Muslim took the oath of allegiance to us and the people took the oath to us with the condition that, whoever betrayed us, (the shedding of) his blood was lawful. Then he betrayed us and we passed judgment on him as he had on others for us. Our gratitude in acknowledging his role for us did not prevent us from doing justice to him."

According to Isḥāq b. Ibrāhīm al-Mawṣilī—al-Faḍl b. al-Rabīʿ—his father; I heard al-Manṣūr say that he had heard his father say that his father, ʿAlī b. ʿAbdallāh, had said, "The lords of this world are the most generous, and the lords of the next world are the Prophets."

According to Ibrāhīm b. ʿĪsā: Al-Manṣūr was angry with Muḥammad b. Jumayl al-Kātib,[468] who came from al-Rabadhah,[469] and he ordered him to be thrown to the ground. He proved his innocence, and he ordered him to be raised up. He looked at his drawers and saw that they were made of linen. He ordered him to

465. *Qur'ān*, XXXIV: 54.

466. Al-Manṣūr had Abū Muslim, architect of the ʿAbbāsid revolution in Khurāsān, executed in 137/755 in al-Madā'in. Here he is concerned to justify his action.

467. I.e., al-Manṣūr.

468. He was in charge of the *kharāj* (land tax) of al-Kūfah in 155/772 and later served al-Hādī before and during his caliphate (see al-Ṭabarī, III, 519; al-Jāhshiyārī, 124–25, 167).

469. A small town in the Ḥijāz; see Yāqūt, *Muʿjam*, III, 24. The site has recently been excavated with interesting results by the Saudi Department of Antiquities.

be thrown down and given fifteen blows with a stick, saying, "Do not dress in linen drawers, for that is extravagant."

According to Muḥammad b. Ismā'īl al-Hāshimī—al-Ḥasan b. Ibrāhīm[470]—his *shaykhs*: When Abū Ja'far had killed Muḥammad b. 'Abdallāh in Medina and his brother Ibrāhīm at Bākhamrā[471] and Ibrāhīm b. Ḥasan b. Ḥasan[472] rebelled in Egypt and was brought to him, he wrote a letter to the descendants of 'Alī b. Abī Ṭālib in [434] Medina telling them about Ibrāhīm b. al-Ḥasan b. al-Ḥasan and his rebellion in Egypt and saying that Ibrāhīm would not have acted without their consent and that they were conspiring to seek power and seeking the breaking of relations and disobedience; they had failed in their opposition to the Banū Umayyah when they challenged them for power and they were feeble in seeking revenge so that the sons of his father had risen up in anger on their behalf against the Banū Umayyah, sought revenge for them, and shed their blood and wrested power from their hands, and he quoted in the letter the poem of Subay' b. Rabī'ah b. Mu'āwiyah al-Yarbū'ī:[473]

Were it not for my protection of you when you were incapable,
for I protected and defended you through God's help,
Your affairs were lost, and I knew no reliable people for them,
and everything that God does not protect is wasted.
Name those who scattered the people from around you
and those at the mention of whom fingers are bent (i.e., the best).
We never ceased to confer on you all the time
the favors whose usefulness is apparent.
There never ceased to exist among you people of treachery and dissension,

470. Probably the son of the 'Alid leader Ibrāhīm b. 'Abdallāh. He was arrested after the defeat of the rebellion. He later played an important part in the rise to power of al-Mahdī's *wazīr*, Yaqūb b. Dāwūd. See below pp. 461–64.

471. The village between al-Baṣrah and al-Kūfah where Ibrāhīm's army was defeated by the 'Abbāsids; see al-Ṭabarī, III, pp. 301–14.

472. As Houtsma notes, his leadership of a revolt in Egypt is not found in al-Tabarī or other sources, it is probable that he was a supporter of 'Alī b. Muḥammad, who led an unsuccessful uprising in Egypt at the same time as the rebellions of Muḥammad and Ibrāhīm in 145/762.

473. I can find nothing more about this poet.

a traitor to God and a cutter-off of kinship.
When we have been absent from you and you witnessed
great deeds, there were good satisfactory witnesses.[474]
We looked after you and you looked after your own affairs,
and things are abasing and exalting.[475]
Do the feet of men come high to their chests?
Do the hoofs go high above the hump (of the camel)?
Men among you are conspiring for headship,
as frogs move under the pond.

According to Yaḥyā b. al-Ḥasan b. ʿAbd al-Khāliq: The salaries of the secretaries and tax collectors in the days of Abū Jaʿfar were three hundred *dirhams*, and this continued to be the case until the days of al-Ma'mūn. The first man who allowed an increase in
[435] salaries was al-Faḍl b. Sahl.[476] As for the time of the Umayyads and ʿAbbāsids, the salaries remained at three hundred or below. Al-Ḥajjāj used to pay Yazīd b. Abī Muslim three hundred *dirhams* each month.

According to Ibrāhīm b. Mūsā b. ʿĪsā b. Mūsā: The postmasters in all outlying districts used to write to al-Manṣūr during his caliphate every day about the price of wheat and corn and seasoning and the price of all foods and all the decisions the *qāḍī* had made in their district, and what the governor had done and what wealth was returned to the treasury and items of news. After they had said the sunset prayer, they used to write to him about what happened each day and they used to write to him about what happened each night when they said the morning prayer. When their letters arrived, he looked at them and, if he saw that the prices were as usual, he did nothing but, if he saw that something had changed, he wrote to the governor and the tax collector there and asked about the reasons for the price change, and when the reply came about the reason he was gently concerned about it until prices returned to normal. If he had doubts about a judgment

474. This verse appears to be corrupt and against the spirit of the poem.

475. Possibly a reference to *Qur'ān*, LVI: 3. "Many will it bring low, many will it exalt."

476. Al-Faḍl b. Sahl was *wazīr* and chief adviser to al-Ma'mūn in the early years of his caliphate. Yazīd b. Abī Muslim was a freedman and the foster brother of al-Ḥajjāj, who became governor of Ifrīqiyah.

the *qāḍī* had made, he wrote to him about that and asked those who were in his presence about his conduct and, if he disapproved of anything that was done, he wrote to him, rebuking him and criticizing him.

According to Isḥāq al-Mawṣilī—al-Sabbāḥ b. Khāqān al-Tamīmī—a man of his family—his father: Al-Walīd was mentioned to al-Manṣūr when he was settling in Baghdad and leaving Medina and finishing with Muḥammad and Ibrāhīm, the sons of ʿAbdallāh, and they said, "God curse the apostate unbeliever." In the assembly were Abū Bakr al-Hudhalī, Ibn ʿAyyāsh al-Mantūf, and al-Sharqī b. al-Quṭāmī,[477] all of them members of his *ṣaḥābah*, and Abū Bakr al-Hudhalī said that he was told by a paternal cousin of al-Farazdaq[478] that al-Farazdaq said, "I came into the presence of al-Walīd b. Yazīd,[479] and his boon companions were with him and he had had a morning drink and he said to Ibn ʿĀ'ishah,[480] 'Sing the song of Ibn al-Zibaʿrā:[481] [436]

Would that my *shaykh*s at Badr had witnessed
the fear of al-Khazraj[482] of falling spears.
We killed a double number of their lords.
We put right on the bend of Badr (i.e., the defeat), and it became straight.'

Ibn ʿĀ'ishah said, 'I will not sing this, O Commander of the Faithful,' but he replied, 'Sing it, or I will cut out your tonsils,' so he sang it and al-Walīd said, 'Well done,' and by God he was of

477. Occasionally used as a source by al-Ṭabarī (once in section I, twice in section II). He is recorded in the *Fihrist*, 195, among the traditionists.

478. Tammām b. Ghālib al-Tamīmī, d. ca. 110/728, one of the most famous poets of the Umayyad period and a rival of Jarīr. See *Aghānī*, Būlāq, II, 19; Beirut, XXI, 299; and *EI*², s.v. "al-Farazdaḳ."

479. Umayyad caliph, 125–26/743–44.

480. Muḥammad b. ʿA'ishah, d. ca. 125/744, famous singer at the court of the Umayyad caliph al-Walīd b. Yazīd. See *Aghānī*, Būlāq, II, 62; Beirut, II, 170.

481. ʿAbdallāh b. Zibaʿrā al-Sahmī, Qurashī poet who abused the Muslims. He was converted to Islam at the conquest of Mecca and was received by the Prophet; see *Aghānī*, Būlāq, XIV, 11; Beirut, XV, 138. The poem is also quoted by Ibn Hishām, *Sīrah*, 616.

482. One of the tribes of Medina that supported the Prophet Muḥammad This is an anti-Islamic poem, attacking the military prowess of the Prophet's supporters at the battle of Badr, hence Ibn ʿA'ishah's reluctance to sing it and al-Manṣūr's comment.

the faith of Ibn al-Ziba'rā the day he recited this poem. Al-Manṣūr cursed him and his companions cursed him, and he said, 'Praise be to God for his generosity and his unity.'"

According to Abū Bakr al-Hudhalī: The governor of Armenia[483] wrote to al-Manṣūr that the army had mutinied against him and broken the locks of the treasury and taken what was in it, and al-Manṣūr said in his letter, "Leave our office in disgrace, for if you were intelligent they would not have mutinied and if you were strong they would not have plundered."

According to Isḥāq al-Mawṣilī—his father: A joker rebelled against Abū Ja'far in Palestine and he wrote to his governor there, "His blood will be on your blood if you do not send him to me," so he made great efforts to find him, captured him, and sent him off. He was ordered to be brought into the caliph's presence and when he stood before him Abū Ja'far said to him, "You have preyed on our governors. I will scatter about more of your flesh than remains on your bone," and he replied, and he was an old man with a weak, thin, unimpressive voice:

Do you train your wife after she has become decrepit?
The training of the decrepit man is wearisome.[484]

[437] His words were not clear to al-Manṣūr so he asked Rabī' what he was saying, and he replied that he had said:

The slave is your slave and the wealth is your wealth,
and is your punishment deflected from me?

He said, "O Rabī', I have forgiven him so let him go, take care of him, and give him good care."

He said: A man complained to al-Manṣūr about his tax gatherer (*'āmil*), saying that he had taken a part of his estate and added it to his property, so he wrote to his official in the note of the complainer, "If you prefer justice, peace will be your companion. Do justice to this complainer for his wrong."

He said: A man of the common people wrote a note to him requesting the building of a mosque in his area, and he wrote on

483. *Ṣāḥib Armaniyyah*, used here of the governor.
484. Freytag, *Proverbia*, II, 666, n. 277.

his note, "One of the portents of the Day of Judgment is the proliferation of mosques, so increase your paces (toward a distant *masjid*), and your reward will be increased."

He said: A man of the Sawād complained about one of the tax collectors in a note that was sent up to al-Manṣūr, who replied, "If you are telling the truth, bring him held up by the upper front of his shirt. We give you permission to do that."

According to 'Umar b. Shabbah—Abū al-Hudhayl al-'Allaf:[485] Abū Ja'far said, I was told that al-Sayyid Ibn Muḥammad (al-Ḥimyarī)[486] died in al-Karkh or in Wāsiṭ and they did not bury him and, if that story is true, indeed I would burn it down. It is said that the true story was that he died in the time of al-Mahdī in al-Karkh of Baghdad and that they avoided burying him and that al-Rabī' was sent to take charge of his affair, and he ordered that, if they were obstructive, their houses should be burned, but Rabī' was diverted from them.

According to al-Madā'inī: When al-Manṣūr had finished with Muḥammad and Ibrāhīm and 'Abdallāh b. 'Alī and 'Abd al-Jabbār b. 'Abd al-Raḥmān and went to Baghdad and things became calm for him, he quoted this verse:

You often spend the night on a sword edge of tribulation, [438]
but God will suffice against that which you feared.

He said: 'Abdallāh b. al-Rabī' recited to me that al-Manṣūr had recited after the killing of these:

There is many an affair that will not harm you,
but the heart still palpitates for fear of them.

According to al-Haytham b. 'Adī: When al-Manṣūr heard of the scattering of the sons of 'Abdallāh b. Ḥasan[487] through the lands, fleeing from his punishment, he quoted:

My lance is a strong wood (*nab'*), which neither the pinching and
pressing

485. D. 226/840–41, a Mu'tazilī scholar from al-Baṣrah; see *Fihrist*, 386–87.

486. Ismā'īl b. Muḥammad, a poet well known for his pro-'Alid sympathies. The date of his death is not known; see *Aghānī*, Būlāq, VII, 2; Beirut, VII, 224.

487. The 'Alid rebels of 145/762 Muḥammad and Ibrāhīm.

of the straightening instrument, nor grease, nor fire can soften.
When I take a fearful man under my protection, his grazing places are safe.
And when I make a safe man fearful for his safety, the house looks not spacious enough for him.
Come to me and lower some of your eyes,
for I am to every man the protector from his neighbor.

According to ʿAlī b. Muḥammad—Wāḍiḥ, freedman of Abū Jaʿfar: Abū Jaʿfar ordered me to buy him two soft pieces of cloth, so I bought them for a hundred and twenty *dirhams* and brought them to him. He asked me how much they were and I said, "Eighty *dirhams*." He replied, "Good! Ask for a reduction, for, if the goods arrive to us and then are returned to their owner, that breaks him down!" So I took the two pieces from their owner, and on the next day I brought the two of them with me to him, and he asked me what I had done and I said that I had returned them to him and that he had given me a reduction of twenty *dirhams*. He said, "You have done well; cut up one of them as a shirt, and make the other into a gown for me." I did that and he wore the shirt for fifteen days and did not wear anything else.

According to a freedman of ʿAbd al-Ṣamad b. ʿAlī—ʿAbd al-Ṣamad b. ʿAlī: Al-Manṣūr used to order his family to dress well to show their prosperity by wearing brocade and perfume. If he saw that any of them had failed to do that or had not done enough, he
[439] would say, "O so-and-so, I do not see the gleam of musk in your beard,[488] and I see it shining in the beard of so-and-so," and in this way he used to urge them to use more perfume so that he might be enhanced with the common people by their appearance and the sweetness of their breath and that he might enhance them (his family) among them (the people). If he saw any of them in plain cloth, he abused him.[489]

According to Aḥmad b. Khālid: Al-Manṣūr used to ask Mālik b. Adham[490] much about the story of ʿAjlān b. Suhayl, brother of

488. The perfuming of beards was a luxury of the ʿAbbāsid court.
489. The text seems to be corrupt here.
490. Al-Bāhilī; he was one of the Umayyad generals in Iran defeated by the

Ḥawtharah b. Suhayl.[491] We were sitting with 'Ajlān when Hishām b. 'Abd al-Malik passed and someone said, "The cross-eyed man has passed," and he asked, "Whom do you mean?" "Hishām," he answered. "You are calling the Commander of the Faithful with a derisive nickname, and, by God, were it not for your kinship, I would cut off your head," and al-Manṣūr said, "That is a man with the likes of whom life and death have a use (a meaning)."

According to Aḥmad b. Khālid—Ibrāhīm b. 'Īsā: Al-Manṣūr had a servant with pale, brownish skin, acceptably skillful, and al-Manṣūr said to him one day, "What race are you?" and he replied, "Arab, O Commander of the Faithful," and he asked, "Which Arabs?" and he replied, "From Khawlān. I was captured from Yemen by one of our enemies, who castrated me, and I became a slave and passed to a member of the Umayyad family and then to you." The caliph replied, "You are certainly an excellent page, but no Arab ever enters my palace to serve my harem. Go out, may God forgive you, and go wherever you wish."

According to Aḥmad b. Ibrāhīm b. Ismā'īl b. Dāwūd b. Mu'ā-wiyah b. Bakr,[492] who was one of the courtiers (ṣaḥābah): Al-Manṣūr attached a man from al-Kūfah called al-Fuḍayl b. 'Imrān[493] to his son Ja'far and appointed him as his secretary and put him in charge of his affairs. He had the same position with regard to him as Abū 'Ubaydallāh had to al-Mahdī. Abū Ja'far had wished   [440] that the oath of allegiance should be taken to Ja'far after al-Mahdī. Umm 'Ubaydallāh, Ja'far's nurse, plotted against al-Fuḍayl b. 'Imrān and told stories against him to al-Manṣūr and hinted that al-Fuḍayl had homosexual inclinations forward Ja'far. Al-Manṣūr sent his freedman al-Rayyān and Hārūn b. Ghazwān, the freed-man of 'Uthmān b. Nahīk,[494] to al-Fuḍayl, who was with Ja'far

---

'Abbāsıd armies under Qaḥṭabah. In 'Abbāsıd tımes he fought on the Byzantıne frontıer. See Crone, *Slaves,* 168–69.

491. Al-Bāhılī as well. He was sent by Marwān to reınforce Ibn Hubayrah ın Iraq agaınst the 'Abbāsıd armıes and repeatedly urged Ibn Hubayrah to adopt a more active strategy; he was executed after the fall of Wāsıṭ (Crone, *Slaves,* 143). The story again shows Abū Ja'far's admıratıon for the Umayyads and their supporters.

492. A secretary and poet of the reıgns of al-Manṣūr and al-Mahdī; see *Fihrıst,* 176.

493. Otherwıse unknown.

494. For 'Uthmān, see note 400, above, on hıs brother 'Īsā.

in Ḥadīthah of Mosul[495] and said, "When you see al-Fuḍayl, kill him wherever you meet him." He wrote an edict for them and he wrote to Jaʿfar, telling him what he had ordered them to do and he told them not to hand the letter over to Jaʿfar until they had carried out the execution. They left and, when they reached Jaʿfar, they sat at his gate waiting for permission to go in, and al-Fuḍayl came out to them. They seized him and took out al-Manṣūr's letter. Nobody opposed them and they cut off his head on the spot, and Jaʿfar did not know until they had finished. Al-Fuḍayl was an upright and God-fearing man and, when al-Manṣūr was told that he was completely innocent of what he was accused of and that he had been hasty with him, he sent a messenger and promised him ten thousand *dirhams* if he reached him before he was killed, and the messenger arrived before his blood was dry.

According to Muʿāwiyah b. Bakr—Suwayd, freedman of Jaʿfar: Jaʿfar sent for him and said, "Woe to you. What does the Commander of the Faithful say about the killing of a pious and God-fearing Muslim who has committed no crime or offense?" to which Suwayd replied, "He is the Commander of the Faithful and he does what he wishes and he knows best what he is doing." Jaʿfar said, "O sucker of your mother's clitoris! I am speaking to you in the language of the elite, and you reply in the language of the common people. Take him by the legs and throw him into the Tigris." He said, "I was seized and said, 'I want to talk to you,' so he said, 'Leave him!' and I said, 'Do you think your father will be answerable for Fuḍayl only? When does he answer for him when he had already killed his paternal uncle ʿAbdallāh b. ʿAlī and ʿAbdallāh b. al-Ḥasan and other descendants of the Prophet
[441] wrongly, and he had killed countless men of this world, before he was responsible for the death of Fuḍayl, (who was only) a rat who nipped Pharaoh's balls.'[496] He laughed and said, 'Leave him to the curse of God!'"

According to Qaʿnab b. Muḥriz[497] Abū Muḥammad b. ʿĀʾidh,

495. About thirty miles southeast of Mosul, on the east bank of the Tigris just above its junction with the Upper Zāb; see Yāqūt, *Muʿjam*, II, 230; Le Strange, *Lands*, 90–91.

496. See *Glossary*, CCXXIV.

497. Al-Bāhilī. Al-Ṭabarī cites him on one other occasion.

freedman of ʿUthmān b. ʿAffān: Ḥafṣ al-Umawī the poet was known as Ḥafṣ b. Abī Jumʿah,[498] freedman of ʿAbbād b. Ziyād, whom al-Manṣūr had appointed literary instructor (*mu'adib*) to al-Mahdī in his audiences. He was a panegyrist of the Umayyads in Umayyad times and in the time of al-Manṣūr, and he did not hold it against him and he remained with al-Mahdī all the time that al-Mahdī was heir apparent but died before al-Mahdī succeeded to the caliphate. Among his poems in praise of the Umayyads was the following:

Where are the two chiefs of ʿAbd Shams,[499] where are they?
    Where are their men of ability and nobility?
You did not compensate them for their kindness to you
    with what you have done, you the family of ʿAbd al-Muṭṭalib.[500]
O inquirer about them,
    they were shoots of palm trees, shining above the wood.
If you foolishly cut off their roots,
    what a time that is turned upside down.
Pour what milk you like into your basin.
    You will drink that milk as sour residue.

It is said that Ḥafṣ al-Umawī came in to al-Manṣūr and he spoke to him and asked information about him. He asked him who he was and he replied, "Your freedman, O Commander of the Faithful," and he said, "A freedman of mine like you I do not know." He answered, "The freedman of a servant of yours, ʿAbd Manāf, O Commander of the Faithful." The caliph approved of his reply and knew that he was a freedman of the Umayyads and attached him to al-Mahdī and said to him, "Take him for yourself."

Among the elegies for al-Manṣūr was the poem of Salm al-Khāsir:[501]

498. There is no section on him in the *Kitāb al-Aghānī*

499. Progenitor of the Umayyads.

500. Father of al-ʿAbbās and grandfather of the Prophet Muḥammad and ʿAlī b. Abī Ṭālib.

501. Salm b. ʿAmr, a poet of the ʿAbbāsid court, prominent in the reign of Hārūn; see *Aghānī*, Beirut, XIX, 214.

I wonder how the two announcers could announce his death.
How could the two lips speak of his departure?
A king who, if one day he faced time,
time would fall down dead.
[442] Would that a hand that had scattered dust on him
came back without any one finger on it.
When the countries acknowledged his absolute rule
and both man and jinn[502] cast down their eyes from fear of it,
Where is the lord of al-Zawrā'[503] to whom it (the country)
has entrusted sovereignty for twenty-two years?[504]
The man is like a kindling stick
when it is surrounded by sparks of fire.
Prohibition does not divert his will,
and intelligent people cannot weaken his rope.
The reins of power have been handed over to him,
so that he can lead his enemies without reins.
Eyes are lowered before him, and you see
hands on chins for fear of him.
He gathered together the borders of his kingdom and then became
beyond their farthest edge and this side of the nearest part.
A Hāshimī in readiness who does not carry the burden
on the back of a runaway foolish camel,
A man of moderation who makes the fearful forget his fear
and determination that causes every heart to fly.
Souls have left scared from him.
What remained in the bodies were only the spirits.

The names of his children and wives: Among his children were al-Mahdī, whose name was Muḥammad, and Ja'far the Elder, and their mother was Arwā, daughter of Manṣūr and sister of Yazīd b. Manṣūr al-Ḥimyarī. Her *kunyah* was Umm Mūsā. This Ja'far died before al-Manṣūr. There were also Sulaymān, 'Īsā and Ya'qūb, whose mother was Fāṭimah, daughter of Muḥammad,

---

502. Lit. "the two heavy ones", see Lane, s.v., *thql*.
503. A name of Baghdad, allegedly because the *qiblah* was bent or crooked and did not face Mecca. See Le Strange, *Baghdad*, 11.
504. The number of years of Abū Ja'far's caliphate.

one of the descendants of Ṭalḥah b. ʿUbaydallāh,[505] and Jaʿfar the Younger,[506] whose mother was a Kurdish slave whom al-Manṣūr had purchased and taken as a concubine, and her son was known as Ibn al-Kurdiyyah (son of the Kurdish woman). There was Ṣāliḥ al-Miskīn, whose mother was a Greek slave girl called Qālī al-Farrāshah. Al-Qāsim died before al-Manṣūr, aged ten, and his mother was a slave girl known as Umm al-Qāsim, who had a garden by the Syrian Gate that is known as the Garden of Umm al-Qāsim to the present day.[507] There was ʿĀliyah,[508] whose mother was an Umayyad woman; al-Manṣūr gave her in marriage to Isḥāq b. Sulaymān b. ʿAlī b. ʿAbdallāh b. al-ʿAbbās.[509] [443]

According to Isḥāq b. Sulaymān—his father: My father said to me, "I am marrying you, O my son, to the most noble of people, ʿĀliyah, daughter of the Commander of the Faithful," and I asked who were our equals, and he answered, "Our enemies, the Umayyads."

Information about His Wills[510]

According to al-Haytham b. ʿAdī: Al-Manṣūr made a will for al-Mahdī when he set out for Mecca in Shawwāl of this year (4 August–1 September, 775). He had stopped at Qaṣr ʿAbdawayh and stayed some days in the castle there. Al-Mahdī was with him, and he gave him his testament. While he was staying in Qaṣr

505. One of the companions of the Prophet, killed at the Battle of the Camel in 36/656.

506. Little is known of Jaʿfar the Younger, and he seems to have played no part in politics He died in 186/802.

507. Not noticed in Le Strange.

508. Not known elsewhere.

509. Brother of Muḥammad (note 29) and Jaʿfar (note 35). He was probably younger than his brothers and only became prominent in the reign of Hārūn, when he held a number of governorates, including Sind, Egypt, al-Baṣrah, and Armenia. He disappears from the record after 194/810. As a governor he seems to have been rather ineffectual but is recorded in the *Fihrist* as an early patron of translators. Daughters of the ʿAbbāsid caliphs in this period were usually married within the family.

510. The various versions of al-Manṣūr's wills and their interpretation are discussed in detail in Dietrich, "Das politische Testament." He also provides a German translation on which I have drawn.

ʿAbdawayh, a shooting star fell on 28 Shawwāl (31 August, 775) after it began to get light, and its track remained clear until sunrise. He bequeathed him his wealth and authority (*sulṭān*), and he did that every day of his stay there, morning and evening, and he did not let up from that, and the two of them parted with emotion. When the day came when he wanted to leave, he called al-Mahdī and said to him, "There is nothing that I have not handed over to you. I will pass on to you some good rules of conduct but, by God, I do not think you will continue with a single one of them." He had a container in which he kept the notebooks (*dafātīr*) of his knowledge, and it was locked and he trusted no one to open it and he kept its keys in the sleeve of his shirt. Ḥammād al-Turkī used to bring him that container when he called for it, and if Ḥammād was away or had gone out it was entrusted to Salamah al-Khādim. He said to al-Mahdī, "Look after this bag and keep it, for in it is the knowledge of your forebears of the past and future until the Day of Resurrection. If things start going badly, look in the larger notebook and, if you find what you want there, (well and good)
[444] but, if not, look in the second and the third until you reach the seventh. If it weighs heavily on you, look in the small notebook, and you will find in it what you need; but I do not think you will do it.

"Look after this city[511] and be careful not to exchange it for another, for it is your house and your glory. For you I have gathered in it such wealth that, if the *kharāj*[512] were to be interrupted for ten years, you would have enough for the salaries of the army and the expenses and allowances of the children and the needs of the frontiers. So keep it and you will not cease to be powerful as long as your treasury remains full, but I do not think you will do this.

"I am commending to you the members of your family (*ahl al-bayt*). Show them honor, give them precedence, give them great benefits, increase their status, submit the people to their authority, and put them in charge of pulpits. Their glory and renown will glorify you, but I do not think you will do this.

"Look after your freedmen and do good to them, bring them

511. Baghdad.
512. Meaning tax receipts in general.

near you, and cherish them for they are your support in adversity if it befalls you, but I do not think you will do this.

"I commend to you generous treatment to the people of Khurāsān, for they are your helpers (*anṣār*) and your party (*shī'ah*) and have spent their wealth in the service of your state and shed their blood for you. You will not drive out love for you from their hearts if you are good to them and forgive whoever among them commits a blunder, rewarding them for what they do and providing for the families and children of those of them who die, but I do not think you will do this.

"Take care over the building of the eastern city (of Baghdad) in case you do not complete it, but I do not think you will do this.

"Be careful not to ask for help from a man of the Banū Sulaym,[513] and I think you will do this.

"Be careful not to bring women to advise you in your affairs,[514] and I think you will do this."

According to sources other than al-Haytham: Al-Manṣūr summoned al-Mahdi when he left for Mecca and said to him, "O Abū 'Abdallāh,[515] I am setting out and I will not return, for we are [445] God's and return to him. I am asking for a blessing on what I am going to do. This sealed book contains my testament. If you hear that I have died and power has passed to you, look into it. I have a debt and I would like you to pay it and be responsible for it." He replied, "I will do it, O Commander of the Faithful." He said, "It is three hundred thousand *dirhams* and some more, and I do not consider it lawful to pay it from the treasury of the Muslims, so take responsibility for it and for any more like it," and he replied, "I will do it."

He said, "This palace is not yours; it is mine and I built my palace with my money and I would like you to give your share in it to your younger brothers," and he replied, "Yes."

He said, "My personal slaves are yours, so assign them to them

---

513. A reference to Ya'qūb b. Dāwūd, future vizier of al-Mahdī, who was a mawlā of Sulaym. According to the account, p. 225, below, he was at this time an unknown prisoner, an indication that this part of the testament is a later addition.

514. Probably a reference to the influence later wielded by al-Khayzurān, wife of al-Mahdī and mother to al-Hādī and Hārūn al-Rashīd.

515. Al-Mahdī.

(your brothers), for you will be in a position where you can spare them and your brothers' needs are greater."

He said, "As for the estates (*ḍiyā'*), I am not enjoining this (i.e., division with his brothers) on you, but, if you were to do that, I would like it," and he said, "I will do it."

He said, "Hand over to them what I have asked you of this, and you will have a share with them in the estates."

He said, "Hand over the baggage and clothes to them," and he replied, "I will do it."

He said, "May God make the caliphate good for you and the benefit will be yours. Fear God in what he has conferred on you and in what I have given you charge over."

He went to al-Kūfah and stayed in al-Ruṣāfah and then left joyfully for the greater and lesser pilgrimages. He drove camels for sacrifice and marked them and distinguished them on their necks. This was in the last days of Dhū al-Qa'dah (September 2–October 1, 775).

According to Abū Ya'qūb b. Sulaymān—Jamrah al-'Aṭṭārah, perfumer to Abū Ja'far:[516] When al-Manṣūr decided to go on the pilgrimage, he summoned Rayṭah,[517] daughter of Abū al-'Abbās and wife of al-Mahdī, who was at that time in al-Rayy, before he set out and bequeathed her what he wished and gave her his instructions and handed over the keys of the treasuries to her. He instructed her and made her swear and confirm the oath that she
[446] would not open one of those treasuries or show it to anyone except al-Mahdī and that not until she was sure of his death, and when that was certain she and al-Mahdī should go together without a third party being present and open the treasury.

When al-Mahdī came from al-Rayy to the City of Peace, she handed over the keys to him and informed him how al-Manṣūr had enjoined her not to open it or show it to anyone until she was certain of his death. When al-Mahdī heard of the death of al-Manṣūr and that the caliphate had passed to him he opened the

516. Abū Ya'qūb is otherwise unknown. 'Aṭṭārah means "a female perfumer," the third example of a female narrator; see above, note 337.

517. Rayṭah was the daughter of al-Saffāḥ who married her cousin, the future caliph al-Mahdī, in 144/761–62. She is described as Umm 'Alī and was still alive in 170/786 at the accession of Hārūn, but otherwise little is known of her.

door, and Rayṭah was with him, and there was a big, long chamber in which there was a collection of corpses of the Ṭālibids, and in their ears were pieces of paper on which were written their genealogies. Among them were children and young men and old men in large numbers. When al-Mahdī saw that, he ordered that a grave be dug for them, and they were buried in it and a tombstone was put over them.

According to ʿĪsā b. Isḥāq b. ʿAlī—his father: I heard al-Manṣūr as he was setting off to Mecca in the year 158, saying to al-Mahdī that he was saying adieu to him, "O Abū ʿAbdallāh, I was born in the month of Dhū al-Ḥijjah and succeeded in the month of Dhū al-Ḥijjah, and it occurs to me that I may die in Dhū al-Ḥijjah of this year and that has persuaded me to make the pilgrimage. Fear God in the affairs of the Muslims that I have entrusted you with, for He will give you relief from the things that will distress you and sadden you (or he said, a relief and refuge) and will provide you with peace and a good outcome when you do not anticipate it. Remember, O my son, the Prophet Muḥammad in His community (*ummah*), that God may look after your affairs. Beware of shedding [447] blood unlawfully, for it is a grave offense to God and an unavoidable and lasting disgrace in this world. Keep to the permitted things, for in that is your reward in the future and your safety in the present.

"Apply the established penalties (*ḥudūd*) and do not go beyond them or you will perish. God knows if something benefits His religion and restrains us from disobeying Him better than the penalties He would have stipulated in His book. Know that for the powerful defense of His Sulṭān, God, in His book, has ordered double the punishment and retribution on those who stir up corruption (*fasād*) on the earth with the severe punishment He reserves for him when He says, 'The punishment of those who wage war against God and His Prophet and strive with might and main for mischief through the land (is execution or crucifixion).'[518]

"Authority, my son, is the strong rope of God and a firm bond and the unshakable religion of God. Preserve it and protect it and strengthen it and defend it. Strike down the heretics in it and

518. *Qur'ān*, V. 33.

those who would apostasize from it. Kill those who leave it, by applying penalties and punishments. Do not exceed what God laid down about it in the perfect and accurate Qur'ān. Give judgment justly and do not be unfair, for that is the best means to prevent discord, to settle enmity, and to get the best remedy.

"Refrain from taking the *fay'*, for you have no need of it on top of what I have left you. Inaugurate your work with a grant to the family and generosity to the kinsmen. Beware of self-indulgence and wasting your subjects' wealth, fortify the frontiers and establish the borders; make the roads safe. Extend your favor to the best people, improve the livelihood of the common people, and keep them calm by bringing them benefits and defending them from disaster. Keep account of your wealth and put it in the treasury and beware of waste. Nobody is secure from misfortunes,
[448] and (future) events cannot be relied on, for that is the nature of time.

"Prepare men and horses and soldiers as far as you are able. Take care not to put off today's work until tomorrow, lest matters pile up on you and they are lost. Be diligent in settling matters that come up at the proper time, first come, first served. Make an effort to get ready for them and prepare men at night to know what will happen in the day and prepare men in the day to know what will happen at night. Take matters in hand yourself; do not get impatient, do not be idle, and do not be faint-hearted. Think the best of your Lord but the worst of your tax collectors and secretaries. Hold yourself in wakefulness. Investigate those who spend the night at your gate and grant permission to the people (to see you) readily. Investigate those strangers who come to you and entrust them to a sleepless eye and undallying soul. Do not sleep, as your father has not slept since he succeeded to the caliphate, and sleep has not entered his eyes without his heart being awake. This is my testament to you and God is my Successor in charge of you."

Then he said farewell to him, and each of them wept in front of the other.

According to 'Umar b. Shabbah—Sa'īd b. Huraym: When al-Manṣūr went on the pilgrimage in the year in which he died, al-Mahdī bade him farewell and he said, "O my son, I have gathered for you more wealth than any caliph before me and I have gathered for you more freedmen than any caliph before me and I have built for you a city the likes of which there has not been in Islam. I am only afraid for you of two men, ʿĪsā b. Mūsā and ʿĪsā b. Zayd.[519] As for ʿĪsā b. Mūsā, he has given me assurances and guarantees that I have accepted from him and, by God, even if he only spoke empty words, I am not afraid for you of him, so put him out of your mind. As for ʿĪsā b. Zayd, if you spend this money, kill these freedmen, and destroy this city so that you can gain control of him, I would not criticize you." [449]

According to ʿĪsā b. Muḥammad—Mūsā b. Hārūn: When al-Manṣūr reached the last halt on the road to Mecca, he looked inside the house he was staying in and there was written in it:

In the name of God, the Merciful, the Compassionate.
Abū Jaʿfar, your death is drawing near, and your years
Are coming to a close. There is no escape from the decree of God.
Abū Jaʿfar, is there a wizard[520] or astrologer
With you today who can hold back the pain of death?

He summoned the man in charge of maintaining the halting places and said to him, "Did I not give you orders that no vandal should enter the building?" and he replied, "O Commander of the Faithful, no one has entered it since it was finished." He said, "Read what is written inside the house!" and the man replied, "I do not see anything, O Commander of the Faithful." He summoned the chief chamberlain and said, "Read what is written inside the house!" and he replied, "I do not see anything inside the house." Al-Manṣūr then dictated the two verses and they were written down. Then he turned to his chamberlain and said, "Recite me a verse from the Book of God that will make me long for God," and he recited, "In the Name of God, the Merciful, the Compassionate. And soon will the unjust assailants know to what vicissitudes

519. Son of Zayd b. ʿAlī who rebelled against the Umayyads in al-Kūfah in 122/740. He played an active role in the ʿAlid rebellions of 145/762 and subequently went into hiding, becoming leader of the small clandestine group of the Zaydiyyah (see above, note 137) and refusing the blandishments of al-Mahdī and Yaʿqūb b. Dāwūd. He died of natural causes toward the end of al-Mahdī's reign (see Iṣfahānī, *Maqātil*, especially pp. 405, 411, 416–19).

520. A soothsayer or pre-Islamic holy man among the Arabs; see *EI*², s.v. "Kāhin."

their affairs will take them."[521] He ordered that his jaws be pinched and said to him, "Could you not think of anything other than this verse to recite?" and he replied, "O Commander of the Faithful, the Qur'ān has been erased from my mind except for this verse." He gave orders to move from that lodging, seeing what had occurred as an evil omen, and he rode off on horseback. When he was in the *wādī* called Saqar, which was the last lodging on the road to Mecca, his horse stumbled and crushed his back. He died and was buried at Bi'r Maymūn.

[450] According to Muḥammad b. ʿAbdallāh, freedman of the Banū Hāshim[522]—one of the *ʿulamā'* and people of *adab*: A voice called to Abū Jaʿfar from his palace in the city and he heard it say:

By the Lord of Stillness and Movement,
    death has different nets.
Remember, O myself, that if you do evil
    and if you have good intentions, everything will be yours.
The night and day do not take turns,
    nor do the stars of the sky revolve in the heavens
Except to transfer authority from one king,
    when his power ceases, to another
Until they bring it to a King
    Who shares the glory of His authority with no one,
Who is the Creator of the sky and earth,
    the establisher of the mountains, the Controller of the heavens.

Abū Jaʿfar said, "By God, it is close to the time of my death."

According to ʿAbdallāh b. ʿUbaydallāh[523]—ʿAbd al-ʿAzīz b. Muslim:[524] I came in to al-Manṣūr one day and greeted him, and he was lost for words and confused in his answer. I got up when I

521. *Qur'ān*, XXVI: 227.

522. Not known elsewhere.

523. B. al-ʿAbbās b. Muḥammad b. ʿAlī. An ʿAbbāsid, grandson of al-ʿAbbās b. Muḥammad, al-Manṣūr's brother; see note 58, above. He led the pilgrimage four times in al-Ma'mūn's reign and is last recorded as governor of Yemen in 217/833.

524. Al-ʿUqaylī, brother of Isḥāq and Bakkār (see note 114, above). His family had been staunch supporters of Marwān, the last Umayyad caliph, and he himself appears below, p. 197, showing his loyalty to Marwān's son. He died in 167/783–84.

saw him like that, intending to leave him, but he said to me after a while, "I saw as a dreamer sees a man reciting these verses to me:

O little brother, be modest in your wishes.
It is as if your day has come to you
And time has visited you with
the vicissitudes it has visited you with.
And, if you wish to be a base and humble slave, you are that;
you were made sovereign of what you were made sovereign of,
But command has passed to others.

The cause of my worry and grief, which you see, is what I heard and saw," and I said, "It was a good thing you saw, O Commander of the Faithful," but it was not long after that he set out on the pilgrimage and died on the way there. [451]

In this year the oath of allegiance was taken to al-Mahdī as caliph, and he was Muḥammad b. ʿAbdallāh b. Muḥammad b. ʿAlī b. ʿAbdallāh b. al-ʿAbbās, in the early dawn of the night when Abū Jaʿfar al-Manṣūr died, which was Saturday, 6 Dhū al-Ḥijjah, 159 (October 7, 775, a Sunday), as it is reported by Hishām b. Muḥammad and Muḥammad b. ʿUmar. According to al-Wāqidī, the oath was taken to him in Baghdad on Thursday, 18 Dhū al-Ḥijjah (October 19), of this year. Al-Mahdī's mother was Umm Mūsā, daughter of Manṣūr b. ʿAbdallāh b. Yazīd b. Shammar al-Ḥimyarī.

The Caliphate of al-Mahdī

The Events of the Year 158 (cont'd)

(NOVEMBER 11, 774–OCTOBER 30, 775)

Muḥammad b. ʿAbdallāh b. Muḥammad b. ʿAlī b. ʿAbdallāh b. al-ʿAbbās: A description of the oath of allegiance that was taken to al-Mahdī as caliph when his father al-Manṣūr died at Mecca.

According to ʿAlī b. Muḥammad al-Nawfalī—his father: In the year that Abū Jaʿfar died I left (on the Pilgrimage) by the Baṣrah road and Abū Jaʿfar had left by the Kūfah road, and I met him at Dhāt ʿIrq[525] and accompanied him. Whenever he rode, I put myself in his way and greeted him. He was seriously ill and on the brink of death. When he reached Bi'r Maymūn, he stayed there and we entered Mecca and I completed the lesser pilgrimage. I used to visit Abū Jaʿfar frequently in his camp and stay there until shortly after midday, and then I left and the Hāshimites did [452] likewise. His illness began to worsen and become acute. On the night that he died, none of us knew and I performed the morning prayer in the Masjid al-Ḥarām (in Mecca) at daybreak and then

525. Modern Ḍarība, the point where pilgrims coming overland from Iraq don the *iḥrām*. See Yāqūt, *Muʿjam*, IV, 107.

rode out in my two robes,[526] with my sword belted on top of them. I went with Muḥammad b. ʿAwn b. ʿAbdallāh b. al-Ḥārith[527] who was one of the lords and *shaykh*s of the Banū Hāshim. At the time, he was wearing two rose-colored garments that he had donned for *iḥrām* with his sword belted on them.

He said: The *shaykh*s of the Banū Hāshim used to like rose-colored garments for the *iḥrām* because of a tradition of ʿUmar b. al-Khaṭṭāb and ʿAbdallāh b. Jaʿfar and the words of ʿAlī b. Abī Ṭalib about it.[528] When we reached the bottom of the *wādī*, we met al-ʿAbbās b. Muḥammad and Muḥammad b. Sulaymān with horses and men on their way into Mecca. We went over to them and greeted them and went on, and Muḥammad b. ʿAwn said to me, "What do you think about the role of those two men and of their entering Mecca?" "I reckon that the man has died," I replied, "and that they want to secure Mecca." And so it proved to be.

While we were going along we came across a man of unclear form in two ragged garments (for *iḥrām*), and we were still in the half-light of early dawn. He came between our two beasts and addressed us saying, "The man, by God, has died," and then he disappeared.[529] For our part, we went on until we came to the camp. When we entered the large tent we used to sit in every day, there was Mūsā b. al-Mahdī sitting in the place of honor by the tent pole, whereas al-Qāsim b. al-Manṣūr was at the side of the tent. Previously, when we met al-Manṣūr at Dhāt ʿIrq, whenever he mounted his camel, al-Qāsim would come and ride in front of him, between him and the Chief of Police, and the people would
[453] be ordered to bring their petitions to him. When I saw him at the side of the tent and Mūsā in the place of honor, I knew that al-Manṣūr had died. While I was sitting there, al-Ḥasan b. Zayd came up and sat down beside me so that his thigh rested against mine, and people came until they filled the tent, among them Ibn ʿAyyāsh al-Mantūf. While we were like that I heard a faint sound of weeping and al-Ḥasan said to me, "Do you think that the man

526. The *iḥrām*, the ritual dress for the pilgrimage; see *EI*², s.v. "Iḥrām."

527. Despite al-Nawfalī's comment on his seniority, he is not recorded elsewhere. He was a descendant of al-Ḥārith b. al-ʿAbbās, hence a distant cousin of the ruling branch of the ʿAbbāsid family.

528. See Hinds and Crone, *God's Caliph*, 84.

529. Presumably an apparition or ghost.

had died?" and I replied, "I do not think that, but perhaps he is very weak or has lost consciousness." The next thing we knew was that suddenly, Abū al-ʿAnbar, the black servant of al-Manṣūr, came to us with his outer garments torn in front and behind and dust on his head, crying, "Alas for the Commander of the Faithful!" Every single person who was in the tent stood up and rushed for the tents of Abū Jaʿfar, wanting to go in, but the servants prevented them, pushing them in the chest, and Ibn ʿAyyāsh al-Mantūf said, "Glory be to God! Have you never witnessed the death of a caliph? Sit down, may God have mercy on you!" The people sat down and al-Qāsim stood up and rent his clothes and put dust on his head, but Mūsā, who was a young lad, remained seated in his place, not budging.

Then al-Rabīʿ came out with a scroll in his hand. He let the end of it fall to the ground and took the top of it and read:

> In the name of God, the Merciful, the Compassionate. From ʿAbdallāh al-Manṣūr, Commander of the Faithful, to the Banū Hāshim, his supporters, the people of Khurāsān, and the generality of the Muslims who survive him.

Then he dropped the scroll from his hand and wept and the people wept, and then he picked up the scroll and said, "It is easy for you to weep but this is a covenant that the Commander of the Faithful has made and we must read it to you, may God have mercy on you, so listen!"

The people fell silent and he carried on with the reading: [454]

> I hereby write this document of mine while I am alive in the last day of this world and the first of the next. I give you greeting and ask God not to make strife among you after me or "cover you in confusion in party strife, giving you a taste of mutual vengeance—each from the other."[530] Oh Banū Hāshim! Oh people of Khurāsān!

and then he began commending al-Mahdī to them and reminding them of the oath of allegiance to him and exhorting them to uphold his state and remain faithful to his covenant to the end of the document.

530. *Qur'ān*, VI: 65.

According to al-Nawfalī—his father: This was something that al-Rabīʿ had concocted. Then he looked at the faces of those present and approached the Hāshimites and took the hand of al-Ḥasan b. Zayd,[531] saying, "Stand up, Abū Muḥammad, and take the oath of allegiance!" Al-Ḥasan stood up with him, and al-Rabīʿ took him to Mūsā and sat him down before him. Al-Ḥasan took Mūsā's hand and turned to the people and said, "O people, the Commander of the Faithful al-Manṣūr had beaten me and confiscated my wealth and al-Mahdī interceded on my behalf, and he (al-Manṣūr) restored me to favor and he asked that my wealth be returned but he refused that, so al-Mahdī gave it back out of his own money and doubled it, giving two items for every one. Who could be more likely than I to take the oath of allegiance to the Commander of the Faithful, without reservation, with good spirit and a sincere heart?" Then he gave Mūsā the oath of allegiance to al-Mahdī and shook his hand. Next al-Rabīʿ came to Muḥammad b. ʿAwn, giving him precedence on account of his age, and he took the oath. Then he came to me and raised me up, and I was the third (to take the oath).[532] Then the rest of the people took the oath, and, when he had completed that, he entered the tent and remained there a little while. Then he came out to us, the body of the Hāshimites, and ordered us to stand, so we all stood up with him, and we were a great gathering of people from Iraq, Mecca, and Medina, who had come on the pilgrimage. We went in and there was al-Manṣūr on his bier in his shroud with his face uncovered, and we carried him three miles to Mecca. It is as if I could see him now, looking at him from near the leg of the bier as
[455] we carried him, and the wind was blowing and ruffling the hair on his temples because he had let his hair grow long in order to shave it off,[533] and the dye had faded from his beard. So we brought him to his grave and lowered him into it.

He said: I heard my father say that the first thing that earned

---

531. Al-Ḥasan was a leading member of the ʿAlid family; hence his pledge of loyalty was very important.

532. The narrator, Muḥammad al-Nawfalī, came from a branch of Quraysh, Nawfal, having been a brother of Hāshim and ʿAbd Shams, and this accounts for his position of honor.

533. Shaving the hair is part of *iḥrām*; he would have grown his hair to make the subsequent shaving more noticeable.

'Alī b. 'Īsā b. Māhān a high position was that, on the night when Abū Ja'far died, they tried to make 'Īsā b. Mūsā take a renewed oath of allegiance to al-Mahdī; it was al-Rabī' who undertook that, but 'Īsā b. Mūsā refused. The military commanders who were present began to push forward and backward, and 'Alī b. 'Īsā b. Māhān rose up, drew his sword, and came to him and said, "By God, you will take the oath or I will cut your head off!" When 'Isa saw that, he took the oath and the people took it after him.

According to 'Īsā b. Muḥammad—Mūsā b. Hārūn: Mūsā b. al-Mahdī and al-Rabī', the freedman of al-Manṣūr, despatched Manārah,[534] the freedman of al-Manṣūr, with news of the death of al-Manṣūr and with the oath of allegiance to al-Mahdī, and afterward they sent al-Ḥasan al-Sharawī[535] with the staff of the Prophet and his mantle,[536] which the caliphs had inherited. Abū al-'Abbās al-Ṭūsī[537] sent the seal of the caliphate with Manārah. Then they left Mecca. 'Abdallāh b. al-Musayyab b. Zuhayr[538] carried the *ḥarbah* (ceremonial spear) in front of Ṣāliḥ b. al-Manṣūr, as he used to do in the lifetime of al-Manṣūr, and al-Qāsim b. Naṣr b. Mālik,[539] who was in charge of the *shurṭah* of Mūsā al-Mahdī at that time, broke it. 'Alī b. 'Īsā b. Māhān interfered because of the grievance he had against 'Īsā b. Mūsā and what had been done by him to the Rāwandiyyah[540] and openly accused them and

534. He is also described as being one of al-Manṣūr's agents (*'ummāl*), but little else is known of him; see Crone, *Slaves*, 192.

535. He was a freedman of Muḥammad b. 'Alī, al-Manṣūr's father, and later became governor of Mosul.

536. The staff (*qaḍīb*) and the mantle (*burdah*) were among the insignia of the caliphate. The *qaḍīb* was lost in the later Middle Ages, but it is believed that the *burdah* passed eventually to the Ottomans and is now kept in the Topkapı Palace in Istanbul.

537. He was keeper of the seal at this time; see above, note 21.

538. Son of al-Manṣūr's long-serving *ṣāḥib al-shurṭah* (above, note 24). He was later governor of Egypt for a year in Hārūn's reign and *ṣāḥib al-shurṭah* for al-Ma'mūn (Crone, *Slaves*, 187).

539. There seems to have been a continuing rivalry between the family of al-Musayyab b. Zuhayr al-Ḍabbī and Mālik b. al-Haytham al-Khuzā'ī for command of the *shurṭah*. Al-Qāsim himself was later *ṣāḥib al-shurṭah* to Hārūn for a short time but was overshadowed by his powerful uncle 'Abdallāh b. Mālik. For the family, see Kennedy, *'Abbasid Caliphate*, 80–81.

540. It is not clear why 'Īsā was so unpopular with sections of the Khurāsāniyyah, but the ruthless repression of the Rāwandiyyah, who were Khurāsānīs, in 141/758–59 seems to have been a contributory factor.

talked about their journey, one of the leaders being Abū Khālid al-Marwarrūdhī. The matter was on the point of becoming serious
[456] and reaching alarming proportions so that they put on arms. Muḥammad b. Sulaymān took action about that and dealt with the matter with other members of his family, but Muḥammad was the best of them at it; the disturbance died down and became calm. He wrote to al-Mahdī about it, and he wrote back removing ʿAlī b. ʿĪsā from command of Mūsā b. al-Mahdī's guard and putting Abū Ḥanīfah Ḥarb b. Qays[541] in his place, and the state of the army quieted down. Al-ʿAbbās b. Muḥammad and Muḥammad b. Sulaymān came to al-Mahdī, al-ʿAbbās b. Muḥammad arriving first. Manārah reached al-Mahdī on Tuesday, 15 Dhu al-Ḥijjah (16 October, 775, a Monday), greeted him as caliph, offered his condolences, and handed the letters over to him. The people of the City of Peace took the oath of allegiance to him.

According to al-Haytham b. ʿAdī—al-Rabīʿ: When al-Manṣūr was on the pilgrimage during which he died, at al-ʿUdhayb[542] or one of the other halts on the road to Mecca, he had a dream. Al-Rabīʿ was in the other side of his litter. He was frightened by it and he said, "O al-Rabīʿ, I think I will die on this trip of mine and that you must secure the oath of allegiance to Abū ʿAbdallāh al-Mahdī."

Al-Rabīʿ continued: I said to him, "God will preserve you, O Commander of the Faithful, and Abū ʿAbdallāh will reach what you love in your lifetime, if God wills." His illness increased at that, and he said, "Hasten me to the Ḥaram and safety of my Lord, and I will escape from my sins and self-indulgences." He continued to feel like this until he reached Bi'r Maymūn, and I said to him, "This is Bi'r Maymūn, so you have entered the Ḥaram," and he said, "Thanks be to God," and he died the very same day.

Al-Rabīʿ continued: I ordered the tents to be pitched and the pavilions[543] to be prepared, and I attended to the Commander of

541. He had been one of the assassins of Abū Muslim (al-Ṭabarī, III, 110, 114). He never became a prominent figure and is last recorded escorting a prisoner at the beginning of Hārūn's reign in 171/787–88.

542. An oasis that was the stage after Qādisiyyah on the pilgrimage road from al-Kūfah to Mecca; see Yāqūt, *Muʿjam*, IV, 92; Morony, *Iraq*, 153.

543. I have translated *khiyam* as tents and *fasāṭīṭ* as pavilions, but there is no clear distinction, except that *fasāṭīṭ* were probably the larger tents for general gatherings.

the Faithful and dressed him in the *ṭawīlah* and the *durrāʿah*,[544] and I propped him up. Over his face I put a thin veil so that you [457] could see his form but not perceive his condition. I brought his family close to the veil so that it was not obvious what had happened to him, but his form could be seen. Then I went in and stood in a place from which I could pretend to them that he was talking to me. After that I came out and said, "The Commander of the Faithful is recovering, by the Grace of God, and sends you his greeting and says, 'I desire that God may safeguard your affairs, crush your enemies, and delight your friends, and I desire that you should renew the oath of allegiance to Abū ʿAbdallāh al-Mahdī so that no enemy or oppressor can make trouble among you,'" and all the people said, "May God give success to the Commander of the Faithful; we will hasten to do that." He[545] went in and stayed for a bit and then came out and said, "Come on with the oath!" so all of them swore, and there was not a single one among the courtiers (*khāṣṣah*), principal men (*awliyā'*),[546] and chiefs present who did not swear to al-Mahdī. He went in again and came out weeping with his chest rent and slapping his face, and one of those present said, "Our curses on you, O son of a sheep!" meaning al-Rabīʿ, for when his mother who used to suckle him died, he was suckled by a sheep. A hundred graves were dug for al-Manṣūr, and they were all filled in so that the position of his tomb, which was obvious to the people, was not known, and he was buried in a different one because of fear for him.[547] This was done with the tombs of the caliphs of the ʿAbbāsid family, and no one knew the whereabouts of their tombs. When al-Rabīʿ reached him, al-Mahdī exclaimed, "O slave, did not the majesty of the Commander of the Faithful restrain you from doing what you did to him?" People said that he had beaten him, but this was not true.

One of those who was present on al-Manṣūr's pilgrimage said: I

---

544. Al-Rabīʿ tried to show that Abū Jaʿfar was in a normal condition. Thus he dressed him in *ṭawīlah* (*qalansūwah*) and *durrāʿah* (a coat of mail).

545. The narrative changes to the third person here.

546. *Khāṣṣah* means the elite, or inner circle, and was a more loosely used term than *ṣaḥābah*, which can also be translated as "courtiers," who were a defined and salaried group. *Awliyā'* is also a general term for prominent people.

547. The ʿAbbāsids had exhumed the bodies of the Umayyad caliphs and desecrated their graves; Abū Jaʿfar must have been anxious that the same would not happen to him.

saw Ṣāliḥ b. al-Manṣūr with his father. The people were with him and Mūsā b. al-Mahdī was among his followers, but when the
[458] people returned they were following Mūsā, and Ṣāliḥ was with them.[548]

It was mentioned on the authority of al-Aṣmaʿī: The first person to announce the death of Abū Jaʿfar in al-Baṣrah was Khalaf al-Aḥmar,[549] and that was when we were sitting in the circle[550] of Yūnus,[551] and he passed us and greeted us and said:

"Calamity has prepared to bring forth her first born."

Yūnus said, "What did he say?[552]

You have certainly caused her to bring forth, a huge-necked she-camel.
The death of the Imām is one of the great disasters."

Ibrāhīm b. Yaḥyā b. Muḥammad b. ʿAlī led the pilgrimage in this year. It is said that al-Manṣūr had arranged that.

The governor of Mecca and al-Ṭā'if in this year was Ibrāhīm b. Yaḥyā b. Muḥammad b. ʿAlī b. ʿAbdallāh b. ʿAbbās and of Medina ʿAbd al-Ṣamad b. ʿAlī; ʿAmr b. Zuhayr al-Ḍabbī, brother of al-Musayyab b. Zuhayr, was in charge of al-Kūfah, and it is said that the governor (*ʿāmil*) of it was Ismāʿīl b. Abī Ismāʿīl al-Thaqafī,[553] who was said to be a freedman of the Banū Naṣr of Qays; Sharīk b. ʿAbdallāh al-Nakhaʿī was in charge of the judiciary there, and Thābit b. Mūsā[554] was in charge of the taxation (*kharāj*). Ḥumayd b. Qaḥṭabāh was in charge of Khurāsān and

---

548. This reflects Mūsā's changed status and position in the order of precedence when his father became caliph and he became heir apparent. Such matters of protocol were taken very seriously in the ʿAbbāsid court.

549. Abū Muḥriz Khalaf b. Ḥayyān, 115–80/733–96. His parents were brought from Farghānah as slaves. He was freed and lived in al-Baṣrah, becoming a great expert on ancient Arab poetry; see *EI*², s.v. "Khalaf."

550. *Ḥalqah*, the circle of students and friends gathered round a teacher.

551. Abū Isḥāq Yūnus b. ʿAmr al-Sabīʿī, a Baṣran traditionist who was an important source for sections I and II of the *History* but who contributed no material on the ʿAbbāsid period.

552. Meaning "How does the poem continue?"

553. Al-Ṭabarī quotes him twice as a source for the last days of Umayyad rule in Iraq, but nothing else is known of his career.

554. A tax specialist who was later in charge of the taxation of Iraq, Syria, and the Maghrib in Hārūn's reign; see Yaʿqūbī, *Buldān*, 252; al-Jahshiyārī, 124, 177.

Sharīk b. 'Abdallāh of the judiciary of Baghdad, along with the judiciary of al-Kūfah. It is said that the *qāḍī* of Baghdad on the day al-Manṣūr died was 'Ubaydallāh b. Muḥammad b. Ṣafwān al-Jumaḥī[555] and that Sharīk b. 'Abdallāh was in charge of the judiciary of al-Kūfah specifically. It is also said that Sharīk was in charge of the judiciary of al-Kūfah and of leading its people in prayer. In charge of police in Baghdad on the day al-Manṣūr died is said to have been 'Umar b. 'Abd al-Raḥmān,[556] the brother of   [459] 'Abd al-Jabbār b. 'Abd al-Raḥmān, but some said it was Mūsā b. Ka'b.[557] 'Umārah b. Ḥamzah was in charge of the taxation office of al-Baṣrah and its district, and 'Ubaydallāh b. al-Ḥasan al-'Anbarī was in charge of the judiciary and prayers there with Sa'īd b. Da'laj over the incidents (*aḥdāth*).   In this year, according to Muḥammad b. 'Umar, the people were afflicted by a severe plague (*wabā'*).

---

555. 'Ubaydallāh b. Muḥammad b. 'Abd al-Raḥmān b. Safwān. He had been ın Medına at the tıme of the rebellıon of Muḥammad b. 'Abdallāh ın 145/762 but remaıned ın contact wıth the 'Abbāsids (see al-Tabarī, III, 226). He was later governor of Medına, where he remaıned untıl hıs death ın 160/776–77.

556. Al-Azdī. Hıs brother had been executed by al-Manṣūr for rebellıon, so ıt ıs a bıt surprısıng to fınd hım in thıs position. See Crone, *Slaves*, 173–74.

557. For the problems thıs raıses, see note 193, above.

The Events of the Year

159

(October 31, 775–October 18, 776)

Al-'Abbās b. Muḥammad led the summer raid on Byzantium, reaching Ankara.[558] Al-Ḥasan b. al-Waṣīf[559] was in charge of the vanguard of al-'Abbās's army with the freedmen. Al-Mahdī had assigned a number of commanders from Khurāsān and others to him. Al-Mahdī himself went out and camped at Baradān and remained there until he had despatched al-'Abbās b. Muḥammad and those he sent with him. Al-'Abbās did not give al-Ḥasan b. al-Waṣīf, or anyone else, a separate command. In his raids he conquered a city of the Byzantines and a *maṭmūrah*[560] with it and returned safely, not a single one of the Muslims being injured.

Ḥumayd b. Qaḥṭabah, al-Mahdī's governor of Khurāsān, died in

558. Brooks, "Byzantines and Arabs," 735. It will be seen that my understanding of the passage is somewhat different.

559. This seems to have been his only public role. He appears in al-Ṭabarī, III, as al-Mahdī's personal servant. *Waṣīf* means a slave, a servant, or a page.

560. Brooks takes this to be a subterranean granary, but it could refer more generally to any underground structure, like the rock-cut churches and dwellings still found in Cappadocia.

this year, and al-Mahdī appointed Abū 'Awn 'Abd al-Malik b. Yazīd in his place.

In this year Ḥamzah b. Mālik[561] was appointed governor of Sijistān and Jibra'īl b. Yaḥyā of Samarqand.

In this year al-Mahdī built the mosque of al-Ruṣāfah and built its wall and dug its moat. [460]

In this year al-Mahdī deposed 'Abd al-Ṣamad b. 'Alī from Medina, the city of the Prophet, because he was angry with him, and appointed Muḥammad b. 'Abdallāh al-Kathīrī[562] in his place. Then he deposed him and appointed 'Ubaydallāh b. Muḥammad b. 'Abd al-Raḥmān b. Ṣafwān al-Jumaḥī.

In this year al-Mahdī sent 'Abd al-Malik b. Shihāb al-Misma'ī[563] by sea to the land of Hind and assigned to him 2,000 people of al-Baṣrah from all the troops (*ajnād*) and sent them with him. He sent 1,500 of the volunteers[564] who were settled in frontier garrisons[565] with a commander from the people of Syria called Ibn al-Ḥubāb al-Madḥijī with 700 Syrians. He was accompanied by 1,000 volunteers from the people of al-Baṣrah with their wealth, among them, it is said, al-Rabī' b. Ṣubayḥ,[566] and 4,000 of the Uswāriyyīn[567] and the Sabābijah.[568] 'Abd al-Malik b. Shihāb ap- [461]

561. Son of Mālik b. al-Haytham, brother of 'Abdallāh b. Mālik and uncle of al-Qāsim b. Naṣr; see note 539, above. Ḥamzah was later governor of Khurāsān in 177/793–94 and died in 181/797–98; see Crone, *Slaves*, 181–83.

562. He was again interim governor in the next year but is otherwise unknown.

563. He was briefly governor of Sind two years later. None of the other commanders is known elsewhere.

564. The distinction seems to be between the salaried *ajnād* and the voluntary *muṭawwi'ah*, who fought because they wished to make a contribution to the *jihād*, or Holy War.

565. *Murābiṭāt* means the men who form such a garrison (see Lane, s.v. *rabaṭa*). From the same root comes the better-known *ribāṭ*, meaning a frontier fortress or simply a religious house.

566. According to Ibn al-Athīr, this name should read Ṣubīḥ (see editor's note).

567. So voweled by the editor in the text; the manuscript versions are obviously corrupt. They were Persian cavalrymen who deserted to the Muslims after the conquest of Iraq and settled in al-Baṣrah, where they became like a small tribe and retained their own identity. See Morony, *Iraq*, 198, 207, 213.

568. Again this is reconstructed by the editor from corrupt readings. He relates it to Persian *shabānah*, meaning "night watchmen." The *Addenda*, s.v. *sbj*, suggests the reading *siyābijah* and that it derives from a name given to soldiers originally from Sumatra who emigrated to Iraq in pre-Islamic times; see EI^1, s.v. "Sayābidjah."

pointed al-Mundhir b. Muḥammad al-Jārūdī as leader of the 1,000 volunteers from al-Baṣrah and his own son Ghassān b. ʿAbd al-Malik as leader of the 2,000 men assigned to him from al-Baṣrah. He appointed his son ʿAbd al-Wāḥid b. ʿAbd al-Malik as leader of the 1,500 volunteers from the frontier garrisons. He kept Yazīd b. al-Ḥubāb and his men as a separate unit, and they set out. Al-Mahdī sent Abū al-Qāsim Muḥriz b. Ibrāhīm to supervise their equipment before they left. They set out on their expedition and reached the city of Bārbad[569] in the land of al-Hind in the year 160 (776–77).

In this year Maʿbad b. al-Khalīl died in Sind. He was al-Mahdī's governor there, and he appointed Rawḥ b. Ḥātim in his place[570] on the advice of his *wazīr*, Abū ʿUbaydallāh.

In this year al-Mahdī ordered the release of all those who were in al-Manṣūr's prison, except those who were accused of shedding blood or killing or those who were known for spreading corruption or against whom anyone had a complaint or just claim. They were released, and among those who were released from the dungeon was Yaʿqūb b. Dāwūd,[571] freedman of the Banū Sulaym. Imprisoned with him in that prison was al-Ḥasan b. Ibrāhīm b. ʿAbdallāh b. al-Ḥasan b. al-Ḥasan b. ʿAlī b. Abī Ṭālib.[572]

In this year al-Mahdī transferred al-Ḥasan b. Ibrāhīm from the dungeon he was in to the custody of Nuṣayr al-Waṣīf.[573]

[462] The reasons why al-Mahdī transferred al-Ḥasan b. Ibrāhīm from the dungeon to Nuṣayr:

---

569. The editor suggests that this should read Nārbudda. I have not been able to locate this place.

570. Al-Muhallabī, elder brother of Yazīd; see note 90, above. At the time of the ʿAbbāsid Revolution, he had joined Abū Jaʿfar at the siege of Wāsiṭ, and he served the ʿAbbāsids continuously until his death in Ifrīqiyah in 174/791, becoming, as Ibn Khallikān says, the only man, apart from Abū Mūsā al-Ashʿarī, to hold office under five caliphs. He returned in 165/781–82 to become governor of his family's home town, al-Baṣrah. He had another spell in al-Kūfah (see pp. 237, 239, below) before his final appointmant to Ifrīqiyah in 171/787–88, see also Ibn Idhārī, *Bayān*, 84.

571. His origins and rise and fall are fully dealt with in the following pages. Al-Ṭabarī's version is corroborated with some more detail in al-Jahshiyārī, 155–63.

572. An ʿAlid, son of Ibrāhīm, who led the 145/762 rebellion in al-Baṣrah.

573. For the term Waṣīf, see note 559, above. He later took the news of al-Mahdī's death to al-Hādī in Jurjān (see al-Ṭabarī, III, 545) and is last recorded in 202/817–18, when he took the oath of allegiance to Ibrāhīm b. al-Mahdī.

It is said that the reason for this was that, when al-Mahdī ordered the release of the prisoners as I have mentioned, Ya'qūb b. Dāwūd was imprisoned with al-Ḥasan b. Ibrāhīm in one place and Ya'qūb b. Dāwūd was released but al-Ḥasan b. Ibrāhīm was not. He was disturbed by this and feared for his life, so he searched for a way of escape for himself and release. He secretly communicated with one of his reliable helpers, who dug a tunnel from a place opposite to the place where he was in prison. After Ya'qūb b. Dāwūd had been released, he used to visit Ibn 'Ulāthah,[574] who was al-Mahdī's *qāḍī* in the City of Peace, and stay with him until he became friendly with him. Ya'qūb heard how al-Ḥasan b. Ibrāhīm intended to escape, so he approached Ibn 'Ulāthah and told him that he had some advice for al-Mahdī and asked to be sent to Abū 'Ubaydallāh. Ibn 'Ulāthah asked him what the advice was, but he refused to tell him and kept it to himself. Ibn 'Ulāthah went to Abū 'Ubaydallāh and told him about Ya'qūb and what he said to him. He ordered him to be fetched and, when he entered, he asked to be taken to al-Mahdī to tell him the advice he had, so he was taken to him. When he came in to al-Mahdī, he thanked him for his favor in releasing him and his generosity to him and said that he had some advice for him. Al-Mahdī asked him for it in the presence of Abū 'Ubaydallāh and Ibn 'Ulāthah, but he asked that they leave. Al-Mahdī told him that he had trust in them, but he refused to reveal anything to him until they got up and he was alone with him. Then he told him the information about al-Ḥasan b. Ibrāhīm and his plan and that it would take place that very [463]
night. Al-Mahdī sent a trustworthy man to bring him information, and he told him that Ya'qūb's information was correct. Al-Mahdī ordered that al-Ḥasan be transferred to Nuṣayr. He remained in his custody until he schemed and schemes were made for him and he escaped and could not be found. News about him became public, and he was sought but could not be captured. Al-Mahdī remembered Ya'qūb's guidance to him, and he hoped for guidance from him like that he had been given (before) in his affair.

574. Muḥammad b. 'Abdallāh b. 'Ulāthah; he is said (see below, p. 203) to have been one of the two *qāḍī*s of al-Ruṣāfah. His brother Sulaymān was governor of al-Jazīrah for Marwān b. Muḥammad, the last Umayyad caliph; see Crone, *Slaves*, 171.

He asked Abū 'Ubaydallāh about him, and he replied that he was present, as he had stayed with Abū 'Ubaydallāh. Al-Mahdī summoned him privately and spoke of what he had done with regard to al-Ḥasan b. Ibrāhīm the first time and of his advice to him, and he informed him of what had occurred in his affair. Ya'qūb replied that he did not know where he was but that, if he gave him a safe-conduct he could trust, he would guarantee to bring him so that he could fulfill his safe-conduct and be generous to him and favor him. Al-Mahdī gave him this in his council (*majlis*) and guaranteed it. Ya'qūb said to him, "Refrain, O Commander of the Faithful, from mentioning him and give up searching for him because that frightens him. Leave me and him so that I can entice him and bring him to you." Al-Mahdī agreed to this.

Ya'qūb said, "O Commander of the Faithful, you have extended your justice to your people, treated them fairly, and spread your goodness and favor among them. Their hopes have grown and their expectations have increased. However, there remain some things that, if I drew them to your attention, you would not fail to look into as you do in other affairs. Furthermore, there are things done behind your door without your knowing. If you give me a
[464] way of coming in to you and give me permission to bring them to your notice, I shall do that." Al-Mahdī granted him that and entrusted him with it. He appointed Sulaym, the black eunuch of al-Manṣūr,[575] as his channel of communication with al-Mahdī whenever he wished to enter. Ya'qūb used to go in to al-Mahdī by night and offer him advice on good and fine matters concerning the frontiers, the building of fortresses, the strengthening of raids, and the marrying of single people, the liberating of prisoners and captives, the redemption of debtors, and the distribution of alms to the virtuous. He enjoyed his favor because of that and because he hoped he would secure for him the capture of al-Ḥasan b. Ibrāhīm. He took him as a brother in God and issued a decree (*tawqī'*) to that effect and established him in the *dīwān*,[576] and he was assigned 100,000 *dirhams*, which was the first grant he

575. I have translated *khādim* as eunuch, possibly wrongly. At this date it may well just mean "servant"; cf. *waṣīf*.

576. That is, he was given a regular salary, recorded in the official list, or *dīwān*.

had ever received from it. His status continued to increase and climb upward until he placed al-Ḥasan b. Ibrāhīm in the hands of al-Mahdī, after which his status fell and al-Mahdī ordered that he be imprisoned. 'Alī b. al-Khalīl[577] said about that:

What a wonder is the changing of affairs
pleasing and unpleasing.
Time plays with men
and has running occurrences.
Because of Ya'qūb b. Dāwūd,
the ropes of Mu'āwiyah[578] are fraying.
The disasters from 'Āfiyah[579] have infringed upon Ibn 'Ulāthah
the *qāḍī*.
Say to the *wazīr* Abū 'Ubaydallāh, [465]
"Do you have a future?"
Ya'qūb is looking into affairs, and you are looking sideways.
You introduced him, and he rose above you.
That is the real inauspiciousnes.

In this year al-Mahdī dismissed Ismā'īl b. Abī Ismā'īl from al-Kūfah and its *aḥdāth* (supervision of daily affairs). Opinions differ as to who succeeded him; some say it was Isḥāq b. al-Ṣabbāḥ al-Kindī, then al-Ash'athī,[580] on the advice of Sharīk b. 'Abdallāh, the *qāḍī* of al-Kūfah. 'Umar b. Shabbah says that al-Mahdī appointed 'Īsā b. Luqmān b. Muḥammad b. Ḥāṭib b. al-Ḥārith b. Mu'ammar b. Ḥabīb b. Wahb b. Hudhāfah b. Jumaḥ[581] and ap-

577. Mawlā of Shaybān from al-Kūfah and a poet at the court of Hārūn; Ibn al-Nadīm numbers him among the *Zindiq* poets (*Fihrist*, 804). See *Aghānī*, Būlāq, XIII, 14; Beirut, XIV, 166. He is not quoted elsewhere by al-Ṭabarī.

578. Abū 'Ubaydallāh, al-Mahdī's vizier, whose position was being threatened by Ya'qūb.

579. Ibn Yazīd al-Azdī. He is described as joint *qāḍī* of 'Askar al-Mahdī with Ibn 'Ulāthah. The sense of the poem is that he was supplanting Ibn 'Ulāthah, just as Ya'qūb was supplanting Abū 'Ubaydallāh.

580. I.e., a member of the tribe of Kindah, descended from the great Ash'ath b. Qays al-Kindī, companion of the Prophet and a leading figure in the politics of early Muslim Iraq. The family was still very influential in al-Kūfah in early 'Abbāsid times. Isḥāq was the father of Ya'qūb al-Kindī, known as the "philosopher of the Arabs"; see Crone, *Slaves*, 110–12.

581. A Qurashī, Jumaḥ being a branch of Quraysh. He was later governor of Egypt, 161–62/778–79. It is not clear why al-Ṭabarī gives so complete a genealogy

pointed his brother's son ʿUthmān b. Saʿīd b. Luqmān over the police. It is also said that Sharīk b. ʿAbdallāh was in charge of the prayers and the judiciary and ʿĪsā of the *aḥdāth*, and then Sharīk was appointed alone as governor and put Isḥāq b. al-Ṣabbāḥ al-Kindī in charge of the police. A poet said:

You would not be more than a puppet raised up by Sharīk
even if your hand were to stretch so high as to catch Canopus.[582]

They say that Isḥāq did not thank Sharīk and that Sharīk said to him:

He prays and fasts for the things of this world he hopes for;
he attains them and prays and fasts no more.

According to ʿUmar[583]—Jaʿfar b. Muḥammad, the *qāḍī* of al-Kūfah:[584] Al-Mahdī put Sharīk in charge of the prayers as well as the judiciary and Isḥāq b. al-Ṣabbāḥ in charge of the police. Then he later appointed Isḥāq b. al-Ṣabbāḥ over the prayers and the *aḥdāth*; then he appointed Isḥāq b. al-Ṣabbāḥ b. ʿImrān b. Ismāʿīl b. Muḥammad b. al-Ashʿath as governor of al-Kūfah. He appointed
[466] al-Nuʿmān b. Jaʿfar al-Kindī[585] over the police, but al-Nuʿmān died and he appointed his brother Yazīd b. Jaʿfar over the police.

In this year al-Mahdī deposed Saʿīd b. Daʿlaj from the *aḥdāth* of al-Baṣrah and ʿUbaydallāh b. al-Ḥasan from the prayers and the judiciary of its people, and he appointed ʿAbd al-Malik b. Ayyūb b. Ẓubyān al-Numayrī in place of both of them. He wrote to ʿAbd al-Malik, ordering him to do justice to those people of al-Baṣrah who had been oppressed by Saʿīd b. Daʿlaj. Then in this year the *aḥdāth* were removed from the control of ʿAbd al-Malik b. Ayyūb and given to ʿUmārah b. Ḥamzah. ʿUmārah put a man from al-Baṣrah called al-Miswar b. ʿAbdallāh b. Muslim al-Bāhilī[586] in

---

and none of his forebears seems to have distinguished himself; the identical genealogy is recorded by Ibn al-Kalbī (Caskel, table 24).

582. The poem may be a comment on the different social status of Sharīk and Isḥāq, humble Sharīk appointing the aristocratic Isḥāq as his deputy.

583. B. Shabbah.

584. Not recorded elsewhere.

585. Presumably a relative of his.

586. Probably a cousin of Salm b. Qutaybah b. Muslim al-Bāhilī, whose family was prominent in al-Baṣrah; see above, note 27.

charge of it, and ʿAbd al-Malik was confirmed in charge of the prayers.

In this year Qutham b. al-ʿAbbās was deposed from al-Yamāmah because of (the caliph's) anger, but, when the letter of his deposition arrived in al-Yamāmah, he had died. Bishr b. al-Mundhir al-Bajalī[587] was appointed governor in his place.

In this year Yazīd b. Manṣūr was deposed from Yemen and Rajāʾ b. Rawḥ was appointed in his place.

In this year al-Haytham b. Saʿīd[588] was deposed from al-Jazīrah and al-Faḍl b. Ṣāliḥ was appointed as governor.

In this year al-Mahdī manumitted his slave girl (*umm walad*) al-Khayzurān and married her.[589]

In this year al-Mahdī also married Umm ʿAbdallāh, daughter of Ṣāliḥ b. ʿAlī and sister of al-Faḍl and ʿAbdallāh b. Ṣāliḥ by the same mother. In this year in Dhu al-Ḥijjah (20 September–18 October, 776) fire broke out among the boats in Baghdad by the palace of ʿĪsā b. ʿAlī.[590] Many people were burned, and the boats there with their contents were destroyed by fire.

In this year Maṭar, freedman of al-Manṣūr, was deposed from [467]
Egypt and Abū Ḍamrah Muḥammad b. Sulaymān[591] was made governor in his place.

In this year there was agitation among the Banū Hāshim and their party of the people of Khurāsān, demanding the removal of ʿĪsā b. Mūsā from his position as heir apparent and its transfer to Mūsā b. al-Mahdī. When that became apparent to al-Mahdī, he wrote, it is said, to ʿĪsā b. Mūsā, who was in al-Kūfah, ordering

587. Nothing more is known about him.

588. He is probably to be identified with al-Haytham b. Saʿīd b. Zuhayr, mawlā of al-Manṣūr, who had a *suwayqah* (small market) in west Baghdad by the Round City (Yāqūt, *Muʿjam*, III, 288). It is not clear when he was appointed to al-Jazīrah, and no further information is known about him.

589. Mother of the future caliphs al-Hādī and Hārūn and the princess al-Banūqah. A former slave of Yemeni origin, she became very powerful because of her influence with al-Mahdī. Her position declined in al-Hādī's reign, but she regained much of her influence upon the accession of Hārūn. She died in 173/789.

590. This lay on the west bank of the Tigris, where the ʿĪsā Canal flowed into it, see Le Strange, *Baghdad*, 146. There was a harbor there mostly used by boats coming from al-Baṣrah.

591. Not to be confused with Muḥammad b. Sulaymān the ʿAbbāsid (see note 29, above). He remained governor until 161/778, according to al-Ṭabarī, but is not recorded by al-Kindī (see note 167, above).

him to come to him, but ʿĪsā was suspicious of his intentions and refused to come to him.

According to ʿUmar:[592] When power passed to al-Mahdī, he asked ʿĪsā to resign his position but he refused, so he wanted to coerce him. He appointed Rawḥ b. Ḥātim b. Qabīṣah b. al-Muhallab as governor of al-Kūfah and Khālid b. Yazīd b. Ḥātim in charge of the police. Al-Mahdī was wanting Rawḥ to attack ʿĪsā in a way that nothing could be held against Rawḥ, but he could not find any means of achieving this.

ʿĪsā had left for an estate of his at al-Raḥbah[593] and only used to come into al-Kūfah during two months in the year, in Ramaḍān, when he joined the Friday prayers, and the ʿĪd,[594] after which he returned to his estate, and at the beginning of Dhū al-Ḥijjah to attend the ʿĪd[595] and return immediately to his estate. When he attended the Friday prayers, he used to ride from his house to the doors of the mosque, dismount on the threshold of the door, and pray on the spot, Rawḥ wrote to al-Mahdī saying that ʿĪsā b. Mūsā did not attend Friday prayers or enter al-Kūfah except for two months of the year and, when he did come, he rode until he reached the square by the mosque, which was the praying place of
[468] the people, and then he crossed it to the gates of the mosque and his animals dropped dung in the praying place of the people. No one else did this. Al-Mahdī wrote to Rawḥ, ordering him to block the ends of the lanes that led to the mosque with planks of wood so that the people would dismount there. Rawḥ put the planks at the ends of the lanes, so that the place became known as "the Planks." ʿĪsā b. Mūsā heard about this before Friday, and he wrote to the heirs of Mukhtār b. Abī ʿUbayd,[596] the house of Mukhtār being on the edge of the mosque, and bought it for a high price, refurbished it, and had a bath installed. On Thursday he went there and stayed in it and, when he wanted to go to Friday prayers, he mounted a donkey and rode slowly to the gate of the mosque,

592. B. Shabbah.

593. It is probable that ʿĪsā's secluded residence was the great palace now known as Ukhaydir, in the desert west of al-Kūfah.

594. The *ʿĪd al-Fiṭr*, or Feast of the Breaking of the Ramaḍān Fast on 1 Shawwāl.

595. *The ʿĪd al-Adha*, or Feast of Sacrifice, on 10 Dhū al-Ḥijjah.

596. Mukhtār had led a famous rebellion against the Umayyads in al-Kūfah in 65–67/685–87.

prayed in a corner, and returned to his house. He made al-Kūfah his home and stayed there. Al-Mahdī became insistent with ʿĪsā and said, "If you do not agree to renounce your rights so that I can have the oath of allegiance taken to Mūsā and Hārūn, I will feel justified in treating you as a rebel, but, if you accept, I will compensate you with what will be more advantageous to you and more immediately useful." He agreed and took the oath of allegiance to the two of them, and al-Mahdī ordered ten million *dirhams* for him, or, it is said, twenty million *dirhams*, and numerous estates (*qaṭā'i'*).

According to someone other than ʿUmar: Al-Mahdī wrote to ʿĪsā b. Mūsā when he was intending to depose him, ordering him to come to him, but he was suspicious of his intentions and refused to come so that it was feared that he would rebel. Al-Mahdī sent his uncle al-ʿAbbās b. Muḥammad to him and wrote a letter and informed him what he wanted him to say to ʿĪsā. Al-ʿAbbās reached ʿĪsā with al-Mahdī's letter and his message to him, and he returned to al-Mahdī with his reply to that. After al-ʿAbbās had [469] come to him, he sent Muḥammad b. Farrūkh Abū Hurayrah,[597] the commander, with a thousand of his companions who were enthusiastic in their support (for al-Mahdī). He gave each man a drum and ordered them to beat them in unison as they reached al-Kūfah. He entered the city one night in the early dawn, and his companions beat their drums. ʿĪsā b. Mūsā was extremely frightened by that. Abū Hurayrah came to him and ordered him to set out. ʿĪsā complained that he was ill, but Abū Hurayrah did not accept this and brought him immediately to the City of Peace.

The leader of the pilgrims in this year was Yazīd b. Manṣūr, the maternal uncle of al-Mahdī, on his arrival from Yemen.

According to Aḥmad b. Thābit—anon.—Isḥāq b. ʿĪsā—Abū Maʿshar: Muḥammad b. ʿUmar al-Wāqidī and others also say this: Yazīd b. Manṣūr came from Yemen because of a letter from al-Mahdī ordering him to come to him and appointing him in

597. Al-Azdī. He had been one of the small group of Khurāsānī soldiers who had discovered al-Saffāḥ in al-Kūfah and first proclaimed him caliph (al-Ṭabarī, *History*, III, 36). Immediately before his death, al-Hādī sent him to arrest his brother Hārūn, and, when Hārūn became caliph, he had Muḥammad executed in 171/787–88.

charge of the Pilgrimage and telling him of his longing to see him and have him near.

The governor of Medina in this year was ʿUbaydallāh b. Ṣafwān al-Jumaḥī, Isḥāq b. al-Ṣabbāḥ al-Kindī was in charge of the prayers and the *aḥdāth* at al-Kūfah, Thābit b. Mūsā was in charge of the taxation there, and Sharīk b. ʿAbdallāh of the judiciary. ʿAbd al-Malik b. Ayyūb b. Ẓubyān al-Numayrī was in charge of
[470] the prayers at al-Baṣrah. ʿUmārah b. Ḥamzah was over the *aḥdāth* there, with al-Miswar b. ʿAbdallāh b. Muslim al-Bāhili as his deputy and ʿUbaydallāh b. al-Ḥasan over the judiciary. ʿUmārah b. Ḥamzah was over the districts (*kuwar*) of the Tigris, al-Ahwāz, and Fārs. Bisṭām b. ʿAmr was in charge of Sind,[598] Rajāʾ b. Rawḥ of Yemen, and Bishr b. al-Mundhir of al-Yamāmah. Abū ʿAwn ʿAbd al-Malik b. Yazīd was in charge of Khurāsān, al-Faḍl b. Ṣāliḥ of al-Jazīrah, Yazīd b. Ḥātim of Ifrīqiyah, and Muḥammad b. Sulaymān Abū Ḍamrah of Egypt.

598. His brother Hishām had been governor of Sind in 156–57/772–74, and he himself was appointed to Azerbaijān in 161/777–78. See Crone, *Slaves*, 167–68.

The Events of the Year 160

(October 19, 776–October 8, 777)

The events of this year:

Among the events of this year was the rebellion of Yūsuf b. Ibrāhīm, he was the one who was called Yūsuf al-Barm,[599] in Khurāsān. He and those who followed him and shared his opinions repudiated al-Mahdī because of the position he was alleged to be in and his conduct in that position. It is said that many people joined him and Yazīd b. Mazyad was sent against him and met him in battle until they fought hand to hand and Yazīd took him prisoner and sent him to al-Mahdī with a number of his principal supporters. When they were brought to al-Nahrawān, Yūsuf al-Barm was carried on a camel with his face toward the tail of his camel, and his supporters were also on camels. They were taken into al-Ruṣāfah in this position and brought to al-Mahdī. He ordered Harthamah b. Aʿyan to cut off Yūsuf's hands and legs and then to behead him and his supporters, and they were crucified on the Upper Bridge over the Tigris at the ʿAskar al-Mahdī end. [471]

599. For this rebellion, see Daniel, *Khurāsān*, 166–67.

He only ordered Harthamah to kill him because he had killed a brother of Harthamah's in Khurāsān.[600]

In this year ʿĪsā b. Mūsā arrived with Abū Hurayrah on Thursday, 6 Muḥarram (Thursday, October 24, 776), according to al-Faḍl b. Sulaymān. He stayed in a house belonging to Muḥammad b. Sulaymān on the banks of the Tigris in ʿAskar al-Mahdī. For some days he stayed visiting al-Mahdī, frequently going in by the entrance he was used to using and not meeting with any opposition, hostility, or indifference, and some of the courtiers became friendly with him. Then one day he came to the palace before al-Mahdī's audience and came into an audience being held by al-Rabīʿ in a small room (*maqṣūrah*) with a door. The chiefs of the (ʿAbbāsid) party had gathered that day to depose him and attack him, and they did that when he was in the room where al-Rabīʿ held his audience. The door of the room was locked in front of them, so they beat on the door with their maces and their staffs until they smashed it and almost broke it down. They cursed him with the worst of curses and besieged him there. Al-Mahdī appeared to disapprove of what they were doing, but this did not deter them from what they were doing but rather they intensified their attack on him. He and they remained in this position for some days until senior men from his family made it public in the presence of al-Mahdī and they insisted on deposing him and cursed him to his face, Muḥammad b. Sulaymān being the most hostile of them toward him. When al-Mahdī saw their opinion of ʿĪsā and their hatred of him and his position as heir apparent, he called on them to accept Mūsā as heir. He went along with their opinion and agreement and urged ʿĪsā to respond to him and them by giving up the oath to himself that was on the necks of the people and releasing them from it. He refused, saying that he was restrained
[472] by an oath on his money and his family.[601] Al-Mahdī sent him a number of legal scholars (*fuqahā*) and judges, among them Muḥammad b. ʿAbdallāh b. ʿUlāthah, al-Zanjī b. Khālid al-Makkī,[602]

---

600. Daniel regards this as the "ostensible reason," but there seems to me no cause to doubt al-Ṭabarī's account.

601. I.e., an oath with provision that he would give away his money and divorce his wives if he broke it; see p. 186, below, where ʿĪsā's letter of resignation contains such penalty clauses.

602. Nothing more seems to be known of him.

and others, and they gave him a legal opinion as they saw it. (He agreed to his deposition).[603] Eventually al-Mahdī decided to buy the oath that he had on the necks of the people for what would be a satisfaction and compensation to him for what he was paying out for the breaking of his oath. This was ten million *dirhams* and the estates of the Upper Zāb and Kaskar, and ʿĪsā accepted this. Since al-Mahdī had begun negotiations about deposing him until he had agreed to it, ʿĪsā had remained confined with him in the House of the *Dīwān*[604] in al-Ruṣāfah until he accepted the deposition and the surrender on Wednesday, 26 Muḥarram (Wednesday, 13 November, 776), after the afternoon prayer. He took the oath of allegiance to al-Mahdī and to Mūsā after him on the morning of Thursday, 27 Muḥarram (Thursday, 14 November, 776), toward midday. Then al-Mahdī received the members of his family in a pavilion that Muḥammad b. Sulaymān had given him that was pitched in the Courtyard of the Gates.[605] He received their oaths of allegiance to himself and to Mūsā b. al-Mahdī after him one by one until the last of them, and then he went out to the Friday Mosque in al-Ruṣāfah and sat on the pulpit. Mūsā climbed up so that he was below him and ʿĪsā stood on the first step of the pulpit. Al-Mahdī thanked God and praised him and prayed for the Prophet. Then he explained why he had called together the people of his House and his Party, his commanders, his helpers (*anṣār*) and others of the people of Khurāsān. He told them about the deposition of ʿĪsā b. Mūsā and the transfer of the rights he had over the people to Mūsā, son of the Commander of the Faithful, about their choice of him and their pleasure in him and how he saw their response to that, what he hoped from their interest and [473]
friendship and what he feared from their differences in intention and disagreements in their words. ʿĪsā had resigned his precedence and released them from the oath to him that was on their necks. His rights in this had passed to Mūsā, son of the Commander of the Faithful, with the agreement of the Commander of the Faith-

603. The editor suggests that these words from Ibn al-Athīr's version should be inserted; al-Ṭabarī, III, 472, n. *b*.

604. *Dār al-Dīwan*, presumably the building where the *dīwān* records (see note 401, above) were kept, but it is not recorded by the geographers.

605. *Saḥn al-Abwāb*, it seems that this was in the caliph's palace in al-Ruṣāfah.

ful and the members of his family and his party. Mūsā was the agent of the Book of Allāh and the *sunna* of His Prophet among them with the best and most just conduct.

(He continued,) "So take the oath of allegiance, you who are present and make haste to do what others have made haste to do before. All goodness lies in consensus and all evil in division. I ask Allāh for us, and for you, good fortune through His mercy and action in obedience to Him and what is pleasing to Him, and I ask the forgiveness of Allāh for me and for you."

Mūsā sat down below him separately on the pulpit so as not to leave a gap between him and those who came up to take the oath of allegiance to him and shake his hand and so that his face should not be hidden. ʿĪsā remained standing in his place and a letter was read to him detailing his resignation, his withdrawal from his position as heir apparent, and his releasing of the people from the oath of allegiance to him that was on their necks. That was his own doing, and he was doing it obediently without force, willingly without anger, lovingly without duress. ʿĪsā agreed to that and went up to swear allegiance to al-Mahdī and shook his hand and then retired. The family of al-Mahdī took the oath in order of age, swearing allegiance to al-Mahdī and then to Mūsā, shaking both their hands until the last of them had finished. Those of the courtiers (*aṣḥāb*) and the leading military commanders and men of the (ʿAbbāsid) party who were present did likewise. Then al-Mahdī came down and went to his house, leaving his maternal uncle Yazīd b. Manṣūr in charge of taking the oath from those who were left of the upper and lower classes (*khāṣṣah wa-ʿāmmah*). He administered it until all the people had finished. Al-Mahdī handed over to ʿĪsā what he had given him and satisfied him with for the resignation of the position of heir apparent. For him he
[474] wrote a letter of resignation witnessed by all the people of his house, his courtiers and his party, his secretaries and the soldiers in his *dīwān*s, as a proof against ʿĪsā and a block to any claims or pretensions he might have to what he had given up.

This is a copy of the conditions that ʿĪsā wrote for himself:

> In the name of God, the Merciful, the Compassionate. This is a letter to the servant of Allāh al-Mahdī Muḥammad, Commander of the Faithful, and to the heir apparent

of the Muslims, Mūsā, son of al-Mahdī, to the members of his family, to all his commanders and troops of the people of Khurāsān, and to all the Muslims in eastern and western parts of the earth wherever they may be. I wrote it for al-Mahdī Muḥammad, Commander of the Faithful, and for the heir apparent of the Muslims, Mūsā b. Muḥammad b. ʿAbdallāh b. Muḥammad b. ʿAlī concerning the assigning to him of the covenant that belonged to me until the words of the Muslims came together, their affair was harmonized, and their desires were united to accept appointing Mūsā, son of al-Mahdī Muḥammad, Commander of the Faithful, as heir apparent. I have acknowledged that the writing of that is binding on me and that the writing in it is mine. I have entered into what the Muslims have entered into concerning the choice of Mūsā, son of the Commander of the Faithful, and the oath of allegiance to him and have abandoned the oath of allegiance to me that was on their necks, and given you freedom from that, in fullness without embarrassment on your behalf, or any of your number or the generality of the Muslims. There is nothing either old or new of that which gives me any claims, demands, proofs, arguments, or obedience from anyone of you or from the generality of the Muslims. There is no oath of allegiance (due to me) in the lifetime of Muḥammad, Commander of the Faithful, or after him, or after the heir apparent of the Muslims, Mūsā, as long as I live until my death. I have sworn allegiance to Muḥammad al-Mahdī, Commander of the Faithful, and to Mūsā son of the Commander of the Faithful after him, and I [475] have granted to them and to the mass of the Muslims of the people of Khurāsān and others absolution from the conditions that applied to me in this matter that I have abandoned. I have made a pact with Allāh to persist in this. I will not release any of His creatures from any pact or agreement or oath or assurance (they have made) to hear and obey and support al-Mahdī Muḥammad, Commander of the Faithful, and his heir apparent, Mūsā, son of the Commander of the Faithful, either secretly or openly, by word or by deed, by intention, by force, by urgent request, for better or for worse. (I shall act) in friendship to the two of them and those they appoint to office and hostility to those who are hostile to them, whoever it might be, as if we were still in this position that I have abandoned.

If I deviate from or change or alter or interfere with or act contrary to anything I have promised in this agreement or if I call on others to disobey anything I have made incumbent on myself in this letter to al-Mahdī Muḥammad, Commander of the Faithful, and his heir apparent, Mūsā, son of the Commander of the Faithful, and to the mass of the Muslims, or do not fulfill it, every wife I have married at the time I wrote this letter or will marry in the next thirty years is divorced three times, finally and completely, every slave I have now or will own in the next thirty years is free before Allāh, and all my wealth, coin or goods or loans or land, whether great or small, long held or newly acquired, or that I shall acquire in the next thirty years from today, will be alms (*ṣadaqah*) for the wretched and the governor will distribute it as he sees fit. I will walk barefoot from the City of Peace to the old house of Allāh[606] that is in Mecca, dedicated and obliged, for thirty years. There will be no expiation for me and no escape for me except fulfillment of it, and God will ensure the fulfillment of it as the responsible witness, and God is a
[476] sufficient witness. The witness to ʿĪsā b. Mūsā of his acceptance of what is in these conditions is four hundred and thirty members of the Banū Hāshim, of the freedmen, of the courtiers (*ṣaḥābah*) of Quraysh, the ministers, secretaries, and judges. This was written in Ṣafar, 160 (18 November—16 December, 776), and sealed by ʿĪsā b. Mūsā.

A poet said:

Abū Mūsā hated death,
but in death was escape and honor.

606. The Kaʿbah.

He cast off power and appeared dressed in
a very long garment of blame that goes down till his feet are not seen.

In the year 160 'Abd al-Malik b. Shihāb al-Misma'ī reached the city of Bārbad with those volunteers and others who had set out with him. They attacked the city the day after their arrival and besieged it for two days. They then prepared a mangonel and attacked it with all their equipment. Then the people gathered together and spurred each other on with the Qur'ān and praising Allāh, and Allāh allowed them to take it by force. Their horsemen entered it from all sides and forced them to take refuge in their stronghold. They lit fires with oil, and some of them were burned while others attacked the Muslims but Allāh killed them all. More than twenty Muslims were martyred and Allāh gave (the city) as booty (*fay'*) to them.

The sea became rough so that they could not sail away on it, so they stayed until it improved and they were afflicted with a disease in their mouths called scurvy (*ḥumām qurr*), and about a thousand of them died, including al-Rabī' b. Ṣubayḥ. Then they left when it was possible and reached the shore of Fārs at a place called Baḥr Ḥamrān.[607] The wind rose up on them there during the night, and most of their ships were wrecked. Some of them [477] were drowned and some escaped. They brought with them some of their prisoners, among them the daughter of the king of Bārbad, to Muḥammad b. Sulaymān, who was at that time governor of al-Baṣrah.

In this year Abān b. Ṣadaqah was appointed secretary and minister (*wazīr*) to Hārūn b. al-Mahdī.

In this year Abū 'Awn was deposed from Khurāsān on account of (the caliph's)[608] anger and Mu'ādh b. Muslim was put in his place.

In this year the summer expedition (against the Byzantines)

607. Not known to the geographers.

608. According to Ibn al-Athīr, this was because he failed to defeat the rebel al-Muqanna'. That the caliph still retained a high opinion of him is shown by the anecdote, pp. 256–57, below.

was led by Thumāmah b. al-Walīd al-ʿAbsī.[609]

In this year al-Ghamr b. al-ʿAbbās al-Khathʿamī[610] led a raid on the Syrian (Mediterranean) sea.

In this year al-Mahdī returned the family of Abū Bakrah from their genealogy in Thaqīf to their position as clients of the Prophet of God.[611] The reason for this was that a man of Abū Bakrah complained of injustice to al-Mahdī and claimed to be related to him because of his position as a freedmen of the Prophet of God. Al-Mahdī replied, "You have established this genealogy and traced back this descent only when you felt you needed to and you required to become close to us." Al-Ḥakam said, "O Commander of the Faithful, if anybody has denied that, we will acknowledge it. I am asking you to return me and the clan of Abū Bakrah to our descent from the freedman of the Prophet of God and to order that the family of Ziyād b. ʿUbayd be expelled from the genealogy to which Muʿāwiyah had attached them, contrary to the judgment of the Prophet: 'The child belongs to the bed and to the adulterer the stone.' They should be returned to their descent from ʿUbayd among the freedmen of Thaqīf."[612]

Al-Mahdī ordered that all the branches of the family of Abū
[478] Bakrah and the family of Ziyād should be returned to their genealogy. He wrote to Muḥammad b. Sulaymān a letter that he ordered should be read out in the Great Mosque (in al-Baṣrah) to

609. He was to lead the expedition for the next two years. For his background, see Crone, *Slaves*, 105–6.

610. Yaʿqūbī, *Buldān*, 253, says that he had a property in Baghdad and calls him *ṣāḥib al-baḥr*, "the lord of the sea."

611. Abū Bakrah Nufayʿ (or Nafīʿ) b. Masrūḥ was a slave man of Thaqīf by origin, but he became a mawlā (client here, rather than freedman) of the Prophet. His mother, Sumayyah, later married ʿUbayd, so he and Ziyād were half-brothers (see note 612). His descendant is claiming that this bond entitles him to be considered as a member of the Prophet's kin. The issue was important because genealogy decided the level of pension paid by the *dīwān*.

612. Ziyād was Muʿāwiyah's right-hand man in Iraq. At first he was accepted as the son of ʿUbayd, a mawlā of Thaqīf and his wife Sumayyah, but it was widely believed that Sumayyah had been unfaithful and that Ziyād's true father was Abū Sufyān, Muʿāwiyah's father. As a sign of his gratitude, Muʿāwiyah acknowledged the link and had Ziyād accepted as an Umayyad. Al-Mahdī removed his descendants to the humbler position of mawālī of Thaqīf. The descendant of Abū Bakrah is arguing that this is a precedent and that the caliph can alter people's genealogical status if he believes that to be right.

the effect that the family of Abū Bakrah should be returned to their status as freedmen of the Prophet and their descent from Nufay' b. Masrūḥ.[613] There should be returned to those who acknowledged that genealogy their wealth in al-Baṣrah, which he ordered should be restored to them the same as those in a similar position whose wealth had been restored to them. It should not be returned to those who denied that. He appointed as investigator and examiner of them al-Ḥakam b. Samarqand.[614]

Muḥammad put into effect the orders that had come about the family of Abū Bakrah, except those of them who were not present. As for the family of Ziyād, what strengthened the opinion of al-Mahdī about them was what 'Alī b. Sulaymān reported that his father told him: "I was in the presence of al-Mahdī when he was investigating complaints (*maẓālim*), when a man from the family of Ziyād called al-Ṣughdī b. Salm b. Ḥarb came to him and he asked, 'Who are you?' and he replied, 'Your cousin (*ibn 'amm*),' so he asked, 'Which cousin?' and he traced his genealogy back to Ziyād.[615] Al-Mahdī said, 'O son of Sumayyah the adulteress, since when are you my cousin?' and he was very angry with him, and he was squeezed in the neck and thrown out and the people rose."

He said: When I went out, 'Īsā b. Mūsā or Mūsā b. 'Īsā followed me and said, "By God, I wanted to send after you because the Commander of the Faithful turned to us after you had gone out and said, 'Who knows anything about the family of Ziyād?' and, by God, none of us knew a thing about it. Do you have any information, O Abū 'Abdallāh?" I continued to tell him about Ziyād and the family of Ziyād until we reached his house by the Muḥawwal Gate, where he asked me by God and kinship to write all of it down so that he could go to the Commander of the Faithful and tell him about it on my authority. So I wrote it down and sent it to him, and he went to al-Mahdī and informed him about it. Al-Mahdī ordered that a letter be written to Hārūn al-Rashīd, [479]
who was his governor of al-Baṣrah,[616] ordering him to write to

613. See note 611, above.

614. He is not recorded elsewhere.

615. If Ziyād had been accepted as an Umayyad, his descendant would have been a (very distant) cousin of the caliph.

616. The situation seems to have been that the young Hārūn had some theoret-

the governor to remove the family of Ziyād from the *dīwān* of Quraysh and the Arabs[617] and to examine the descendants of Abū Bakrah about their position as clients of the Prophet. Those who accepted it were to retain their wealth, but, if they traced their descent to Thaqīf, it should be confiscated. They were examined and all of them accepted their status as freedmen except three, and their wealth was confiscated. After that the family of Ziyād bribed the chief of the *dīwān* to restore them to their previous position. Khālid al-Najjār[618] said about this:

To me :(the brothers) Ziyād, Nāfiʿ, and Abū
Bakrah are one of the most amazing wonders.
One is a Qurashī, he says, the next
a client and the third, as he alleges, an Arab.

A copy of the letter sent by al-Mahdī to his governor of al-Baṣrah ordering that the family of Ziyād be returned to their genealogy:

In the name of God, the Merciful, the Compassionate. The most just thing that the governors of the Muslims themselves, their courtiers, and their general public undertake in their affairs and their judgments is acting among them (the Muslims) in accordance with the Book of God and in surrendering to the desires other than it leads to with it. They should persevere with it and take pleasure in it in their likes and dislikes because of what is in it about the establishment of the legal punishments of God, the knowledge of His law, the following of His wishes, and the obtaining of His rewards, and His good recompense. Whatever goes in conflict with it, in rejecting it
[480] and in surrendering to the desires other than it, leads to all sorts of going astray and depravity in this world and the next.

It was the decision of Muʿāwiyah b. Abī Sufyān to adopt Ziyād b. ʿUbayd, the slave of the family of ʿAllāj of Thaqīf

ical authority over al-Basrah but appointed an executive governor to administer the city.

617. Following Ibn al-Athīr here, see al-Ṭabarī, III, 479, n. *b*.

618. Nothing more is known of him.

and to accord him what the mass of the Muslims after him and many in his own time refused him[619] because of their knowledge of Ziyād and his father and his mother. (Those who refused him were) persons of good will, virtue, law (*fiqh*), piety, and knowledge. Muʿāwiyah did not follow that because of piety, or good guidance, or observing the guiding *Sunnah*, or the example of the past *imāms* of truth, but because of his desire for the destruction of his faith and his afterlife and his determination to contradict the Book and the *Sunnah*. He admired Ziyād for his determination and effectiveness and what he hoped from his assistance and his support to strengthen him in his resorting to the falsehood in his conduct, ways, and wicked works. The Prophet of God said, "The child belongs to the bed and to the adulterer the stone,"[620] and he said, "He who claims descent from someone other than his father, or to be related to someone other than his master, upon him is the curse of God and His angels and of all the people. God will not accept either repentance or ransom from him." By my life, Ziyād was not born in the lap of Abū Sufyān, nor in his bed, nor was ʿUbayd a slave of Abū Sufyān, nor was Sumayyah his slave girl. They were not his property, and he did not own them by any means.

All those who know traditions and anecdotes remember what Muʿāwiyah said to Naṣr b. Ḥajjāj b. ʿIlāṭ al-Sulamī[621] and those freedmen of the Banū'l-Mughīrah al-Makhzūmī who were with him,[622] and how they wanted to adopt him and accept his claim. Muʿāwiyah prepared a stone under one of his cushions and threw it at them, and they said to him, "Should we regard as permissible what you have done for Ziyād while you do not make permissible to us what we have done to our relative (Naṣr)?"

619. I.e., the status of a member of Quraysh.

620. Crone and Hinds, *God's Caliph*, 88, claim that this is the first time a caliph ever quoted a prophetic tradition in a public statement.

621. Naṣr was the beautiful lad of Medina with whom a certain woman was infatuated. ʿUmar b. al-Khaṭṭāb drove him out of Medina.

622. No further information is available about them.

Upon that Muʿāwiyah said to them "The judgment of the Prophet of God is better for you than the judgment of
[481] Muʿāwiyah." Thus in his judgment about Ziyād and his adopting him, and what he did for him and how he promoted him, Muʿāwiyah contradicted the order of God, Great and Glorious, and pursued in this matter his own desire, forsaking truth and avoiding it. God, Great and Glorious, says, "Who is more led astray than he who follows his own desires without the guidance of God, for God does not give guidance to a wrong-doing people."[623]

And He said to David, to whom he had given judgment and Prophecy and wealth and the caliphate, "O David, we did indeed make you a vicegerent (*khalīfah*) on the earth," to the end of the verse.[624]

The Commander of the Faithful asks God to safeguard his soul and his faith and protect him from pursuing his own desires and to grant him success in all his affairs as He wishes and accepts, for He is listening and close.

The Commander of the Faithful has decided that he will return Ziyād and those who are descended from him to their mother and their well-known genealogy; he assigns them to their father, ʿUbayd, and their mother, Sumayyah. He is following the words of the Prophet of God and what truthful people and rightly guided *Imām*s have agreed upon. He does not hold permissible what Muʿāwiyah has ventured that contradicts the Book of God and the *Sunnah* of his Prophet. The Commander of the Faithful is the person most entitled to do that and to apply it because of his kinship with the Prophet of God and his following in his tracks, his keeping alive of his *Sunnah* and his rejection of the customs (*sunan*) of others that deviate and outrage truth and good guidance.

God, Great and Glorious, has said, "Apart from Truth, what remains but error? How then are ye turned away?"[625]

623. *Qur'ān*, XXV: 50.
624. *Qur'ān*, XXXVIII: 26.
625. *Qur'ān*, X: 32.

> Know that this is the decision of the Commander of the Faithful about Ziyād and the matter of the children of Ziyād, so attach them to their father, Ziyād b. 'Ubayd, and their mother, Sumayyah. Force them about that and make it known to those of the Muslims in your area, so that they may know it and it may be accepted among them. The Commander of the Faithful has written to the *qāḍī* of al-Baṣrah and the master of their *dīwān* about that. Peace be upon you and the mercy of God and His blessings.

Mu'āwiyah b. 'Ubaydallāh wrote this in the year 159 (31 October, 775–18 October, 776). When the letter reached Muḥam- [482]
mad b. Sulaymān, he set about putting it into effect, but then representations were made on their behalf and he did not proceed. 'Abd al-Malik b. Ayyūb b. Ẓubyān al-Numayrī had been sent a letter like the one to Muḥammad, but he did not put it into effect because of his relationship to Qays and his dislike of any of his people, leaving it for another group.[626]

In this year the death of 'Ubaydallāh b. Ṣafwān al-Jumaḥī occurred. He was governor of Medina, and Muḥammad b. 'Abdallāh al-Kathīrī was appointed in his place, but he remained there only a short time before he was removed and Zufar b. 'Āṣim al-Hilālī was appointed in his place. Al-Mahdī appointed 'Abdallāh b. Muḥammad b. 'Imrān al-Ṭalḥī[627] in charge of the judiciary in Medina in this year.

In this year 'Abd al-Salām al-Khārijī[628] rebelled and was killed.

In this year Bisṭām b. 'Amr was deposed from Sind and Rawḥ b. Ḥātim was made governor.

Al-Mahdī led the pilgrims in this year. When he left his city, he

---

626. Numayr and Quraysh were of the Qays group, thinly represented in al-Baṣrah, and 'Abd al-Malik did not want to lose the family of Ziyād.

627. B. Ibrāhīm b. Muḥammad b. Ṭalḥah b. 'Ubaydallāh, a descendant of Ṭalḥah b. 'Ubaydallāh, the Prophet's companion and one of the first Muslims. This may be why al-Ṭabarī singles him out for notice, for he does not seem to have been famous for any other reason (see Caskel, Table 21, for the full genealogy).

628. B. Hāshim al-Yashkūrī. Ibn al-Athīr adds that he was killed near Mosul, and al-Khalīfah, *Tārīkh*, 702, quotes al-Mahdī's letter refuting his claims. For further details, see text, p. 492.

appointed his son Mūsā as his deputy and with him left Yazīd b. Manṣūr, the maternal uncle of al-Mahdī, as his vizier and administrator of his affairs. In this year his son Hārūn and a group of people of his household set out with al-Mahdī. Among those who accompanied him was Ya'qūb b. Dāwūd because of the position he had with him. When he reached Mecca, al-Ḥasan b. Ibrāhīm b. 'Abdallāh b. al-Ḥasan, for whom Ya'qūb had asked al-Mahdī for a safe-conduct, came to him with his safe-conduct. Al-Mahdī gave him the best of gifts and rewards and assigned him wealth from the state lands (*ṣawāfī*) in the Ḥijāz.

[483] In this year, al-Mahdī took off the cover (*kiswah*) of the Ka'bah and replaced it with a new one. This was because the keepers of the Ka'bah, it is said, told him that they were afraid that it would be destroyed by the weight of the covers that were on it. He ordered that the covers that were on it should be stripped off so that it was completely bare. Then he ordered that the whole house be covered with perfume (*khalūq*). It is said that, when they reached Hishām's cover, they found it was made of very thick brocade and they found that the covers of those before him were mostly of textiles from Yemen.

This year it is said that al-Mahdī distributed a great deal of money to the inhabitants of Mecca and that he did the same to the people of Medina. It is said that the amount he distributed on this journey was investigated and it was found to be thirty million *dirhams*, which he brought with him. Three hundred thousand *dīnārs* came to him from Egypt and 200,000 from Yemen, and it was all distributed. One hundred and fifty thousand garments were also distributed. He extended the mosque of the Prophet of God and ordered the removal of the enclosure (*maqṣūrah*) that was in the mosque of the Prophet, so it was removed.[629] He wanted to reduce the height of the pulpit of the Prophet of God and return it to its original state, removing from it what Mu'āwiyah had added. It is said on the authority of Mālik b. Anas[630] that he took advice about this and he was told that there

629. The enclosure for prominent people (*maqṣūrah*) was disapproved of by the pious because all Muslims should be considered equal before God.

630. D. 179/796. The great traditionist and legal scholar, author of the *Muwaṭṭā* and founder of the Mālikī legal school; see EI^2, s.v. "Mālik b. Anas."

were nails that joined the wood that Muʿāwiyah had added to the original ancient wood and that it was not safe to take out these nails because the vibration would break it, so he abandoned the idea.

During the days he was staying in Medina he ordered that five hundred of the men of the Anṣār[631] should be recruited and that they should be a guard and helpers (*anṣār*) to him in Iraq. They were to be given their food in addition to their salaries and, on their arrival with him at Baghdad, they were given a property (*qaṭīʿah*),[632] which was known after them.

During his stay there, he married Ruqayyah the ʿUthmānī, daughter of ʿAmr.[633]

In this year Muḥammad b. Sulaymān brought ice to al-Mahdī, [484]
which reached him in Mecca. Al-Mahdī was the first of the caliphs to have ice brought to him in Mecca.

In this year, al-Mahdī returned to his family and others the plots (*qaṭāʾiʿ*) that had been confiscated from them.

Isḥāq b. al-Ṣabbāḥ al-Kindī was in charge of the prayers and the *aḥdāth* in al-Kūfah in this year, and Sharīk was in charge of the judiciary there. Muḥammad b. Sulaymān was in sole charge of al-Baṣrah and its *aḥdāth* and its separate offices, the districts (*kuwar*) of the Tigris, Baḥrayn, and ʿUmān and the districts of Ahwāz and Fārs. ʿUbaydallāh b. al-Ḥasan was in charge of the judiciary of al-Baṣrah in this year. Muʿādh b. Muslim was in charge of Khurāsān, al-Faḍl b. Ṣāliḥ of al-Jazīrah, Rawḥ b. Ḥātim of Sind, Yazīd b. Ḥātim of Ifrīqiyah, and Muḥammad b. Sulaymān Abū Ḍamrah of Egypt.

---

631. In this case, descendants of the original *anṣār* of Medina, the helpers of the Prophet are meant, not the Khurāsāniyyah, who are often referred to as the *anṣār* of the ʿAbbāsids; see note 63, above.

632. Le Strange, *Baghdad*, 222, notes a Bridge of the Anṣār on the East Bank of the Tigris in Baghdad.

633. Probably daughter of ʿAbdallāh b. ʿAmr, a grandson of the caliph ʿUthmān. After al-Mahdī's death, Ruqayyah became the wife of al-Ḥusayn b. ʿAlī, the unsuccessful ʿAlid rebel of 169/785–86.

The
Events of the Year
161
(October 9, 777–September 27, 778)

The events of this year:

Among the events of this year was the rebellion of Ḥakīm al-Muqanna'[634] in Khurāsān, from one of the villages of Marw. It is said that he used to teach the transmigration of souls and applied it to himself. He led many people astray and became powerful and moved to Transoxania. Al-Mahdī sent a number of commanders to fight him, among them Mu'ādh b. Muslim, who was at that time in charge of Khurāsān. With him were 'Uqbah b. Muslim,[635] Jibra'īl b. Yaḥyā, and Layth, freedman of al-Mahdī.[636] Then al-Mahdī put Sa'īd al-Ḥarashī[637] in sole command of the war against

634. For the most recent discussion of al-Muqanna', with full references, see Daniel, *Khurāsān*, 137–47.

635. This name should probably read 'Uqbah b. Salm, on whom see note 72, above.

636. He was later appointed governor of Sind (see below, p. 505; Ya'qūbī, *Tā'rīkh*, II, 465; Crone, *Slaves*, 192.

637. Not to be confused with Sa'īd b. 'Amr b. Aswad al-Ḥarashī, who was governor of Khurāsān for the Umayyads 103–4/721–22 (cf. Crone, *Slaves*, 144–45, who attempts to link the two). Al-Kindī, *Governors*, 122, reveals that the family at

him and attached the commanders to him. Al-Muqanna' began to gather food in preparation for a siege in a castle in Kishsh.[638]

In this year Naṣr b. Muḥammad b. al-Ash'ath al-Khuzā'ī[639] apprehended 'Abdallāh b. Marwān[640] in Syria and brought him to al-Mahdī, before he was appointed governor of Sind, and al-Mahdī imprisoned him in the Muṭbaq.[641] [485]

Abū al-Khaṭṭāb mentioned: 'Abdallāh b. Marwān b. Muḥammad, whose *kunyah* was Abū al-Ḥakam, was brought to al-Mahdī when he was holding a public audience in al-Ruṣāfah, and he said, "Who knows this man?" and 'Abd al-'Azīz b. Muslim al-'Uqaylī stood by him and said to him, "Abū al-Ḥakam?" and he replied, "Yes, the son of the Commander of the Faithful," and he said, "How have you been since I saw you?" Then 'Abd al-'Azīz turned to al-Mahdī and said, "Yes, Commander of the Faithful, this is 'Abdallāh b. Marwān." The people were amazed at his boldness, but al-Mahdī did not take any action against him.

When al-Mahdī imprisoned 'Abdallāh b. Marwān he laid a trap for him. 'Amr b. Sahlah al-Ash'arī[642] came and claimed that 'Abdallāh b. Marwān had killed his father and he was brought before 'Āfiyah the *Qāḍī*, who gave judgment that he should be killed for 'Amr's father, and proof was established against him. When the judgment was about to be carried out, 'Abd al-'Azīz b. Muslim al-'Uqaylī came to 'Āfiyah the *Qāḍī*, passing through the people until he reached him, and said, "'Amr b. Sahlah alleges that 'Abdallāh b. Marwān killed his father. By God he is lying, for I alone killed him, on the orders of Marwān, and 'Abdallāh is

---

one time consisted of slaves of Ziyād b. 'Abd al-Raḥmān al-Qushayrī (Naṣr b. Sayyār's governor of Nīshāpūr). His father, Dāwūd, was a Turk, while his mother was maternal aunt of the king of Ṭabaristān. He later campaigned in Ṭabaristān and is last recorded in 189/805, when he came to meet Hārūn al-Rashīd on his visit to al-Rayy. He was given extensive properties in eastern Baghdad by al-Mahdī, including a market and a square, perhaps as a reward for defeating al-Muqanna'.

638. In Transoxania between Samarqand and the Oxus, known since A D the fifteenth century as Shahr-i Sabz. See Le Strange, *Lands*, 469–70.

639. Son of the Khurāsānī commander Muḥammad b. al-Ash'ath al-Khuzā'ī. He was later governor of Sind and died there in 164/780–81 (Crone, *Slaves*, 185).

640. Son and heir apparent of Marwān b. Muḥammad, the last Umayyad caliph. He died in prison in 170/786–87.

641. The state prison within the walls of the Round City in Baghdad; see Le Strange, *Baghdad*, 27.

642. Nothing is known of this man or his father.

innocent of his blood." The case against 'Abdallāh b. Marwān was dropped, and al-Mahdī did not take any action against 'Abd al-'Azīz b. Muslim because he killed him on the orders of Marwān.

In this year Thumāmah b. al-Walīd led the summer expedition[643] and camped in Dābiq, and the Byzantines assembled an army while he was heedless. When his scouts and spies came and told him, he did not pay any attention to what they said. He went out against the Byzantines, who were commanded by Michael, with
[486] the advance guard, and a number of the Muslims were killed. 'Īsā b. 'Alī was posted (*murābiṭ*) at the fortress of Mar'ash[644] at that time. The Muslims did not make a summer raid this year because of that.

In this year al-Mahdī ordered the building of castles (*quṣūr*) on the road to Mecca[645] more extensive than the castles that Abū al-'Abbās had built from Qādisiyyah to Zubālah, and he ordered that Abū al-'Abbās's castles should be enlarged, and he left the staging posts that Abū Ja'far had built as they were. He ordered the building of reservoirs (*maṣāni'*) at each watering place and the renewal of the milestones and cisterns (*birak*) and the building of watering troughs with the reservoirs. He put Yaqṭīn b. Mūsā in charge of this, and he continued with it until the year 171 (June 22, 787–June 10, 788). Yaqṭīn's successor in this was his brother Abū Mūsā.

In this year al-Mahdī ordered the enlargement of the great mosque in al-Baṣrah, and it was extended in front in the direction of the *qiblah* and on the right in the direction of the square of the Banū Sulaym. He put Muḥammad b. Sulaymān, who was at that time governor of al-Baṣrah, in charge of the work.

In this year al-Mahdī ordered the demolition of the enclosures (*maqṣūrah*) in all the mosques and the shortening of the pulpits

---

643. Brooks, "Byzantines and Arabs," 735.

644. Modern Maraş, in southeastern Turkey. It was one of the main Muslim bases on the south side of the Taurus mountains; see Le Strange, *Palestine*, 502–3.

645. With the establishment of 'Abbāsid power in Iraq, the pilgrimage road from al-Kūfah and al-Baṣrah to Mecca became increasingly important, and water supply was a constant problem; see below, p. 501. This was aggravated by the fact that the pilgrimage fell in high summer during the reigns of al-Mahdī and Hārūn. This was one of a series of measures to improve the position that culminated in the work of Zubaydah in the reign of Hārūn.

and their reduction to the size of the pulpit of the Prophet of God. He wrote about that to the provinces and it was done.

In this year al-Mahdī ordered Ya'qūb b. Dāwūd to send trusted agents to all the regions, and this was done. No letter was allowed to be sent on behalf of al-Mahdī to a governor until Ya'qūb b. Dāwūd had written to his trusted agent to send it.

In this year the status of Abū 'Ubaydallāh, the vizier of al-Mahdī, was humbled. Ya'qūb attached to himself a large number of the legal experts of al-Baṣrah and of the people of al-Kūfah and Syria. He appointed as chief of the Baṣrans and organizer of their business Ismā'īl b. 'Ulayyah al-Asadī[646] and Muḥammad b. Maymūn [487] al-'Anbarī.[647] He appointed 'Abd al-A'lā b. Mūsā al-Ḥalabī[648] as chief of the people of al-Kūfah and the people of Syria.

The reason why the position of Abū 'Ubaydallāh with al-Mahdī changed:

We have already mentioned the reasons for his appointment in the days of al-Manṣūr and how al-Mansūr attached him to al-Mahdī when he sent him to al-Rayy at the time when 'Abd al-Jabbār b. 'Abd al-Raḥmān rebelled against al-Manṣūr.[649]

According to Abū Zayd 'Umar b. Shabbah—Sa'īd b. Ibrāhīm—Ja'far b. Yaḥyā—al-Faḍl b. al-Rabī': The freedmen used to denounce Abū 'Ubaydallāh to al-Mahdī and attack him in his presence. The letters of Abū 'Ubaydallāh used to convey to al-Manṣūr whatever business he wished, and the freedmen were closeted with al-Mahdī and used to inform him about Abū 'Ubaydallāh and incite him against him.

Al-Faḍl said: The letters of Abū 'Ubaydallāh used to come to my father one after the other complaining about the freedmen and what he suffered from them. He continued to mention it to al-Manṣūr and tell him about his position, and he extracted letters from him to al-Mahdī ordering him to stop listening to slander about him.

646. 116–93/734–809. An important authority for Section I of al-Ṭabarī's history. Ibn al-Nadīm numbers him among the traditionists (*Fihrist*, 549).

647. Not known elsewhere.

648. Not known elsewhere; his name al-Ḥalabī suggests that he came from Aleppo.

649. In 141/758–59. For the fall of Abū 'Ubaydallāh, see also al-Jāḥiẓ, 150–57, and Sourdel, *Vizirat*, I, 99–103.

He said: When Abū ʿUbaydallāh saw the influence of the freedmen over al-Mahdī and how they were alone with him, he approached four educated and knowledgeable men from different tribes and attached them to al-Mahdī so that they were among his courtiers, so as not to let the freedmen be alone with him. Then when Abū ʿUbaydallāh spoke to al-Mahdī on some business of his, one of these four men raised objections concerning the busi-
[488] ness that he was speaking about. Abū ʿUbaydallāh passed over it in silence and did not argue with him and left. He ordered that the man be kept from seeing al-Mahdī, so he was kept from him. News of this reached my father.

He said: My father went on the pilgrimage with al-Manṣūr in the year in which he died, and my father undertook what he undertook on behalf of al-Mahdī with regard to the oath of allegiance and its renewal from the household of al-Manṣūr and his commanders and freedmen. When he arrived, I met him after sunset and accompanied him while he went past his dwelling place and left the house of al-Mahdī and went to Abū ʿUbaydallāh and he said, "O my little son, he is friend (*ṣāḥib*) of the man,[650] and it is necessary that we should not deal with him as we used to deal with him about it, nor should we call him to account for the help we gave him in his business."

We went on until we reached Abū ʿUbaydallāh's gate, and he remained standing while I prayed the evening prayer. The chamberlain came out and said, "Enter," so he stretched his legs and I stretched mine. (The chamberlain) said, "I only gave you permission to enter, O Abū al-Faḍl," and my father replied, "Go and tell him that al-Faḍl is with me," and turning to me he said, "This is also related to that."

He said: The chamberlain came out and gave permission for us to enter together so we went in, my father and I. Abū ʿUbaydallāh was in the front of the reception room, on a prayer mat leaning with his elbow on a cushion and I said (to myself), "He (usually) stands up for my father when he comes in," but he did not stand up for him. And I said, "He will sit erect when he approaches him," but he did not do it. And I said, "He will summon a prayer

650. I.e., al-Mahdī; now that Abū ʿUbaydallāh's master is caliph, he must be treated with respect.

rug for him," but he did not do it. My father sat down before him on the carpet while he was leaning. He began to ask him about his journey, his travel, and his conditions, and my father waited for him to ask about what he had done in the business of al-Mahdī and the renewal of the oath of allegiance, but he avoided it and, when my father began to mention it, he said, "News of you has reached me." Then my father began to get up and he said, "I see that the gates are closed so you may stay," and my father replied, "The gates cannot be closed to me." But he answered, "Yes, they have been closed."

My father thought that he was wanting to detain him so that he [489] could rest after his journey and to ask him so he said, "I will stay." Abū 'Ubaydallāh said, "O so-and-so, go and prepare a place for Abū al-Faḍl to spend the night in the house of Muḥammad b. 'Ubaydallāh." When my father saw that he was wanting him to leave the house he said, "The gates cannot be closed in front of me." Then he made up his mind and rose.

When we left the house, my father turned to me and said, "O my little son, you are most stupid," and I said, "What is my stupidity?" and he replied, "You should have said to me, 'You should not have come and, when you did come and we were not admitted, you should not have gotten up until you had prayed the evening prayer and you should have gone away and not entered. When you entered and he did not stand up for you, you should have returned and not stayed with him.' The right course of action was entirely what I did. But, by the one and only God, Whose oaths are binding, I will use my rank and spend my wealth to satisfy myself from Abū 'Ubaydallāh."

He said: He began to make strenuous efforts but he could not find any way of getting at the object of his hate, despite using great stratagems. Then he remembered al-Qushayrī,[651] whom Abū 'Ubaydallāh debarred (from entering the caliph's presence). He sent to him and when he came he said, "You already know what Abū 'Ubaydallāh has done to you, and he has done the most evil sorts of things to me. I have conspired against him with all my power, but I have not found any way to get at him. Do you

651. I cannot identify him further.

have any ideas about his business?" He replied, "Abū 'Ubaydallāh can only be got at in one way, which I will tell you. It is said that Abū 'Ubaydallāh is the most ignorant of men in his trade, but Abū 'Ubaydallāh is the most skillful of people, or it is said that
[490] he is suspect in his adoption of the Faith, but Abū 'Ubaydallāh is the most upright of men; if the daughters of al-Mahdī were in his lap, that would be their safe place. Or it is said that he is inclined to contradict the Sulṭān, but Abū 'Ubaydallāh cannot be attacked through that; yet he is only showing some inclinations toward Qadar. He cannot be attacked through that to the extent of drawing an accusation against him, but he can be attacked for all this through his son."

Al-Rabī' took him in his arms and kissed him between the eyes. Then he began to conspire against the son of Abū 'Ubaydallāh and, by God, he continued to scheme and make insinuations to al-Mahdī and accused him with regard to one of al-Mahdī's harem until suspicion of Muḥammad b. Abū 'Ubaydallāh was established in al-Mahdī's mind. He ordered that he should be summoned and Abū 'Ubaydallāh was brought out, and he said, "Muḥammad, recite!" and he began to recite, but he was unable to speak the Qur'ān. The caliph said, "Mu'āwiyah, did you not tell me that your son has learned all the Qur'ān?" He replied, "O Commander of the Faithful, I did tell you, but he left me years ago and in that period when he kept his distance from me, he has forgotten the Qur'ān." He said, "Get up and come near to God by killing him!" and he began to stand up and collapsed. Al-'Abbās b. Muḥammad said, "I think, Commander of the Faithful, that you should excuse the old man."

He said: He did so and he ordered that he (the son) be taken out and beheaded.

He said: Al-Mahdī was suspicious of him in his heart and al-Rabī' said to him, "You have killed his son, so it is not desirable that he should be with you or that you should trust him," and he filled al-Mahdī with anxiety and his affair turned out as it turned out and al-Rabī' achieved what he wanted; he was avenged and his power increased.

According to Muḥammad, son of Abū 'Abdallāh Ya'qūb b. Dāwūd—his father: Al-Mahdī beat a man of the al-Ash'arīs and caused him pain. Abū 'Ubaydallāh felt solidarity with the man

because he was a freedman of theirs and he said, "Death would be better than that, O Commander of the Faithful," and al-Mahdī said to him, "O Jew, get out of my camp (*'askar*),[652] God curse you!" and he said, "I do not know where I shall go if not to the fire (of hell)," and my father said, "O Commander of the Faithful, how fitting that such a thing should be prepared," and he said to me, [491]
"Glory be to God, O Abū 'Abdallāh."

In this year, al-Ghamr b. al-'Abbās made a naval raid (on the Byzantine Empire).

In this year Naṣr b. Muḥammad b. al-Ash'ath was appointed to Sind in place of Rawḥ b. Ḥātim and he set out there until he reached it, when he was deposed and replaced by Muḥammad b. Sulaymān, who sent 'Abd al-Malik b. Shihāb al-Misma'ī. He arrived there and came upon Naṣr unawares. He gave him permission to set out, so he set out until he stopped on the shore about six *farsakh*s from al-Manṣūrah. Naṣr b. Muḥammad then received his diploma of appointment to Sind and returned to his post. 'Abd al-Malik had been there for eighteen days and he did not block his way, and so he returned to al-Baṣrah.

In this year al-Mahdī appointed 'Āfiyyah b. Yazīd al-Azdī as *qāḍī*. He and Ibn 'Ulāthah were both *qāḍī*s in 'Askar al-Mahdī in al-Ruṣafah. The *qāḍī* in the eastern city (*madīnat al-sharqiyyah*) was 'Umar b. Ḥabīb al-'Adawī.[653]

In this year al-Faḍl b. Ṣāliḥ was deposed from al-Jazīrah and 'Abd al-Ṣamad b. 'Alī was appointed in his place.

In this year 'Īsā b. Luqmān was made governor (*'āmil*) of Egypt.[654]

In this year Yazīd b. Manṣūr was appointed governor (*wālī*) of the Sawād of al-Kūfah, Ḥassān al-Sharawī of Mosul, and Bisṭām b. 'Amr al-Taghlibī of Azerbaijān.

---

652. Al-Ruṣāfah in Baghdad was sometimes called 'Askar al-Mahdī, the Camp of al-Mahdī, and it may be what is meant here.

653. It is not clear what is meant here. The Sharqiyyah quarter lay on the west bank of the Tigris to the east of the Round City. According to Le Strange (*Baghdad*, 90–91), it originally had its own Friday mosque and *qāḍī*, so it could have been referred to as a *madīnah*. The other possibility is that this should read, *madīnat al-gharbiyyah* ("the western city"), meaning the Round City and its suburbs on the west bank, as opposed to al-Ruṣāfah on the east.

654. Al-Kindī, *Governors*, 128.

In this year he deposed Abū Ayyūb, who was called Sulaymān al-Makkī, from the *dīwān* of taxes (*kharāj*), and Abū al-Wazīr 'Umar b. al-Muṭarrif was appointed in his place.[655]

In this year Naṣr b. Mālik died of hemiplegia, which afflicted him. He was buried in the cemetery of the Banū Hāshim and al-
[492] Mahdī prayed over him. In this year Abān b. Ṣadaqah was transferred from Hārūn b. al-Mahdī to Mūsā b. al-Mahdī and appointed as his *wazīr* and secretary. Yaḥyā b. Khālid b. Barmak was appointed to his position with Hārūn b. al-Mahdī. In this year al-Mahdī deposed Muḥammad b. Sulaymān Abū Ḍamrah from Egypt in Dhū al-Ḥijjah (August 30–September 27, 778) and appointed as governor (*wālī*) Salamah b. Rajā'.[656]

Mūsa b. Muḥammad b. 'Abdallāh al-Hādī led the pilgrimage this year, and he was heir apparent to his father.

The governor of al-Ṭā'if, Mecca, and al-Yamāmah in this year was Ja'far b. Sulaymān. Isḥāq b. al-Ṣabbāḥ al-Kindī was in charge of the prayers and the *aḥdāth* at al-Kūfah and Yazīd b. Manṣūr of the Sawād there.

---

655. Nothing is known of either of these: 'Umar's appointment is confirmed by al-Jahshiyārī (166). He married Ya'qūb b. Dāwūd's brother's daughter and is last recorded on the pilgrimage of 169/786.

656. His appointment is not noted by al-Kindī, and nothing more is known of him.

The Events of the Year 162

(September 28, 778–September 16, 779)

The events of this year:

Among these was the killing of ʿAbd al-Salām al-Khārijī at Qinnasrīn. It was said: This ʿAbd al-Salām b. Hāshim al-Yashkūrī rebelled in al-Jazīrah, and his following there became numerous and his power became intense. He was met by a number of al-Mahdī's commanders, among them ʿĪsā b. Mūsā al-Qāʾid (the Commander).[657] He killed him with a number of those who were with him, and he routed a number of the commanders. Al-Mahdī sent troops against him, and he afflicted disaster on more than one commander, among them Shabīb b. Wāj al-Marwarrūdhī.[658] Then he assigned to Shabīb a thousand horsemen and gave each one of them a thousand *dirhams* for supplies. Then he sent them to meet Shabīb, and they came to him and Shabīb set out on the

---

657. B. ʿAjlān al-Khurāsānī, not to be confused with ʿĪsā b. Mūsā the ʿAbbāsid. He had taken part in the mutiny of Khurāsānī troops in Ifrīqiyah in 148/765 (Ibn Idhārī, *Bayān*, 73), but little more is known of him.

658. He had been present at the proclamation of al-Saffāḥ as caliph in 132/750 and was one of the four assassins of Abū Muslim. His name implies that he originally came from Marw al-Rūdh in Khurāsān.

tracks of ʿAbd al-Salām. He fled from them until he reached Qinnasrīn,[659] where Shabīb met him and killed him.

[493] In this year al-Mahdī established the registry departments[660] and appointed his freedman ʿUmar b. Bazīʿ[661] in charge of them. ʿUmar b. Bazīʿ appointed al-Nuʿmān b. ʿUthmān Abū Ḥāzim[662] in charge of the registry of the taxation of Iraq.

In this year al-Mahdī ordered that payments be made to the lepers and people of the prisons in all districts.[663]

In this year Thumāmah b. al-Walīd al-ʿAbsī was appointed to command the summer expedition, but he did not carry it out.

In this year the Byzantines attacked Ḥadath and destroyed its walls.[664] Al-Ḥasan b. Qaḥṭabah led the summer expedition with thirty thousand regular troops, beside volunteers. He reached Ḥammah al-Adhrūliyyah[665] and wrought great destruction and damage in Byzantine lands, without capturing a fortress or meeting an army. The Byzantines called him "the sea monster." It is said that al-Ḥasan only came to this al-Ḥammah (hot spring) to soak in it because of the skin complaint (*waḍaḥ*) he had. Then he withdrew with the people safely. Ḥafṣ b. ʿĀmir al-Sulamī[666] was *qāḍī* in his army and in charge of the booty (*fay'*) that was collected.

He said: In this year Yazīd b. Usayd al-Sulamī raided through

---

659. Ancient Chalcis, south of Aleppo in northern Syria, an important center at the time of the Muslim conquests; it was at this time in full decline, Aleppo becoming the regional center; see Yāqūt, *Muʿjam*, VI, 403–4; Le Strange, *Palestine*, 486–87.

660. *Dawāwin al-azimmah*. Morony, *Iraq*, 66–68, 512, explains that these dīwāns were registries where records of all decisions were stored. According to him, Ziyād b. Abīhi was said to have been the first Muslim official to use them, in the reign of Muʿāwiyah, which seems to conflict with the statement here that they were established by al-Mahdī.

661. Nothing is known of his origins, but he seems to have been a freedman. In 168/784–85 he was replaced by ʿAlī b. Yaqṭīn, but a year later he succeeded al-Rabīʿ as vizier to the caliph Mūsā al-Hādī, which is probably why he does not seem to have held office under Hārūn; see al-Ṭabarī, III, 582–83, 598; al-Jahshiyārī, 144, 146, 160, 166, 173.

662. Nothing more is known of him.

663. Presumably this relates to the payment of alms, though why the people of the prisons (*ahl al-sujūn*) were so favored is not clear.

664. Brooks, "Byzantines and Arabs," 735–36. My interpretation differs somewhat from his.

665. Dorylaion, modern Eskişehir, on the main road across Asia Minor, between the frontier and Constantinople.

666. Nothing more is known about him.

the pass of Qālīqalā,[667] took booty, and conquered three fortresses and took many prisoners and captives.

In this year ʿAlī b. Sulaymān[668] was deposed from Yemen and ʿAbdallāh b. Sulaymān[669] was appointed in his place.

In this year Salamah b. Rajāʾ was deposed from Egypt and ʿĪsā b. Luqmān was appointed governor (*wālī*) in Muḥarram (September 28–October 27, 778),[670] and was then deposed in Jumādā II (February 23–March 23, 779). Wāḍiḥ, freedman of al-Mahdī, was appointed governor but was deposed in Dhū al-Qaʿdah (July 20–August 18, 779) when Yaḥyā al-Ḥarashī[671] was appointed.

In this year the Muḥammirah[672] appeared in Jurjān, led by a man called ʿAbd al-Qahhār. He conquered Jurjān and killed many people. ʿUmar b. al-ʿAlāʾ[673] launched a raid against him from Ṭabaristān and killed ʿAbd al-Qahhār and his companions.

Ibrāhīm b. Jaʿfar b. al-Manṣūr[674] led the people on the pilgrim- [494]

---

667. Byzantine Theodosopolis, modern Erzurum, in the extreme eastern part of Anatolia.

668. Al-ʿAbbāsī, son of Sulaymān b. ʿAlī and brother of Muḥammad (note 29, above) and Jaʿfar (note 35) He became governor of northern Syria and al-Jazīrah soon after this and seems to have remained in that area until removed from office by al-Hādī in 169/786. He was also briefly governor of Egypt 169–70/786, after which he disappears from the record; see al-Kindī, *Governors*, 131.

669. Al-Rabaʿī, no relation of his predecessor, ʿAlī; he is known only for his appointment to Yemen.

670. Al-Ṭabarī's account differs here from that of al-Kindī, *Governors*, 121–22, who has ʿĪsā arriving in Dhū al-Ḥijjah 161, that is, a month before al-Ṭabarī says he was appointed. They agree on the year of his dismissal and on the appointment of Wāḍiḥ, but al-Kindī has him deposed in Ramaḍān, a month later than al-Ṭabarī. They both agree that Yaḥyā al-Ḥarashī was the next governor.

671. Brother of Saʿīd (see note 637, above). He had a reputation for determined administration of justice and ruthless establishment of law and order. He subsequently had a varied career as governor of Rūyān and Ṭabaristān, Armenia (twice), and Mosul; he is last heard of as governor of al-Jibāl in 184/800 (al-Ṭabarī, III, 500, 503, 517, 520, 649; Yaʿqūbī, *Tārīkh*, II, 517; al-Kindī, *Governors*, 122).

672. So called because they wore red; they were part of a popular revolutionary movement in Jurjān, devoted to the memory of Abū Muslim. Despite this defeat, they were to reappear in Hārūn's reign; see Daniel, *Khurāsān*, 147.

673. He was by origin a butcher in Qazvīn, in northern Iran, who distinguished himself by raising a troop to oppose the rebellion of Sunbādh (al-Ṭabarī, *History*, III, 119–20). He subsequently became an expert on the affairs of Ṭabaristān and led numerous campaigns there. He is said to have forced the local ruler to surrender, but he was killed in the province at the end of al-Mahdī's reign (al-Ṭabarī, 136, 137, 500, 520, 521, *ʿUyūn*, 229; Balādhurī, *Futūḥ*, II, 46).

674. Son of Jaʿfar the Elder (see note 49).

age in this year. Al-ʿAbbās b. Muḥammad had asked al-Mahdī for permission to go on the pilgrimage after that, and al-Mahdī reproved him for not asking permission before he had appointed anyone for the pilgrimage, so that he could appoint him to it, and he said, "O Commander of the Faithful, I delayed that on purpose because I did not want the appointment."

The governors of the *amṣār* were the same as in the previous year, with ʿAbd al-Ṣamad b. ʿAlī in al-Jazīrah, Saʿīd b. Daʿlaj in Ṭabaristan and al-Rūyān and Muhalhil b. Ṣafwān[675] in Jurjān.

675. Freedman of al-Manṣūr. He is recorded in 137/754–55 fighting Khārijites in al-Jazīrah and disappears from the record after he was dismissed from Ṭabaristān (p. 216, below).

The Events of the Year

163

(SEPTEMBER 17, 779–SEPTEMBER 5, 780)

The events of this year:

Among the events of this year was the destruction of al-Muqanna'. This was because Sa'īd al-Ḥarashī besieged him in Kishsh and the siege tightened and, when he felt near death, he drank poison, and his women and family drank it too and, it is said, they all died. The Muslims entered his castle and cut off his head and sent it to al-Mahdī while he was in Aleppo.

In this year al-Mahdī ordered all the armies of the people of Khurāsān and others to furnish troops for the summer expedition. He set out and camped at al-Baradān for about two months, drawing up his army and making preparations and paying the troops. He gave gifts there to the members of his family who had set out with him.

'Īsā b. 'Alī died on the last day of Jumādā II (March 11, 780) in Baghdad. The next day al-Mahdī left for al-Baradān, setting out on the summer expedition. He left Mūsā b. al-Mahdī as his deputy in Baghdad, and his secretary at that time was Abān b. Ṣadaqah; 'Abdallāh b. 'Ulāthah was the keeper of his seal; 'Alī b. 'Īsā was

[495] the commander of his guard; and ʿAbdallāh b. Khāzim[676] was his chief of police.

According to al-ʿAbbās b. Muḥammad: When al-Mahdī sent al-Rashīd on the summer expedition in the year 163, he set out to escort him, and I was with him. When he was opposite Qaṣr Maslamah,[677] I said, "O Commander of the Faithful, we owe Maslamah a debt of gratitude, for when Muḥammad b. ʿAlī[678] went to him, he gave him four thousand *dīnār*s, saying, 'O my cousin, here are two thousand for your debt and two thousand for your subsistence and, when you have exhausted it, do not be inhibited with us (in asking for more).'" When I told him the story, he ordered that those of the children of Maslamah who were there and his freedmen be brought into his presence and he ordered that they be given twenty thousand *dīnār*s and that salaries (*rizq*) be paid to them. Then he said, "O Abu al-Faḍl, we have recompensed Maslamah and done justice to him." I replied, "Yes, O Commander of the Faithful, you have done more."

According to Ibrāhīm b. Ziyād—al-Haytham b. ʿAdī: Al-Mahdī sent Hārūn al-Rashīd on the raid against the Byzantines, and attached al-Rabīʿ the Chamberlain and al-Ḥasan b. Qaḥṭabah to him.

According to Muḥammad b. al-ʿAbbās:[679] I was sitting in my father's audience in the house of the Commander of the Faithful when he was in command of the guard when al-Ḥasan b. Qaḥṭabah greeted me and sat on the cushion (*firāsh*) that my father used to sit on and asked me about him. I told him that he was riding and then he said to me, "O my dear one, tell him that I have come and

676. B. Khuzaymah al-Tamīmī. The text reads Ḥāzim, but this is corrected in the *Addenda*. Son of Khāzim (note 111, above), he was *ṣāḥib al-shurṭah* to al-Hādī for many years and was consequently out of office under Hārūn but emerged after his death as one of al-Amīn's chief supporters; see Crone, *Slaves*, 181.

677. Castle of Maslamah, more commonly called Ḥiṣn ("fortress") Maslamah. It lay to the north of the Euphrates in al-Jazīrah, between Ḥarrān and al-Raqqah. Maslamah was a son of the Umayyad caliph ʿAbd al-Malik who never became caliph himself but established a great reputation as a soldier on the Byzantine frontier. He built a formidable fortress there and developed irrigation systems, much admired by the geographers (Yāqūt, *Muʿjam*, II, 265, Le Strange, *Lands*, 105).

678. The ʿAbbāsid, father of al-Saffāḥ and al-Manṣūr.

679. Probably a mistake for al-ʿAbbās b. Muḥammad (see above and note 58).

give him greetings from me and tell him that I would like him to say to the Commander of the Faithful, 'Al-Ḥasan b. Qaḥṭabah says, O Commander of the Faithful, may God make me a sacrifice for you. You have sent Hārūn on a raid and attached me and al-Rabīʿ to him. I am the foremost of your military commanders and al-Rabīʿ is the foremost of your freedmen, and it does not seem good to me that we should both leave your gate together; either you send me on on the raid with Hārūn and al-Rabīʿ stays behind or you send al-Rabīʿ and I remain at your gate.'"

He said: My father came and I gave him the message and he went into al-Mahdī and told him. He replied, "By God, he has made a good excuse, not like the cupper, son of the cupper" (meaning ʿĀmir b. Ismāʿīl,[680] who had excused himself from setting out with Ibrāhīm and he was angry with him and confiscated his wealth). [496]

According to ʿAbdallāh b. Aḥmad b. al-Waḍḍāḥ—his grandfather Abū Budayl:[681] Al-Mahdī sent al-Rashīd on a raid and he sent with him Mūsā b. ʿĪsā b. Mūsā, ʿAbd al-Malik b. Ṣāliḥ b. ʿAlī, and two of his father's freedmen, al-Rabīʿ the Chamberlain and al-Ḥasan the Chamberlain.[682] Two or three days after he set out, I came in to him (al-Mahdī), and he said, "Why were you kept back from going with the heir apparent and especially with your two brothers (meaning al-Rabīʿ the Chamberlain and al-Ḥasan the Chamberlain)?" and I replied, "The Commander of the Faithful gave me orders and my place is in the City of Peace until he gives me permission," and he said, "Go and catch up with him and the two of them and say what you require." I said, "I do not need any equipment, if the Commander of the Faithful decides to give me permission to leave." He asked, "When do you intend to

680. Probably ʿĀmir b. Ismāʿīl al-Muslī. There seems to be no information about the incident in question, but the Ibrāhīm referred to may have been Ibrāhīm b. Ṣāliḥ al-ʿAbbāsī, who was governor of Syria for some years (see note 351, above). A cupper is one who draws blood by application of a hot cup to the surface of the skin, an ancient medical technique; the term is used here as an insult, a cupper being of dubious social status.

681. Al-Waḍḍāḥ b. Ḥabīb, quoted by al-Ṭabarī four times in all. His father had governed al-Rayy for the Umayyads (Crone, *Slaves*, 167).

682. Possibly to be identified with al-Ḥasan al-Waṣīf, who had been on a previous raid on Byzantium in 159/779; see note 559, above.

leave?" I replied, "Tomorrow morning." So I took leave of him and set out and caught up with the people.

He said, I began to observe al-Rashīd when he was going out to play polo, and I observed Mūsā b. ʿĪsā and ʿAbd al-Malik b. Ṣāliḥ and they were laughing at him, so I went to al-Rabīʿ and al-Ḥasan—we were never apart—and I said, "May God not reward you two well on behalf of him who sent you or him whom you were sent with!" They said, "Now then, what is the news?" I replied, "Mūsā b. ʿĪsā and ʿAbd al-Malik b. Ṣāliḥ were laughing at the son of the Commander of the Faithful. Could you not prepare an audience for those two so that they can visit him in it, and for the military commanders who were with him, on Friday, and not on other days as he wishes?"

While we were on this journey, the two of them sent for me in the night, and when I came to them there was a man with them, [497] and they said to me, "This is the page of al-Ghamr b. Yazīd,[683] and we have found him with the Book of the State (*Kitāb al-Dawlah*).[684] I opened the book and I looked in it for the years of al-Mahdī, and it said ten years. I said, "There is nothing on earth more amazing than you two! Do you think that this page's information will remain hidden and that this book will be concealed?" and they replied, "Certainly not!" and I continued, "If the Commander of the Faithful's years are cut short, as it says, are you not the first to announce his own death to him?"

He said: They looked stupid, by God, and were covered with confusion and said, "What ought to be done?" and I said, "O young man, fetch ʿAnbasah," meaning the bedouin (*'aʿrābī*) copyist, freedman of the family of Abū Budayl. When he was brought, I said, "With writing like this writing and a page like this page, instead of ten years, insert forty years and insert it on the page."

He said: By God, if I had not seen ten in this and forty in that, I would have had no doubt that the writing was that writing and the page was that page.

He said: Al-Mahdī sent Khālid b. Barmak with Hārūn al-Rashīd, who was at that time heir apparent, when he sent him to raid

683. B. ʿAbd al-Malik, an Umayyad prince.

684. There seems to be no more information about what was clearly a work of prophecy.

Byzantium. He sent with him al-Ḥasan and Sulaymān, sons of Barmak, and he sent Yaḥyā b. Khālid with him in charge of the administration of the army, his expenses, his secretariat, and the managing of his affairs, and all Hārūn's business was in his hands. Al-Rabīʿ the Chamberlain was appointed with Hārūn to go on the raid on behalf of al-Mahdī, and (the differences) between al-Rabīʿ and Yaḥyā were on account of that. He used to ask their advice and act accordingly. God enabled them to make many conquests and bestowed great favor on them in that expedition; Khālid achieved in Samālū what no one had achieved before.

Their astrologer was called the Barmakid, giving a blessing for [498]
and out of respect for him.

When al-Mahdī sent Hārūn on the summer expedition he sent him on, he ordered that the secretaries of the *abnāʾ al-daʿwah* should be sent in to him so that he could inspect them and choose one of them for him.

Yaḥyā said: They sent me in to him with them, and they stood in front of him and I stood the last of them. He said to me, "Yaḥyā, come near!" so I came near. Then he told me to sit down, so I sat down and knelt before him. He said to me, "I have scrutinized the sons of my party (*abnā shīʿatī*) and the people of my state (*dawlatī*), and I have chosen from them a man for Hārūn my son whom I can attach to him to supervise the organization of his army and take charge of his secretariat, and my choice has fallen on you and I think you are the best person for that because you have been his tutor and his special adviser, and I have appointed you in charge of his secretariat and the organization of his army."

He said: I thanked him for that and kissed his hand and he ordered that I be given a hundred thousand *dirhams* as subsistence for my journey, and I was sent to that army when I was sent to him.

He said: Al-Rabīʿ sent Sulaymān b. Barmak on a mission to al-Mahdī and sent a delegation with him. Al-Mahdī was generous to his mission and favored him and was good to the delegation who were with him. Then they went on their way.

In this year was the journey of al-Mahdī with his son Hārūn. Al-Mahdī deposed ʿAbd al-Ṣamad b. ʿAlī from al-Jazīrah and appointed Zufar b. ʿĀṣim al-Hilālī in his place.

The reasons for his deposition:

It was said: On this journey of his, al-Mahdī traveled along the Mosul road. ʿAbd al-Ṣamad b. ʿAlī was in charge of al-Jazīrah and, when al-Mahdī left Mosul and went in to the land of al-Jazīrah, ʿAbd al-Ṣamad did not meet him or prepare victuals for him, or
[499] repair the bridges. Al-Mahdī resented him for that and, when he met him, he scowled at him and made his displeasure plain. ʿAbd al-Ṣamad sent delicacies to him, but he was not pleased with them and returned them and became more angry with him. He ordered him to be punished because of the organization of the victuals for him, but ʿAbd al-Ṣamad made light of it and did not worry. He continued to do more things al-Mahdī hated until they stopped at Ḥiṣn Maslamah. He summoned him and there was an argument between them; al-Mahdī spoke angrily to him about it and ʿAbd al-Ṣamad answered back. He could not bear it and ordered that he be imprisoned and deposed him from al-Jazīrah, and he remained in prison during that journey and after he returned until he was restored to favor. Al-ʿAbbās b. Muḥammad organized the victualing until he reached Aleppo and the good news came to him of the killing of al-Muqannaʿ.

When he was there, he sent ʿAbd al-Jabbār the Muḥtasib[685] to collect those *Zindīq*s[686] who were in that district, so he did that and brought them to him when he was in Dābiq. He killed a number of them and crucified them. Some of their books were brought to him and they were cut up with knives.

He reviewed his army there and gave orders for the journey. He despatched all those of his family who had joined him with his son Hārūn to Byzantium. Al-Mahdī escorted his son Hārūn until he had gone through the Pass and reached the Jayḥān,[687] and there he chose the site of the city that was called al-Mahdiyyah.[688] He bade farewell to Hārūn by the Jayḥān.

---

685. Not known elsewhere.

686. See note 199, above, whether the *Zindīqs* of Aleppo were the same as the *Zindīqs* of Iraq is not clear, and it is possible that they were pagan Sabians from nearby Ḥarrān.

687. Ancient Pyramus, modern Ceyhan. It flows into the Mediterranean in Cilicia, southern Turkey; see Le Strange, *Palestine*, 62.

688. The first foundation of the city later known as Hārūniyyah (modern Haruniye) in southern Turkey on the eastern edge of the Cilician plain; see Le Strange, *Palestine*, 449–50.

Hārūn traveled until he stopped in one of the Byzantine districts[689] in which there was a castle called Samālū.[690] He besieged it for thirty-eight days. He set up mangonels against it, so that God conquered it after ruining it and after thirst and hunger had afflicted its inhabitants and after killing and wounds among the Muslims. Its conquest was according to the conditions that they [500] laid down for themselves that they would not be killed or deported or split up. They were granted that and they came out, and he fulfilled [the conditions] for them. Hārūn returned safely with the Muslims, except those who had been killed or wounded there.[691]

In this year and on this journey, al-Mahdī went to Jerusalem and prayed there. With him were al-ʿAbbās b. Muḥammad, al-Faḍl b. Ṣāliḥ, ʿAlī b. Sulaymān, and his maternal uncle Yazīd b. Manṣūr.

In this year al-Mahdī deposed Ibrāhīm b. Ṣāliḥ from Palestine, and Yazīd b. Manṣūr interceded for him until he was reinstated over it.

In this year al-Mahdī gave his son Hārūn charge of all the west and Azerbaijān and Armenia.[692] He appointed as his secretary in charge of taxation Thābit b. Mūsā and in charge of his correspondence Yaḥyā b. Khālid b. Barmak.

In this year Zufar b. ʿĀṣim was deposed from al-Jazīrah and ʿAbdallāh b. Ṣāliḥ b. ʿAlī was appointed in his place. Al-Mahdī had stayed with him on his journey to Jerusalem and admired his house, which he saw in Salamiyah.[693]

In this year he deposed Muʿādh b. Muslim from Khurāsān and appointed al-Musayyab b. Zuhayr to it.

In this year he deposed Yaḥyā al-Ḥarashī from al-Iṣfahān and appointed al-Ḥakam b. Saʿīd[694] in his place.

---

689. *Rusṭāq*, from Middle Persian *rostak*, an administrative district of the Sasanian Empire. The term continued in use in Muslim Iraq, but it is somewhat strange to find it in a Byzantine context.

690. A Byzantine fortress above Ṭarsūs near the Cilician Gates; see Le Strange, *Palestine*, 530.

691. For this expedition, see Brooks, "Byzantines and Arabs," 436–37.

692. This is the first example of the division of the caliphate between two ʿAbbāsid princes, which was to be a recurrent feature of the politics of the dynasty.

693. In central Syria, to the east of Ḥamāh. His house is commented on by the geographers, and his descendants continued to live there for many years. See Le Strange, *Palestine*, 528.

694. He is not recorded elsewhere.

In this year he deposed Saʿīd b. Daʿlaj from Ṭabaristān and Rūyān and appointed ʿUmar b. al-ʿAlāʾ as governor.

[501] In this year he deposed Muhalhil b. Ṣafwān from Jurjān and appointed Hishām b. Saʿīd[695] as governor.

In this year ʿAlī b. al-Mahdī led the people on the pilgrimage. Jaʿfar b. Sulaymān was in charge of al-Yamāmah, Medina, Mecca, and al-Ṭāʾif in this year. Isḥāq b. al-Ṣabbāḥ was in charge of the prayers and the *aḥdāth* in al-Kūfah, and Sharīk was in charge of the judiciary. Muḥammad b. Sulaymān was in charge of al-Baṣrah and its dependencies, the provinces of the Tigris, al-Baḥrayn, ʿUmān, al-Furaḍ (the seaports),[696] and the districts of Ahwāz and the districts of Fārs. Al-Musayyab b. Zuhayr was in charge of Khurāsān and Naṣr b. Muḥammad b. al-Ashʿath of Sind.

695. B. Manṣūr. Not recorded elsewhere, but possibly a brother of the al-Ḥakam above and nephew of Yazīd b. Manṣūr, maternal uncle of al-Mahdī.

696. Presumably on the Gulf somewhere; only mentioned twice in al-Ṭabarī (p. 503, below) and not recorded by the geographers.

The Events of the Year 164

(September 6, 780–August 25, 781)

Among the events of this year was the raid[697] by ʿAbd al-Kabīr b. ʿAbd al-Ḥamīd b. ʿAbd al-Raḥmān b. Zayd b. al-Khaṭṭāb[698] by the pass of al-Ḥadath. Michael the Patrician met him, it is said, with about ninety thousand men, among them Ṭāzādh the Armenian the Patrician.[699] ʿAbd al-Kabīr lost heart before him and prevented the Muslims from fighting and returned. Al-Mahdī wanted to execute him, but intercession was made for him and he was imprisoned in the Muṭbaq.

In this year, al-Mahdī deposed Muḥammad b. Sulaymān from his offices.[700] He sent Ṣāliḥ b. Dāwūd[701] over what Muḥammad b. Sulaymān had had and sent with him ʿĀṣim b. Mūsā al-Khurāsānī

697. Brooks, "Byzantines and Arabs," 737.

698. A descendant of Zayd b. al-Khaṭṭāb, brother of the caliph ʿUmar, which may have been why he was given the honor of leading the expedition.

699. Theophanes gives the names Tazates. Armenians formed a large and increasing proportion of the Byzantine armies of the period.

700. The governorates of al-Baṣrah, Fārs, and the Gulf shores.

701. B. ʿAlī the ʿAbbāsid, son of Dāwūd b. ʿAlī, not to be confused with Ṣāliḥ, brother of Yaʿqūb b. Dāwūd the vizier.

the secretary, in charge of the taxation. He ordered him to arrest
[502] Ḥammād b. Mūsā, the secretary of Muḥammad b. Sulaymān, and 'Ubaydallāh b. 'Umar,[702] his deputy, and his agents, and that they should be investigated.

In this year al-Mahdī built at Greater 'Īsābādh[703] a palace of mud brick before he laid the foundations of his palace of baked brick, which he called Qaṣr al-Salāmah.[704] It was founded on Wednesday at the end of Dhū al-Qa'dah (the month ended on Friday, July 27, 781).

In this year, when he founded this palace, he set out for al-Kūfah on the pilgrimage. He stayed at al-Ruṣāfah of al-Kūfah for some days, and then he set out in the direction of the pilgrimage until he reached 'Aqabah.[705] Water became scarce for him and those with him, and he was afraid that what they carried would not sustain him and those with him. On top of that, he developed a fever so he returned from 'Aqabah. He was angry with Yaqṭīn[706] about the water because he was in charge of the cisterns. During their journey, and on their return, the people were severely afflicted by thirst until they were on the verge of perishing.

In this year Naṣr b. Muḥammad b. al-Ash'ath died in Sind.

In this year he deposed 'Abdallāh b. Sulaymān from Yemen because of his anger. He sent people to meet him and examine his baggage and account for what he had with him. Then he ordered that he should be imprisoned with al-Rabī' when he returned until he gave up the money and jewels and ambergris that he confessed to. He returned it to him and released him and appointed as governor (*'āmil*) in his place Manṣūr b. Yazīd b. Manṣūr.[707]

In this year al-Mahdī sent Ṣāliḥ, son of Abū Ja'far al-Manṣūr,
[503] from 'Aqabah when he left it to Mecca to lead the pilgrimage

702. Nothing more is known about these three.

703. To the east of Baghdad (Yāqūt, *Mu'jam*, IV, 142–43). It is said to have been named after al-Mahdī's son 'Īsā. Its exact location is unknown.

704. Palace of Well-Being: Yāqūt calls it *Qaṣr al-Salām*, Palace of Peace.

705. One of the stages on the desert road from al-Kūfah to Mecca, on the modern Iraq-Saudi Arabian border (Yāqūt, *Mu'jam*, IV, 134).

706. B. Mūsā.

707. Son of Yazīd b. Manṣūr, maternal uncle of al-Mahdī (note 163, above). He was later briefly governor of Khurāsān, 179–80/796.

with the people, and Ṣāliḥ performed the pilgrimage for the people in this year.

The governor (*ʿāmil*) of Medina, Mecca, al-Ṭā'if and al-Yamāmah in this year was Jaʿfar b. Sulaymān, of Yemen Manṣūr b. Yazīd b. Manṣūr. Hāshim b. Saʿīd b. Manṣūr was in charge of the prayers and *aḥdāth* of al-Kūfah and Sharīk b. ʿAbdallāh of the judiciary. Ṣāliḥ b. Dāwūd b. ʿAlī was in charge of al-Baṣrah and its *aḥdāth*, of the districts of the Tigris, al-Baḥrayn, ʿUmān, al-Furaḍ and the districts of Ahwāz and Fārs. Saṭīḥ b. ʿUmar[708] was in charge of Sind, al-Musayyab b. Zuhayr of Khurāsān, Muḥammad b. al-Faḍl of Mosul, ʿUbaydallāh b. al-Ḥasan of the judiciary of al-Baṣrah, Ibrāhīm b. Ṣāliḥ of Egypt, Yazīd b. Ḥātim of Ifrīqiyah, Yaḥyā al-Ḥarashī of Ṭabaristān, Rūyān and Jurjān, Farāshah, freedman of the Commander of the Faithful, of Dunbāwand and Qūmis,[709] Khalaf b. ʿAbdallāh of al-Rayy[710] and Saʿīd b. Daʿlaj of Sijistān.

---

708. Not known elsewhere

709. Farāshah subsequently became governor of Jurjān and was captured and executed by the Ispahbādh of Ṭabaristān at the end of al-Mahdī's reign; see Crone, *Slaves*, 191. Dunbāwand is the earlier form of Damavand, the great peak of the Elburz chain north of Tehran, but it was also the name of a small town at its foot and the surrounding province. Qūmis was the small province to the east, with its capital at Damghān See Yāqūt, *Muʿjam*, II, 275–77, IV, 414–15; Le Strange, *Lands*, 364–68, 371, and map V.

710. Not known elsewhere

The Events of the Year 165

(August 26, 781–August 14, 782)

Among the events of this year was the summer raid of Hārūn, son of Muḥammad al-Mahdī.[711] It is said that his father sent him on Saturday, 18 Jumādā II (February 7, 782, a Thursday), to raid the lands of Byzantium. He attached al-Rabīʿ his freedman to him. Hārūn penetrated deeply into Byzantine territory and conquered Mājidah.[712] The horsemen of Nicetas, Count of Counts,[713] met him. Yazīd b. Mazyad went out to meet him in single combat. Yazīd was forced to dismount,[714] and then Nicetas fell off and
[504] Yazīd struck him so that he was defeated. The Byzantines were put to flight, and Yazīd took posession of their camp and went to the Domesticos, head of the armed forces (*masāliḥ*) in Nicomedia.[715] Hārūn set out with 95,793 men and took 194,450

711. Brooks, "Byzantines and Arabs," 737–38; my interpretation differs somewhat from that of Brooks.

712. In Cappadocia (Honigmann, *Ostgrenze*, 46, 47).

713. Count of the Opsikion Theme.

714. It is not clear whether Nicetas fell off or dismounted intentionally.

715. For conflicting Byzantine versions of these events, see Brooks, *op. cit.*, 738.

*dīnār*s in gold and 21,414,800 *dirhams* in silver for them. He traveled until he reached the Sea of Marmara. The ruler of Byzantium at that time was Augusta, the wife of Leo.[716] This was because her son was a minor, whose father had died when he was in her charge. Messages and ambassadors passed between her and Hārūn, son of al-Mahdī, seeking peace and reconciliation and the paying of ransoms. Hārūn accepted that from her on condition that she fulfill what she promised and that she provide guides and markets on his route. This was because he had come by a way that was difficult and dangerous for the Muslims. She responded to his requests.

The terms of the peace were ninety or seventy thousand *dīnār*s, which she was to pay at the beginning of April[717] and in June every year, and he accepted that from her and she established markets on his route and sent an ambassador with him to al-Mahdī with what she had agreed should be paid as she could in gold and silver and goods.

They wrote an agreement of truce for three years, and the pris- [505]
oners were handed over. Those whom God gave as booty to Hārūn before the Byzantines would pay the *jizyah* were 5,643 people. Fifty-four thousand Byzantines were killed in battle and 2,090 prisoners were killed in captivity. Among the beasts and trained animals that God gave him as booty with their equipment were twenty thousand riding animals, and he slaughtered a hundred thousand head of cattle and sheep. The salaried troops, beside the volunteers and the traders, numbered one hundred thousand. A work horse was sold for a *dirham* and a mule for less than ten *dirhams*, a coat of mail for less than a *dirham*, and twenty swords for a *dirham*. Marwān b. Abī Ḥafṣah[718] said about that:

You have gone around Constantinople of the Byzantines, resting
the spear on it so that its walls were covered with ignominy.

---

716. The Empress Irene.

717. Unusually al-Ṭabarī uses the Christian months Nīsān and Ḥazīrān here. As Brooks and the *Addenda* point out, Nīsān should probably read Kānūn I, being December and making the payments due every half year.

718. Sometimes called al-Akbar, to distinguish him from Abū al-Samṭ Marwān b. Abī al-Janūb, who is also called Ibn Abī Ḥafṣah. See *Aghānī*, Būlāq, IX, 36; Beirut, X, 74.

You just went toward it and lo, its kings came to you
with its *jizyah*, while the pots of war were boiling.

In this year he deposed Khalaf b. ʿAbdallāh from al-Rayy and appointed ʿĪsā, freedman of Jaʿfar,[719] to it.

In this year Ṣāliḥ b. Abī Jaʿfar al-Manṣūr led the pilgrims.

The governors of the *amṣār* were the same this year as in the previous year, except that Rawḥ b. Ḥātim was the governor of the *aḥdāth* and the public prayers at al-Baṣrah. Al-Muʿallā,[720] freedman of the Commander of the Faithful al-Mahdī, was in charge of the districts of the Tigris, al-Baḥrayn, ʿUmān, Kaskar, and the districts of Ahwāz, Fārs, and Kirmān. Al-Layth, freedman of al-Mahdī, was in charge of Sind.

---

719. Nothing more is known of him; see Crone, *Slaves*, 192.

720. Brother of Layth; see text, p. 484. According to *Aghānī*, Beirut, VI, 239–40, he and his brother were bought in al-Kūfah by ʿAlī b. Sulaymān, who gave them to al-Manṣūr, who in turn gave them to al-Mahdī, who freed them. Al-Muʿallā was first given charge of the *ṭirāz* (state textile industry) and post in Khurāsān before being appointed to this vast governorate; see Crone, *Slaves*, 193. The reign of al-Mahdī was the high point of the influence of the freedmen, and this is exemplified in the careers of al-Muʿallā and Layth.

The Events of the Year 166

(August 15, 782–August 4, 783)

The events of this year:

Among these was the return of Hārūn, son of al-Mahdī, and those who were with him from the Sea of Marmara on 17 Muḥar- [506] ram (August 31, 782). The Byzantines came bringing the *jizyah* with them, and it was said that this was 64,000 *dīnār*s by Byzantine accounting, 2,500 Arab *dīnār*s, and 30,000 *raṭl*s[721] of goat's wool.

In this year al-Mahdī took the oath of allegiance from his military commanders to Hārūn after Mūsā, son of al-Mahdī, and named him al-Rashīd.

In this year he deposed 'Ubaydallāh b. al-Ḥasan from the judiciary of al-Baṣrah and appointed Khālid b. Ṭalīq b. 'Imrān b. Ḥuṣayn al-Khuzā'ī[722] in his place, but his appointment was not approved of, and the people of al-Baṣrah asked to be free from him.

In this year he deposed Ja'far b. Sulaymān from Mecca and Medina and the offices he held.

---

721. A dry weight that varied from place to place, probably between 2 and 4 kg.
722. Nothing more is known of him.

In this year al-Mahdī was angry with Ya'qūb b. Dāwūd. The account of al-Mahdī's anger with Ya'qūb:

According to 'Alī b. Muḥammad al-Nawfalī—his father: Dāwūd b. Ṭahmān, that is, Abū Ya'qūb b. Dāwūd, and his brothers were secretaries to Naṣr b. Sayyār,[723] and before him he was secretary to one of the governors of Khurāsān. At the time of Yaḥyā b. Zayd,[724] he was passing information to him and his companions and warning them about what he heard from Naṣr. When Abū Muslim rose in rebellion to avenge the blood of Yaḥyā b. Zayd and to kill his killers and those who spied on him among the companions of Naṣr, Dāwūd b. Ṭahmān came to him confident in what he knew about what occurred between him and Yaḥyā. So
[507] Abū Muslim gave him a safe-conduct and did not molest him in person, but took the money he had acquired in the time of Naṣr and left the houses and estates in Marw that were his inheritance.

When Dāwūd died, his sons emerged as people of culture and knowledge of the Days[725] of people and their histories and their poetry. They looked and found that they had no status with the Banū al-'Abbās, and they did not aspire to their service because of the position of their father in the secretariat of Naṣr. When they saw that, they adopted the faith of the Zaydiyyah[726] and approached the family of al-Ḥusayn[727] and wanted there to be a state (*dawlah*) for them so that they might live in it. Dāwūd used to roam through the land on his own and sometimes with Ibrāhīm b. 'Abdallāh, seeking oaths of allegiance to Muḥammad b. 'Abdallāh. When Muḥammad and Ibrāhīm b. 'Abdallāh came out in rebellion,[728] 'Alī b. Dāwūd, who was older than Ya'qūb, wrote to Ibrāhīm b. 'Abdallāh, and Ya'qūb with a number of his brothers rebelled with Ibrāhīm.

---

723. The last Umayyad governor of Khurāsān.

724. 'Alid, whose father, Zayd b. 'Alī, rebelled unsuccessfully in al-Kūfah in 122/740. Yaḥyā subsequently fled to Khurāsān, where he was arrested and executed.

725. *Ayyām al-nās*, the "Days," were the battles of the pre-Islamic Arabs and the poetry connected with them, essential knowledge for anyone hoping to be considered educated.

726. See above, note 137.

727. That is, the family of al-Ḥusayn b. 'Alī b. Abī Ṭālib, in this case Muḥammad b. 'Abdallāh and his brother Ibrāhīm, the rebels of 145/762.

728. In 145/762.

When Muḥammad and Ibrāhīm were killed, they hid from al-Manṣūr, and he searched for them and captured Yaʿqūb and ʿAlī and imprisoned them in the Muṭbaq for as long as he lived. When al-Manṣūr died, al-Mahdī favored them, along with others, by releasing them, and he let both of them go. Isḥāq b. al-Faḍl b. ʿAbd al-Raḥmān[729] was with them in the dungeon, and they were not separated from him and his brothers who were in prison with him, and because of that there developed a friendship between them. Isḥāq b. al-Faḍl b. ʿAbd al-Raḥmān was of the opinion that the caliphate had passed to the righteous ones of the Banū Hāshim[730] together, and he used to say that after the Prophet the imāmate had not been secure except with the Banū Hāshim and it was not secure at this time except with them. He used to talk continually of the eldest of the Banū ʿAbd al-Muṭṭalib,[731] and he and Yaʿqūb b. Dāwūd used to have discussions about that.

When al-Mahdī released Yaʿqūb, al-Mahdī continued for some time searching for ʿĪsā b. Zayd[732] and al-Ḥasan b. ʿIbrāhim b. [508]
ʿAbdallāh[733] after al-Ḥasan had escaped from prison. One day al-Mahdī said, "If I found a man of the Zaydiyyah with knowledge of the family of Ḥasan and of ʿĪsā b. Zayd and understanding, I would bring him to me on the way of knowledge, so that he could serve as an intermediary between me and the family of Ḥasan and ʿĪsā b. Zayd." Yaʿqūb was suggested to him, and he was brought and taken into his presence. That day he was wearing furs and sheepskin top boots,[734] a turban of *karābīs*,[735] and a coarse white *kisāʾ*.[736] He spoke and conversed with him and found him to be a

---

729. B. al-ʿAbbās b. Rabīʿ b. al-Ḥārith b. ʿAbd al-Muṭṭalib b. Hāshim. He was thus related to both ʿAlids and ʿAbbāsids, since his ancestor al-Ḥārith was a brother of al-ʿAbbās and Abū Ṭālib.

730. That is, both ʿAlids and ʿAbbāsids.

731. Abū Ṭālib, father of ʿAlī, who was older than his brother al-ʿAbbās, ancestor of the ʿAbbāsids. He is arguing that the ʿAlids had precedence over the ʿAbbāsids because of the relative positions of their ancestors among the Banū Hāshim.

732. See note 159, above.

733. See note 470, above.

734. For a fuller description, see Ahsan, *Social Life*, 47.

735. A fine white cotton or linen fabric.

736. An outer cloak, see Ahsan, *Social Life*, 44. The point of this description is that he was wearing white, traditionally associated with the ʿAlids, not the ʿAbbāsid black.

sterling man. He asked him about ʿĪsā b. Zayd, and people said that he promised him that he would be his intermediary with him. Yaʿqūb used to deny that, but people accused him of owing his position with al-Mahdī to the fact that he led him to the family of ʿAlī. His status with al-Mahdī continued to increase and rise until he made him his *wazīr* and entrusted him with the affairs of the caliphate. He sent for the Zaydiyyah, and they were brought to him from all sides and he gave them charge of the affairs of the caliphate in east and west and every great matter and precious work, and the whole world was in his hands. Bashshār b. Burd[737] said about that:

Sons of Umayyah wake up! Your sleep has gone on too long.
Yaʿqūb b. Dāwūd is caliph.
Your caliphate has been ruined, O people! Search
for the caliph of Allāh among the tambourines and lutes.

He said: The freedmen of al-Mahdī were jealous of him and intrigued against him. One thing by which Yaʿqūb gained al-Mahdī's favor was that he asked for a safe-conduct for al-Ḥasan b. Ibrāhīm b. ʿAbdallāh, and he negotiated between al-Mahdī and al-Ḥasan so that he brought them together in Mecca.

When the family of al-Ḥasan b. ʿAlī[738] knew what he had done, they stayed away from him, and Yaʿqūb knew that if they es-
[509] tablished a state he would not survive in it and that al-Mahdī did not put him on an equal footing because of the greatness of the slander brought to him about Yaʿqūb. Yaʿqūb became close to Isḥāq b. al-Faḍl,[739] and he took to discussing affairs with him. Scandal was reported to al-Mahdī about Isḥāq, and it was said to him that the east and west were in the hands of Yaʿqūb and his friends and he had written to them. It was only enough for him to write to them and they would rise in rebellion on one day at the appointed time and hand over the world to Isḥāq b. al-Faḍl. This hardened the heart of al-Mahdī against him.

According to ʿAlī b. Muḥammad al-Nawfalī: One of the servants

737. Celebrated poet. *Aghānī*, Būlāq, III, 19; Beirut, III, 129.
738. This should probably be the family of al-Ḥusayn b. ʿAlī.
739. The sense would seem to be that he turned to Isḥāq because he was not completely accepted by either the Ḥusaynid ʿAlids or al-Mahdī.

of al-Mahdī mentioned to me that, when he was standing at his head one day to whisk away the flies, Ya'qūb came in and knelt before him and said, "O Commander of the Faithful, you know about the disturbed state of Egypt and that you ordered me to search for a man for it to settle its affairs. I continued to investigate until I decided on a man who will put it right." Al-Mahdī asked him who it was and he replied, "Your paternal cousin, Isḥāq b. al-Faḍl." Ya'qūb saw the change in his face, and he rose and left and al-Mahdī followed him with his eyes and then said, "May God strike me dead if I do not kill you!" Then he raised his head to me and said, "Keep quiet about this, damn you!" The freedmen continued to stir him up against Ya'qūb and turn him against him until he decided to withdraw his favor from him.

According to Mūsā b. Ibrāhīm al-Mas'ūdī[740]—al-Mahdī: Ya'qūb b. Dāwūd appeared to me in a dream and it was said to me that I should take him as *wazīr* and when he saw him he said, "This, by God, is the person I saw in my dream," so he appointed him as *wazīr* and he enjoyed the greatest favor with him. He stayed for some time until he built 'Īsābādh and one of his servants, who was a favorite of his, came to him and said to him, "Aḥmad b. Ismā'īl b. 'Alī[741] said to me, 'He has built a park on which he has spent 50 million *dirhams* of the Muslims' money.'" He remembered what the servant had said but forgot that it was [510]
Aḥmad b. Ismā'īl and imagined that it was Ya'qūb b. Dāwūd. When Ya'qūb b. Dāwūd was before him, he took him by the throat and struck him to the ground and he said, "What is your quarrel with me, O Commander of the Faithful?" and he replied, "Were you not the one who said that I spent fifty million *dirhams* on a pleasure park for myself?" and Ya'qūb said, "By God, my ears did not hear it, and the two angels did not write it." This was the first reason for his affair (i.e., his fall from power).

According to my father: Ya'qūb b. Dāwūd had known from al-Mahdī dissoluteness and licentiousness in the mention of women and sexual intercourse. Ya'qūb b. Dāwūd used to describe many things from his own experience in that, and al-Mahdī did like-

740. Not known elsewhere.

741. An 'Abbāsid, son of al-Manṣūr's uncle, Ismā'īl b. 'Alī. He was governor of Mosul, 165–68/781–85 (al-Azdī, 246, 252).

wise. They[742] used to leave al-Mahdī alone at night and say that he would be furious with Ya'qūb in the morning. When it was morning, Ya'qūb went to visit him, and he had heard about this, and, when al-Mahdī saw him, he smiled and said to him, "Have you had a good time?" and he replied, "Yes," and al-Mahdī used to say, "Sit down, by my life, and tell me," and he used to say, "I was alone with my slave girl yesterday and she said and I said . . . ," and he made a story about that and al-Mahdī did the same and they shared the pleasure. News of this reached those who were plotting against Ya'qūb and they were amazed at it.

According to al-Mawṣilī: Ya'qūb b. Dāwūd said to al-Mahdī about some matter he wished, "This, by God, is extravagance," and al-Mahdī answered, "Damn you! Do only people of nobility think extravagance is good? Damn you Ya'qūb, were it not for extravagance you could not tell the generous from the miserly."

According to 'Alī b. Ya'qūb b. Dāwūd—his father: Al-Mahdī sent for me one day and I came in to him, and there he was in a
[511] *majlis* furnished with exquisite rose-colored fabrics, most lofty in fashion, overlooking a garden in which there were trees, and the tops of the trees were level with the floor of the *majlis*. These trees had burst into leaf with roses and peach and apple blossoms, and all these were pink like the furnishing of the *majlis* that he was in. I have not seen anything more beautiful than it. He had with him a slave girl, than whom I have never seen one more beautiful nor more erect in bearing nor more elegant in proportion, wearing clothes of the same color. I have never seen anything better than this ensemble. He said to me, "O Ya'qūb, what do you think of this *majlis* of ours?" and I replied, "Extremely beautiful; may God grant the Commander of the Faithful enjoyment of it and delight in it." He said, "It is yours. Take it with what is in it and this slave girl so that your pleasure in it may be complete," so I prayed God for him, as it should be.

Then he said, "O Ya'qūb, I have a request from you," and so I jumped up and said, "O Commander of the Faithful, is this some

---

742. Ibn al-Athīr explains: Intriguers used to make attacks on Ya'qūb at night (when they were talking with the caliph) and when they dispersed they were of the belief that he (al-Mahdī) would arrest him the next morning.

grievance you have? I take refuge in God from the anger of the Commander of the Faithful." He said, "No, but I would like you to guarantee to me the fulfilling of this request. I did not ask it for the reason you suspect, and I meant only what I said. I would like you to guarantee to me that you will fulfill this request for me." I replied, "It is the order of the Commander of the Faithful, and it is my duty to hear and obey." He said, "[Do you swear] by God?" and I said "by God" three times, and then he said, "by the life of my head?" and I said, "by the life of your head," and he said, "Put out your hand and swear to it," so I put my hand on him and swore to him by it that I would do what he said and fulfill his request.

When he had made certain of me in his mind, he said, "This so-and-so, son of so-and-so of the descendants of ʿAlī: I would like you to save me from trouble with him and make me free of him and do that quickly." I said that I would do it and he said, "Take him to you," and I transferred him to me and I transferred the slave girl and all the furnishings and everything that was in the house, and he ordered 100,000 *dirhams* for me with it. [512]

I took all of it and went with it and, because of my great pleasure in the slave girl, I put her in the *majlis* with a veil between me and her. I sent for the ʿAlawī and brought him in to me and asked him about his position, and he told me about it and, in short, I found him the most intelligent of men and the clearest of them in speech. Among the things he said to me was, "Damn you, Yaʿqūb! You are accountable to God for my blood, and I am one of the descendants of Fāṭimah, daughter of Muḥammad." I said, "No by God; are you the grateful type if you receive a favor?" And he said, "If you do a favor, I will thank you and invoke God's blessing on you and ask forgiveness for you." I said to him, "Which road would you like best?" and he replied "Such-and-such a road." I asked, "Who is there there with whom you are friendly and whose position you trust?" and he said, "So-and-so and so-and-so." I said, "Go to them and take this money and travel with them in safety under the veil of God. Your meeting with them to go out of my house to such-and-such a place that they have agreed on is at such-and-such a time of night."

Now the slave girl had remembered my words against me and sent them with a servant of hers to al-Mahdī and said, "This is your reward from the one whom you preferred over yourself, and he has acted and done this and this...," until she had passed on the whole story.

Al-Mahdī immediately sent men to police those roads and places that Ya'qūb and the 'Alawī had described, and it was not long before they brought this very 'Alawī to him with his two friends and his money, exactly as the slave girl had told. He said, I got up the next day and there was a messenger from al-Mahdī summoning me to his presence. I was free of anxiety and the affair
[513] of the 'Alawī was not weighing on me until I entered to al-Mahdī and I found him on a chair with a mace in his hand, and he said to me, "O Ya'qūb, what is the position of the man?" and I said, "O Commander of the Faithful, God has relieved you of him." He asked if he had died and I replied, "Yes," and he said, "[Do you swear] by God?" and I said, "by God." Then he said, "Stand up and put your hand on my head," so I put my hand on his head and took the oath with it.

He then said, "Page! Bring out to us what is in this chamber," and he opened the door on the very same 'Alawī and his two friends and the money. I remained at a loss and was filled with regret. I was unable to speak and did not know what to say. Al-Mahdī said, "You have made your blood legal for me if I choose to shed it, but imprison him in the Muṭbaq and let him be forgotten." So I was imprisoned in the Muṭbaq, and I was taken to a well in it and lowered into it. I remained there for a very long time and I do not know the number of days. My sight was afflicted and my hair grew long, so that it was flowing like the hair of beasts.

I was in that condition when I was called and I was taken and brought I knew not where and I was told no more than "Greet the Commander of the Faithful!" so I made my greeting and he said, "Which Commander of the Faithful am I?" and I said "al-Mahdī," and he said, "May God have mercy on al-Mahdī," and so I said, "al-Hādī," but he said, "May God have mercy on al-Hādī," and then I said, "al-Rashīd," and he said, "Yes." I said, "I do not doubt that the Commander of the Faithful understands my story and what has befallen me and that my position has been explained to him." He said, "Certainly, I am aware of that and the Commander of the Faithful knew. Ask for what you need." I said, "To settle in Mecca," and he said, "We will grant that; do you have any other requests?" and I replied, "I have no longer enjoyment in anything and no power of communication," and he said, "Go rightly guided." I left and set my face for Mecca.

His son said, "He stayed in Mecca and he was not long there before he died."

According to Muḥammad b. ʿAbdallāh—his father—Yaʿqūb b. Dāwūd: Al-Mahdī did not drink wine, not because he was avoiding sin, but because he did not like it. His companions ʿUmar b. Bazīʿ; al-Muʿalla, his freedman; and al-Mufaḍḍal[743] and his freedmen used to drink in his presence under his eyes. I used to warn him of their drinking and listening to singing,[744] and I used to say, "It was not for this that you made me *wazīr* and not because of this that I became your companion. After the five prayers in the cathedral mosque, should wine be drunk in your presence and should you listen to singing?" He used to say, "ʿAbdallāh b. Jaʿfar listened,"[745] and I said, "This was not part of his virtues. If a man listened to singing every day, would he increase in nearness or in distance to God?" [514]

According to Muḥammad b. ʿAbdallāh—his father: My father, Yaʿqūb b. Dāwūd, besought al-Mahdī to stop listening to singing and pouring wine until it got on his nerves. Yaʿqūb had grown uneasy about his position and repented to God for what he was doing and looked to the future and advanced the intention of leaving his position. He said, "I used to say to al-Mahdī, 'O Commander of the Faithful, by God, drinking wine myself and repenting to God for it would be more pleasing to me than what I am doing. I am riding to you and wish that a sinful hand would strike me down on the way, so excuse me and appoint another, whomever you wish. I wish to get safe with you, I and my children, and, by God, I am afraid in my sleep. You have put me in charge of the affairs of the Muslims and the payment of the army, but this world of yours is not a fair exchange for my hereafter.'" He used to say, "O God, forgiveness, O God purify his heart," and the poet said to him:

---

743. Called al-Waṣīf. He is later recorded among the ʿAbbāsid party on the pilgrimage of 169/786 when the ʿAlid al-Ḥusayn b. ʿAlī rebelled.

744. The Arabic simply has *al-asmāʿ* "listening," specifically to singing.

745. ʿAbdallāh b. Jaʿfar b. Abī Ṭālib: al-Mahdī is citing the example of ʿAlī's nephew to prove that righteous men could listen to singing.

Leave Yaʿqūb b. Dāwūd on one side,
and take to the good wine that has a good smell.

[515] According to ʿAbdallāh b. ʿUmar[746]—Jaʿfar b. Aḥmad b. Zayd al-ʿAlawī[747]—Ibn Sallām[748]: Al-Mahdī gave a slave girl to one of the sons of Yaʿqūb b. Dāwūd, who was feebleminded. After some days he asked him about her and he said, "O Commander of the Faithful, I never saw the likes of her. I have never had such an easy riding steed between me and the ground. . . present company excepted!"[749] Al-Mahdī turned to Yaʿqūb and said to him, "Whom do you think he means? Does he mean me or does he mean you?" and Yaʿqūb said to him, "You can protect a foolish man against anything except himself."

According to ʿAlī b. Muḥammad al-Nawfalī—his father: Yaʿqūb b. Dāwūd used to go into al-Mahdī and spend the night alone with him chatting and conversing. One night when he was with him when most of the night had passed he came out wearing a dyed Hāshimī *ṭaylasān*[750] that was blue and light, and the *ṭaylasān* had been strongly starched and ironed and it rattled. A page took the reins of his riding beast, a gray beast of his. The page had slept and Yaʿqūb went smoothing his *ṭaylasān*, and it rattled. The palfrey shied and Yaʿqūb approached it, and it turned its back on him and kicked him on his leg and broke it. Al-Mahdī heard the noise and came out barefooted and, when he saw what had happened, he made clear his anxiety and solicitude. Then he ordered that he be carried in a chair to his house. The next day al-Mahdī visited him at dawn, and the people heard about that and they came to him in the morning. He returned to him on the next three days and then he ceased his visits and began to send to him asking him how he was. When he was not present, intriguers were able to influence al-Mahdī, and within ten days (nights) his

746. B. Abū al-Ḥayy al-ʿAbsī. He contributes one other report (see 539, below).
747. Probably a grandson of Zayd b. ʿAlī, the unsuccessful rebel of 122/740.
748. Muḥammad b. Sallām al-Jumaḥī 139–231/756–845, author of the surviving *Ṭabaqāt al-Shuʿarāʾ*, contributes six reports on the Umayyads and ʿAbbāsids to the *History*; see *EI*², s.v. "Ibn Sallām."
749. He clearly did not know how to express himself properly.
750. A piece of material worn over the shoulders and hanging down the back, a bit like an academic hood; see Ahsan, *Social Life*, 42–43.

anger against him became apparent, and he left him in his house [516] to be treated and he announced to his companions that no one should have a Ya'qūbī *ṭaylasān* on him or a Ya'qūbī *qalansūwah* or his clothes would be taken from him. Then he ordered that Ya'qūb should be confined in the prison of Naṣr.

According to al-Nawfalī: Al-Mahdī ordered that Ya'qūb's men be deposed from offices in east and west and ordered that his family be arrested and imprisoned and that was done to them.

According to 'Alī b. Muḥammad: When Ya'qūb b. Dāwūd and his family were imprisoned, his agents dispersed and went into hiding and lived as vagabonds; his story and the story of Isḥāq b. al-Faḍl were told to al-Mahdī, and he sent for Isḥāq by night and for Ya'qūb. He was brought from prison, and he said to him, "Didn't you tell me that this man and the people of his family claimed that they had a better right to the caliphate than we, people of the family,[751] and that they had contempt for us?" and Ya'qūb said to him, "I never told you that," and he said, "You are accusing me of lying and contradicting my words!" Then he called for a whip and struck him twelve violent blows and ordered that he be returned to prison.

Isḥāq came and swore that he had never said that and that it was not his business. Among the things he said was, "How would I say that, O Commander of the Faithful, when my ancestor died in the Jāhiliyyah and your ancestor (lit: grandfather) survived after the Prophet of God and was his heir?"[752] He said, "Send him away." The next morning he summoned Ya'qūb and repeated to him the words that he had spoken, and he replied, "O Commander of the Faithful, do not punish me until I remind you and you remember when you were in a pavilion[753] overlooking the river. You were in the garden and I was with you when Abū al-Wazīr[754] came in."

'Alī said: Abū al-Wazīr was the son-in-law of Ya'qūb b. Dāwūd by the daughter of Ṣāliḥ b. Dāwūd. "Abū al-Wazīr told you this

751. I.e., the 'Abbāsid family.
752. Isḥāq's ancestor was al-Ḥārith b. 'Abd al-Muṭṭalib, brother of al-'Abbās; see note 729, above.
753. *Ṭāramah*, a wooden building of circular form with an arched roof.
754. 'Umar b. al-Muṭarrif; see note 655, above.

story on the authority of Isḥāq. He (al-Mahdī) said, "You have told the truth, Ya'qūb, I remember that," and al-Mahdī was ashamed and apologized to him for the beating. Then he returned him to the prison, and he remained a prisoner in the reign of al-
[517] Mahdī and the whole of the reign of Mūsā until Hārūn released him because of the regard he had for him in the life of his father.

In this year Mūsā al-Hādī left for Jurjān. He appointed Abū Yūsuf Ya'qūb b. Ibrāhīm[755] over his judiciary.

In this year al-Mahdī moved to 'Īsābādh and settled there. It was known as Qaṣr al-Salāmah, and the people settled there with him and *dīnārs* and *dirhams* were struck there.[756]

In this year al-Mahdī ordered the establishment of the post between the City of the Prophet[757] and Mecca and Yemen by mule and camel, and the post had not been established there before.

In this year Khurāsān was agitated against al-Musayyab b. Zuhayr, and al-Faḍl b. Sulaymān al-Ṭūsī Abū al-'Abbās was appointed as governor there.[758] Sijistān was attached to him as well, and he appointed Tamīm b. Sa'īd b. Da'laj as his deputy in Sijistān on the orders of al-Mahdī.

In this year Dāwūd b. Rawḥ b. Ḥātim, Ismā'īl b. Sulaymān b. Mujālid, Muḥammad b. Abī Ayyūb al-Makkī and Muḥammad b. Ṭayfūr were arrested for *Zandaqah*.[759] They confessed and al-Mahdī called on them to repent and released them. He sent Dāwūd

---

755. The famous *qāḍī* and author of the surviving *Kitāb al-Kharāj*. He remained *qāḍī* in Baghdad until his death in 182/799.

756. Most early Islamic coins had the names of the places they were minted on them. 'Īsābādh briefly became a center of habitation and government, but it seems to have been abandoned after al-Mahdī's death.

757. Medina.

758. Barthold, *Turkestan*, 205, mentions that Musayyab introduced a new coinage that may have provoked discontent. For further sources and discussion, see Daniel, *Khurasan*, 168, 184 n. 46.

759. All these were sons of prominent members of the regime, which is probably why they were treated so leniently. Rawḥ b. Ḥātim was the celebrated Muhallabī (see note 570, above); Sulaymān b. Mujālid was a member of al-Manṣūr's *saḥābah* who played an important part in the development of Baghdad; Abū Ayyūb al-Makkī was in charge of the *dīwān al-kharāj* at the beginning of al-Mahdī's reign; and Ṭayfūr was probably the Ṭayfūr, freedman of al-Hādī, who was al-Mahdī's half-brother and is recorded as governor of Iṣfahān in 169/785–86; see Crone, *Slaves*, 195.

b. Rawḥ to his father, Rawḥ, who was at that time governor of al-Baṣrah. He was gracious to him and ordered him to educate him.

In this year al-Waḍḍāḥ al-Sharawī brought 'Abdallāh b. Abū 'Ubaydallāh the *wazīr,* that is Mu'āwiyah b. 'Ubaydallāh al-Ash'arī of the people of Syria. He was the one whom Ibn Shabābah conspired against and who was accused of *Zandaqah*. We have already described his affair and his execution.[760]

In this year Ibrāhīm b. Yaḥyā b. Muḥammad was appointed [518] governor of Medina, the City of the Prophet of God; 'Ubaydallāh b. Qutham[761] was in charge of al-Ṭā'if and Mecca.

In this year Manṣūr b. Yazīd b. Manṣūr was deposed from Yemen and 'Abdallāh b. Sulaymān al-Raba'ī was appointed in his place.

In this year al-Mahdī released 'Abd al-Ṣamad b. 'Alī from the prison he was in.

Ibrāhīm b. Yaḥyā b. Muḥammad led the pilgrimage in this year.

In this year the governor (*'āmil*) of al-Kūfah, in charge of the prayers and the *aḥdāth*, was Hāshim b. Sa'īd. Rawḥ b. Ḥātim was in charge of the prayers and *aḥdāth* in al-Baṣrah, and Khālid b. Ṭalīq was in charge of the judiciary there. Al-Mu'allā, freedman of the Commander of the Faithful, was in charge of the districts of the Tigris; Kaskar; the governorates of al-Baṣrah and al-Baḥrayn; and the districts of Ahwāz, Fārs and Kirmān. Al-Faḍl b. Sulaymān al-Ṭūsī was in charge of Khurāsān and Sijistān; Ibrāhīm b. Ṣāliḥ of Egypt; Yazīd b. Ḥātim of Ifrīqiyah; Yaḥyā al-Ḥarashī of Ṭabaristān, Rūyān, and Jurjān; Farāshah, freedman of al-Mahdi, of Dunbāwand and Qūmis; and Sa'd, freedman of the Commander of the Faithful, of al-Rayy.

In this year there was no summer expedition against the Byzantines because of the truce in it.

---

760. The passage raises a problem. On p. 490 of the text al-Ṭabarī relates how Muḥammad b. 'Ubaydallāh was executed, and there is mention of 'Abdallāh. It is not clear whether this is the same incident with a mistake in the name or a separate event that has been lost from the text. Neither al-Waḍḍāḥ nor Ibn Shabābah can be identified further.

761. B. al-'Abbās b. 'Abdallāh b. al-'Abbās, an 'Abbāsid; for his father, see note 149, above. He remained governor until Hārūn's reign.

The
Events of the Year
167
(AUGUST 5, 783–JULY 23, 784)

The events of this year:

Among these was the sending by al-Mahdī of his son Mūsā with a huge number of soldiers and equipment the likes of which, it was said, no one had ever been equipped with before to Jurjān for
[519] the war against Wandāhurmuz[762] and Sharvīn,[763] the two lords of Ṭabaristān. When al-Mahdī organized it for Mūsā, he placed Abān b. Ṣadaqah in charge of his correspondence, Muḥammad b. Jumayl of his army, and Nufayʿ, freedman of al-Manṣūr, as his chamberlain. ʿAlī b. ʿĪsā b. Māhān was in command of his guard and ʿAbdallāh b. Khāzim of his police. Mūsā despatched the troops against Wandāhurmuz and Sharvīn under the command of Yazīd b. Mazyad and he laid siege to them.

In this year ʿĪsā b. Mūsā died in al-Kūfah. The governor of al-

762. One of the native princes of Ṭabaristān. He resisted this Muslim assault in his mountain stronghold and is last recorded visiting Hārūn on his trip to al-Rayy in 189/805. He was the grandfather of Māzyār, the famous opponent of the Muslims during the reign of al-Muʿtaṣim.

763. Neighbor and ally of Wandāhurmuz.

Kūfah at that time was Rawḥ b. Ḥātim, and Rawḥ b. Ḥātim called on the *qāḍī* and a body of the principal people to witness that he had died of natural causes, and then he was buried. It is said that ʿĪsā b. Mūsā died when Rawḥ b. Ḥātim was in charge of al-Kūfah on Tuesday, 26 Dhū al-Ḥijjah (Tuesday, July 20), and Rawḥ was present at his bier. It was said to him, "Go first, you are the governor (*amīr*)." He said, "God will certainly not see Rawḥ praying over ʿĪsā b. Mūsā. Let his eldest child have precedence." They refused to do that and he insisted, and al-ʿAbbās b. ʿĪsā took precedence and prayed over his father. News of this reached al-Mahdī and he was angry with Rawḥ and wrote to him, "News has reached me of your refusal to pray over ʿĪsā. Did you pray for him for yourself or your father or your grandfather?[764] If I had been present that would have been my position, but since I was absent you should have been the first because of your position of authority," and he ordered that he be called to account. He had been in charge of the taxation along with the prayers and the *aḥdāth*. When ʿĪsā died al-Mahdī still held a grudge against him and his children, yet he used to hate having precedence over him because of his seniority.

In this year al-Mahdī stepped up the hunt and search for *Zindīqs* in all areas and executed them. He put ʿUmar al-Kalwādhī[765] in [520] charge of dealing with them. Yazīd b. al-Fayḍ,[766] secretary to al-Manṣūr, was arrested and, it is said, he confessed and was put in prison but escaped and could not be recaptured.

In this year al-Mahdī deposed Abū ʿUbaydallāh Muʿāwiyah b. ʿUbaydallāh from the *Dīwān al-Rasā'il* and appointed his chamberlain al-Rabīʿ to it. He made Saʿīd b. Wāqid his deputy.[767] Abū

---

764. This is probably a reference to the fact that the Muhallabīs had opposed the later Umayyads and worked for their overthrow and that Rawḥ should have paid his respects to ʿĪsā for his part in the cause to which his father and grandfather had contributed, whatever his personal feelings.

765. From Kalwādhā, a small town on the eastern bank of the Tigris just south of Baghdad. Nothing more is known of him.

766. He seems to have remained in hiding and was one of the *Zindīqs* specifically excluded from an amnesty granted at the beginning of Hārūn's reign (see al-Ṭabarī, III, 604).

767. Al-Rabīʿ as *ḥājib* would not have the necessary expertise to run the *dīwān al-rasā'il* (chancery, responsible for sending out letters) himself. Nothing more is known of Saʿīd b. Wāqid.

ʿUbaydallāh continued to enter (into the presence of the caliph) according to his usual grade.

In this year there spread death and coughing and severe plague in Baghdad and al-Baṣrah.

In this year Abān b. Ṣadaqah died in Jurjān. He was secretary to Mūsā in charge of his correspondence (*rasāʾil*). Al-Mahdī sent in his place Abū Khālid al-Aḥwal Yazīd,[768] the deputy of Abū ʿUbaydallāh.

In this year al-Mahdī ordered the expansion of the Ḥarām mosque,[769] and many houses were incorporated into it. He appointed Yaqṭīn b. Mūsā to oversee the building of the extension and he was occupied with the building of it until the death of al-Mahdī.

In this year Yaḥyā al-Ḥarashī was deposed from Ṭabaristān and Rūyān and what he had in that area, and ʿUmar b. al-ʿAlāʾ was appointed to it. Farāshah, freedman of al-Mahdī, was appointed to Jurjān and Yaḥyā al-Ḥarashī was deposed.

In this year the earth darkened in the last nights of Dhū al-Ḥijjah until the day was well advanced.

In this year there was no summer expedition because of the truce there was between the Muslims and the Byzantines.

Ibrāhīm b. Yaḥyā b. Muḥammad led the pilgrimage in this year. He was governor of Medina and, after he had finished the pilgrimage and returned to Medina for a few days, he died, and Isḥāq b. ʿĪsā b. ʿAlī was appointed in his place.

In this year ʿUqbah b. Salm al-Hunāʾī was stabbed in ʿĪsābādh.
[521] He was in the house of ʿUmar b. Bazīʿ and a man took him by surprise and stabbed him with a dagger and he died there.[770]

The governor of Mecca and al-Ṭāʾif in this year was ʿUbaydallāh b. Qutham. Sulaymān b. Yazīd al-Ḥārithī was in charge of

768. A friend of Yaḥyā the Barmakid. When he died the next year, Yaḥyā looked after his son. His son Aḥmad played a central part in the appointment of Ṭāhir as governor of Khurāsān in 205/820.

769. In Mecca.

770. According to al-Yaʿqūbī, *Tārīkh*, II, 478, he was killed in revenge by a youth whose father he had killed when governor of al-Yamāmah (see note 72, above). Muḥammad b. Ḥabīb has him killed in al-Baḥrayn in al-Mahdī's reign (p. 196).

Yemen;[771] ʿAbdallāh b. Muṣʿab al-Zubayrī[772] of al-Yamāmah; Rawḥ b. Ḥātim was in charge of the prayers of al-Kūfah and the *aḥdāth* there; Muḥammad b. Sulaymān was in charge of the prayers and *aḥdāth* of al-Baṣrah, with ʿUmar b. ʿUthmān al-Taymī[773] in charge of the judiciary there. Al-Muʿallā, freedman of al-Mahdī, was in charge of the districts of the Tigris; Kaskar; the governorates (*aʿmāl*) of al-Baṣrah, al-Baḥrayn, and ʿUmān; and the districts (*kuwar*) of Ahwāz, Fārs, and Kirmān. Al-Faḍl b. Sulaymān al-Ṭūsī was in charge of Khurāsān and Sijistān; Mūsā b. Muṣʿab[774] of Egypt; Yazīd b. Ḥātim of Ifrīqiyah; ʿUmar b. al-ʿAlāʾ of Ṭabaristān and Rūyān; Farāshah, freedman of al-Mahdī, of Jurjān, Dunbāwand, and Qūmis; and Saʿd, freedman of the Commander of the Faithful, of al-Rayy.

---

771. He may have been the brother of Muḥammad b. Yazīd al-Ḥārithī who was governor of Yemen 133–34/750–52. Al-Saffāḥ's mother was a Ḥārithī, and several of them were influential in the early ʿAbbāsid state, especially in Yemen, where the family originated (Crone, *Slaves*, 149; Kennedy, *ʿAbbasid Caliphate*, 52–53).

772. A descendant of the Prophet's companion al-Zubayr b. al-ʿAwwām. Beside his political role, he was a significant source for al-Ṭabarī's *History*.

773. Not known elsewhere.

774. See note 193, above.

The Events of the Year 168

(July 24, 784–July 13, 785)

The events of this year:

Among these was the breaking by the Byzantines of the peace that had been made between them and Hārūn b. al-Mahdī as we described above and their treachery.[775] This was in the month of Ramaḍān (March 17–April 15, 785). Between the beginning of the peace and the Byzantines' treachery and their breaking of it were thirty-two months. 'Alī b. Sulaymān, who was at that time governor of al-Jazīrah and Qinnasrīn, sent Yazīd b. Badr b. al-Baṭṭāl[776] with a cavalry force against the Byzantines, and they took booty and were victorious.

In this year al-Mahdī sent Sa'īd al-Ḥarashī to Ṭabaristān with forty thousand men.

[522] In this year 'Umar al-Kalwādhī, master of the *Zindīqs*, died, and in his place was appointed Ḥamdawayh, who was Muḥammad b. 'Īsā of the people of Maysān.[777]

---

775. Brooks, "Byzantines and Arabs," 739–40.
776. Grandson of the Muslim hero, al-Baṭṭāl, n. 223. He is not known elsewhere.
777. Maysān was in southern Iraq north of al-Baṣrah and to the east of the Great

In this year al-Mahdī executed the *Zindīqs* in Baghdad.

In this year al-Mahdī returned his *dīwān* and the *dīwān* of his family to Medina, and he transferred it from Damascus there.[778]

In this year al-Mahdī went out to Nahr al-Ṣilah, below Wāsiṭ. It was only known as Nahr al-Ṣilah (the canal of the grant), it is said, because he wished to assign to his family and others the rents of it and grant them that.[779]

In this year al-Mahdī appointed ʿAlī b. Yaqṭīn[780] to the *Dīwān Zimam al-Azimmah*[781] over ʿUmar b. Bazīʿ.

According to Aḥmad b. Mūsā b. Ḥamzah—his father:[782] The first person to work the Registry Department was ʿUmar b. Bazīʿ in the caliphate of al-Mahdī. This was because, when the *dīwāns* were gathered to him, he thought that he could organize them only by setting up a *zimam* (registry) on every *dīwān*, so he set up the registry departments and appointed a man to every department. To the registry department of the *kharāj*, he appointed Ismāʿīl b. Ṣubayḥ.[783] The Banū Umayyah did not have registry departments.

ʿAlī b. Muḥammad al-Mahdī, who was called Ibn Rayṭah, led the pilgrimage in this year.

Swamp (Yāqūt, *Muʿjam*, V, 242–43; Le Strange, 43). For his efforts against the *Zindiqs*, see al-Nahrawānī, *al-Jalīs al-Ṣāliḥ* (Beirut, 1987), III, 203–7.

778. The *dīwān* of the family was the list of its members and the salaries they were entitled to. It is surprising that it had remained in the old Umayyad capital: its return to Medina (not Baghdad) was intended to emphasize the connection between the ʿAbbāsids and the Family of the Prophet.

779. Yāqūt (*Muʿjam*, V, 321) says that the canal was dug by al-Mahdī and the land brought into cultivation by him but that the revenue was assigned to the people of the Ḥaramayn (Mecca and Medina).

780. Son of Yaqṭīn b. Mūsā (note 271, above). According to al-Ṭabarī, 549, he was executed for *Zandaqah* in 169/786, but Ibn al-Nadīm, *Fihrist*, 224, says he died in 182/798.

781. For *dīwān al-azimmah* (registry departments), see note 660, above. This new *dīwān* seems to have been an attempt to centralize the registries of different departments.

782. Not known elsewhere.

783. Al-Ḥarrānī. He was subsequently to have a long career as secretary for Hārūn and later for al-Amīn and is last heard of in 195/810–11.

The Events of the Year 169

(July 14, 785–July 2, 786)

The events of this year:

Among these was al-Mahdī's departure in al-Muḥarram (July 14–August 12, 785) to Māsabadhān.[784]

[523] The story of his departure:

It is said that at the end of his reign al-Mahdī had intended to give his son Hārūn precedence over his son Mūsā al-Hādī. He sent a member of his family to him when he was in Jurjān in order to decide finally on the oath of allegiance and give al-Rashīd precedence. Mūsā did not comply. Al-Mahdī then sent one of his freedmen to him, but Mūsā refused to come back and beat the messenger. Al-Mahdī departed because of Mūsā, intending to go to Jurjān, but there befell him what befell him.

According to al-Bāhilī[785]—Abū Shākir,[786] one of the secretaries of al-Mahdī in charge of one of the *dīwāns*: ʿAlī b. Yaqṭīn asked

---

784. A district to the east of Baghdad, on the modern Iraq-Iran border (see Yāqūt, *Muʿjam*, V, 41; Le Strange, *Lands*, 202).

785. Abū Bakr: nothing more is known of him.

786. Nothing more is known of this man.

al-Mahdī to have breakfast with him, and he promised that he would and then he decided to come to Māsabadhān and, by God, he gave orders for the journey as if he were driven to it, and ʿAlī said to him, "O Commander of the Faithful, you promised to me that you would have breakfast with me," and he replied, "Bring your breakfast to Nahrawān!" so he brought it and had breakfast in Nahrawān, and then he departed.

In this year al-Mahdī died. The account of the circumstances of his death:

There are different accounts of his death: According to Wāḍiḥ, *qahramān*[787] to al-Mahdī: Al-Mahdī went out to hunt in a village called al-Radhdh in Māsabadhān, and I remained with him until after the afternoon prayer and then I went to my tent, which was far from his. Just before daybreak I rode to do my duties, and I was traveling through the desert and I had separated from the pages who were with me and from my companions when I met a naked black man traveling on a camel. He came near to me and then said to me, "Abū Sahl, may God give you great recompense for [524] your master, the Commander of the Faithful."[788] I contemplated whipping him, but he vanished from in front of me and, when I came to the portico (of the tent), Masrūr[789] met me and said to me, "Abū Sahl, may God grant you great recompense for your master, the Commander of the Faithful." I went in and there I saw him covered with a shroud in a tent (*qubbah*). I said, "I left you after the afternoon prayer and no one was more cheerful in mood or more healthy in body, so what happened?" He replied, "The hounds chased a gazelle and he continued to follow them and the gazelle rushed through the door of a ruined building and the hounds rushed after it and the horse rushed after the hounds, and his back was smashed against the door of the ruin and he died instantly."

According to ʿAlī b. Abī Nuʿaym al-Marwazī:[790] One of al-

787. A *qahramān* was a member of the domestic staff of the court, rather than a political figure; Wāḍiḥ is not otherwise known.

788. A formula meaning that the caliph has died. Compare the specter who announces the death of al-Manṣūr; see above, p. 162.

789. Abū Hāshim Masrūr al-Khādim, a palace servant who became an important figure at the court of Hārūn; see Crone, *Slaves*, 192–93.

790. Marwazī means coming from Marw; this is the only report he contributes.

Mahdī's slave girls sent beastings with poison in it to a rival of hers. He was sitting in the garden after he had left ʿĪsābādh. He called for it (the beastings) and ate from it, and the slave girl was afraid to say that it was poisoned.

According to Aḥmad b. Muḥammad al-Rāzī:[791] Al-Mahdī was sitting in an upstairs room in the palace at Māsabadhān looking down from his vantage point on those below him. A slave girl of his, called Ḥasanah,[792] had picked up two large pears and put them in a *ṣīnīyah*[793] dish and poisoned one that was the best and ripest in its lowest part, and replaced the stem in it and put it in the upper part of the dish. Al-Mahdī used to like pears very much, and she sent it with a servant of hers to a slave girl of al-Mahdī's whom he favored, intending to kill her with that. The servant was taking the dish with that pear in it, intending to give it to the slave girl whom Ḥasanah had sent it to, when al-Mahdī saw her from the vantage point. When he saw her and saw the pear with her, he called her and stretched out his hand to the pear, which
[525] was uppermost in the dish, the poisoned one, and ate it. When it reached his stomach, he screamed, "My stomach!" and Ḥasanah heard the voice and was told the news, and she began to strike her face in lamentation and weep and said, "I wanted to be alone with you and I have killed you, O my lord!" and he died that day.

According to ʿAbdallāh b. Ismāʿīl, master of the riding animals:[794] When we reached Māsabadhān, I came near to his bridle and took hold of it and he showed no sign of illness, by God, but in the morning he was dead, and I saw that Ḥasanah had returned with sackcloth on her collar and Abū al-ʿAtāhiyah[795] said about that:

In the afternoon, the women went in fine fabrics, but in the
morning they had sackcloth on.
Every butter has a butting day against him by time.
You were not to remain, even if you were given life as long as

---

791. Rāzī means coming from al-Rayy; he contributes two other reports.
792. Not known elsewhere.
793. A metal tray used for serving food.
794. *Ṣāḥib al-marākib*, a palace servant not recorded elsewhere.
795. D. 210/825. The celebrated poet. See *Aghānī*, Būlāq, XIV, 56; Beirut, XV, 218; *EI*², s.v. "Abū'l-ʿAṭāhiyah."

Noah was.
Lament for yourself for you have no alternative but to lament.

According to Ṣāliḥ al-Qārī'—'Alī b. Yaqṭīn: We were with al-Mahdī in Māsabadhān and he woke up one day and said, "I have woken up hungry," and he was brought loaves and cold, cooked meat in vinegar. He ate some of it and then said, "I am going into the hall to sleep in it. Do not wake me up until I wake up myself." He went into the hall and slept, and we slept in the house under the portico. We were awakened by his weeping and hurried to him and he said, "Did you not see what I saw?" and we replied that we had not seen anything and he said, "There stood at the door a man who would be easily recognized by me had he been among a thousand or a hundred thousand men and he recited, saying:

It is as if I were in this palace and its people have perished [526]
and its residences and dwelling places are deserted.
The chief of the people has come after glory and
power to a tomb covered with stones.
Nothing remains but his memory and story
and the wailing of his wives cries out for him."

Ten days did not pass before he died. According to Abū Ma'shar and al-Wāqidī he died in the year 169 on the night of Thursday (i.e., Wednesday night by our reckoning) 22 Muḥarram (Thursday, August 4, 785). His caliphate lasted ten years and one and a half months. Someone said that his caliphate was ten years, forty-nine days and that he died at the age of forty-three.

According to Hishām b. Muḥammad: Abū 'Abdallāh al-Mahdī Muḥammad b. 'Abdallāh began to rule on 6 Dhū al-Ḥijjah, 158 (October 7, 775), and reigned for ten years, one month, and twenty-two days and then died in 169, when he was forty-three years old.

A description of his burial place and those who prayed over him:

It is said that al-Mahdī died in one of the villages of Māsabadhān called al-Radhdh, and about that Bakkār b. Ribāḥ[796] said:

796. He is not noticed in *Aghānī* and not quoted elsewhere in al-Ṭabarī.

May the mercy of the Merciful One at all hours (come down)
over a corpse that decayed at Māsabadhān.
The tomb covered a fault-free man
and two palms that hasten to do kindness.

His son Hārūn prayed over him, and there was not a bier to be found to carry him on, so he was carried on a door and buried under a nut tree he used to sit under.

He was tall, of thin build, with curly hair. Opinions differ as to
[527] his coloring; some said that he was brown, and others said that he was white. Some said that he had a white spot in his right eye, and others said that it was in his left eye, and he was born in Īdhaj.[797]

Some of the Doings of al-Mahdī and Stories about Him

According to Hārūn b. Abī ʿUbaydallāh: When al-Mahdī used to sit for the *maẓālim*, he said, "Bring in the judges to me! If I only settle the *maẓālim* with their approval, it is enough."

According to al-Ḥasan b. Abī Saʿīd—ʿAlī b. Ṣāliḥ:[798] Al-Mahdī sat down one day to give rewards, which were distributed in his presence to his intimates (*khāṣṣah*) among his family and his army commanders. The names were read to him and he ordered bonuses of ten thousand and twenty thousand and similar. There came before him one of the commanders, and he said, "This man is reduced by 500," and he asked, "Why have you brought me down, O Commander of the Faithful?" and he replied, "Because I sent you against an enemy of ours and you fled," and he said, "Would it have pleased you more if I had been killed?" Al-Mahdī said, "No," and the commander went on, "By Him Who has generously bestowed the caliphate on you, if I had stood firm, I would

797. On the border between the provinces of Iṣfahān and Khūzistān, in the Zagros mountains. He was born there because his father was involved in the unsuccessful rebellion of ʿAbdallāh b. Muʿāwiyah against the Umayyads in 126–27/743–45 (Yāqūt, *Muʿjam*, I, 266–69).

798. Nothing more is known of al-Ḥasan, who contributes a number of reports to the *History*, of which this is the first. ʿAlī was the son of Ṣāliḥ, Ṣāḥib al-Muṣallā (note 153, above) and so a good source of court gossip.

have been killed." Al-Mahdī was shamed by him and said, "Give him five thousand more."

According to al-Ḥasan—'Alī b. Ṣāliḥ: Al-Mahdī was angry with one of his army commanders and had reproved him several times and said to him, "For how long will you sin against me and I forgive you?" and he replied, "May it continue forever and may God spare you to forgive us," and he repeated it a number of [528]
times, and al-Mahdī was ashamed about him and took him into favor.

According to Muḥammad b. 'Umar[799]—Ḥafṣ, mawlā of Muzaynah—his father: Hishām al-Kalbī[800] was a friend of mine, and we used to meet and tell stories and recite verses to each other. I had seen him in worn-out clothes and rags on a skinny mule, and he and his mule were obviously in need, so I was surprised when one day he met me on a light-colored mule that was one of the caliphal mules, with a saddle and bridle that belonged to the caliphate, and he was riding in fine clothes and good perfume. I showed my pleasure and then said to him, "I see obvious prosperity," and he replied, "Yes, I will tell you about it and keep it a secret. While I was in my house some days ago between the midday and afternoon prayers, al-Mahdī's messenger came to me, so I went to him and entered to him. He was sitting alone without anyone with him, and in his hands he held a letter. He said 'Come near, O Hishām,' so I came near and sat down in front of him, and he continued, 'Take this letter and read it and do not let the odious things in it prevent you from reading it.'

"I looked at the letter and, when I had read some of it, I found it odious and I threw it from my hand and cursed the author. He said, 'I told you that, if you found it odious, you should not throw it away. Read it on my orders until you reach the end.'

"I read it and it was a letter whose author had abused him savagely without sparing anything, and I said, 'O Commander of the Faithful, who is this cursed liar?' and he replied, 'The Lord of al-Andalus.'[801] I said, 'By God, O Commander of the Faithful,

---

799. Al-Wāqidī.

800. The famous historian. Nothing else is known of Ḥafṣ or his father.

801. The Umayyad ruler of Muslim Spain, at this time 'Abd al-Raḥmān b Mu'āwiyah b. Hishām (138–72/756–88).

the shame is on him and his fathers and mothers.' Then I began abusing them. He was pleased with that and said, 'I am asking you to dictate all abuse of them to a secretary.'

"He called one of the confidential secretaries and ordered him
[529] to sit down nearby, and he ordered me to go to him, and the secretary began a reply from al-Mahdī, and I dictated abuse against them in great quantity and did not spare anything until I had finished the letter. I showed it to him, and his pleasure was obvious and he went on to order that the letter be sealed and put in a bag and given to the Master of the Post and he ordered that it be hastened to al-Andalus.

"Then he ordered a cloth in which there were ten of the best robes and ten thousand *dirhams* and this mule with its saddle and bridle, and he gave me that and said to me, 'Keep silent about what you have heard.'"

According to al-Ḥasan—Miswar b. Musāwir: Al-Mahdī's agent (*wakīl*) oppressed me and was angry with me on account of an estate I had, so I went to Sallām, *ṣāḥib al-maẓālim*,[802] and complained about the oppression to him and gave him a written note. He took the note to al-Mahdī, and there were with him his paternal uncle, al-ʿAbbās b. Muḥammad; Ibn ʿUlāthah; and ʿĀfiyah the *Qāḍī*. Al-Mahdī said to me, "Come near," so I came near, and he asked, "What are you saying?" and I replied, "You have oppressed me." He said, "Are you satisfied with one of these two (*qāḍī*s)?"

"Yes," I said and he told me to approach, and I did so until I was touching the cushion, and he said, "Speak!" I said, "May God give the judge peace, he oppressed me on account of this estate of mine." The *qāḍī* then asked, "What do you say, O Commander of the Faithful?" and he replied, "It is my estate and it is in my hands," and I said, "May God give the judge peace. Ask him whether the estate passed to him before he became caliph or after."

He asked, "What do you say, O Commander of the Faithful?" He answered that it came to him after he had become caliph. The

802. Sallām al-Abrash; see note 289, above.

judge said, "Hand it over to him," and he replied, "I have done it," and al-ʿAbbās b. Muḥammad said, "O Commander of the Faithful. Indeed this *majlis* is dearer to me than twenty million *dirhams*."

According to ʿAbdallāh b. al-Rabīʿ[803]—Mujāhid, the poet:[804] Al-Mahdī went out for sport, and with him was ʿUmar b. Bazīʿ, [530] his freedman. We were cut off from the army and the people (courtiers) in the hunt, and al-Mahdī was struck by hunger and said, "Damn you! Do you have anything?" and he said, "No, nothing. I see a hut, and I think it has a vegetable patch." We went in its direction, and there was a Nabaṭī[805] in a cottage and a vegetable patch. We greeted him and he returned the greeting, and we asked if he had anything to eat. He replied, "Yes, I have *rubaythā'* (a kind of small fish) and barley bread," and al-Mahdī asked, "If you have oil you will have done everything," and he said "Yes." "And leeks?" "As you like, and dates." He hurried to the vegetable patch and brought them greens and leeks and onions, and they ate a large and satisfying meal. Al-Mahdī said to ʿUmar b. Bazīʿ, "Say a poem about this," and he said:

He who prepares a meal of *rubaythā'* in oil, barley bread, and leeks
deserves a blow or two for the evil of his action, or three.

Al-Mahdī said, "It is a shame your poem did not go like this:

deserves a *bidrah*[806] or two for the excellence of his action, or three."

The escort and treasury and servants came by, and al-Mahdī ordered that the Nabaṭī be given three *bidrahs* (30,000 *dirhams*), and he went on his way.

According to Muḥammad b. ʿAbdallāh—Abū Ghānim: Zayd al-Hilālī[807] was a noble, generous, and famous man of the Banū Hilāl, and the inscription on his seal read, "He is successful, O

803. B. ʿUbaydallāh al-Ḥārithī, see note 34, above.
804. He is not noticed in *Aghānī* and does not appear again in the *History*.
805. One of the indigenous, non-Arab inhabitants of Iraq.
806. A large sum of money, 10,000 *dirhams*.
807. Despite the caliph's encomium, Zayd has left no other trace in the historical record.

Zayd, who causeth his work to grow,"[808] and news of this reached al-Mahdī, who said, "The inscription on Zayd al-Hilālī's seal reads, 'He is successful, O Zayd, whose work has a good reputation.'"

According to al-Ḥasan al-Waṣīf: In the reign of al-Mahdī we were struck by a wind so strong that we thought that we would be
[531] swept away to the Last Judgment, so I went out to look for the Commander of the Faithful and I found him lying, his cheek on the ground, saying, "O God, preserve Muḥammad in his people! O God, do not let our enemies among the peoples rejoice! O God, if you have taken the world because of my sin, my forelock is in your hands!" We remained only a little time before the wind disappeared and what we were in vanished.

According to al-Mawṣilī—'Abd al-Ṣamad b. 'Alī: I said to al-Mahdī, "O Commander of the Faithful, we people of the family have been made to imbibe into our hearts the love of our freedmen and the giving of precedence to them. What you have in this respect has gone too far. You have given them charge of all your affairs and you have favored them by night and day, and I fear a change of heart among your soldiers and your commanders from the people of Khurāsān."

He replied, "O Abū Muḥammad, the freedmen deserve that. There is no one who combines these qualities except these freedmen. I can hold audience for the common people and summon a freedman of mine and raise him up so that his knee rubs against mine, and then he gets up from that audience and I can ask him to look after my mount and he does so and does not think himself to be above that. They are not proud with me about that, and if I wanted that from anyone else he would say, 'Where is the person whose job it is and the first to answer your call, and where is he who is first to respond to your summons?[809] I would not shove him out of the way.'"

According to 'Alī b. Muḥammad—al-Faḍl b. al-Rabī': Al-Mahdī said to 'Abdallāh b. Mālik, "Wrestle with this freedman of mine," so he wrestled with him and he took him by the neck, and al-

---

808. The inscription was taken from *Qur'ān*, XCI: 9. The sense of the anecdote is not clear.

809. The text here presents some problems: I have incorporated some of the suggestions made in *Gloss.*, s.v. *'ain*, CXXIV–CXXV, where the matter is discussed.

Mahdī said, "Press hard," and, when ʿAbdallāh saw that, he took him by his leg and he fell on his head and he threw him on the ground. ʿAbdallāh said to al-Mahdī, "O Commander of the Faithful, I left you while I was one of the most beloved of men to you, and yet you still side with your freedman against me." He said, "Have you not heard the words of the poet?

Your freedmen should not be oppressed while you behold, [532]
for the oppression of a certain people's freedman is like the cutting off of the nose."

According to Abū al-Khaṭṭāb:[810] When death was approaching al-Qāsim b. Mujāshiʿ al-Tamīmī,[811] of the people of Marw of the village known as Bārān, he wrote a testament for al-Mahdī: "There is no god but He; that is the witness of God, His angels, and those endued with knowledge, standing firm on justice. There is no god but He, the Exalted in Power, the Wise. The religion before God is Islam . . ."[812] to the end of the verse. Then he wrote that al-Qāsim b. Mujāshiʿ bore witness to that and that Muḥammad was his slave and his messenger, that ʿAlī b. Abī Ṭālib was the heir of the Prophet of God and the inheritor of the imāmate after him.[813] The testament was presented to al-Mahdī and, when he reached this point, he threw it away and did not look at it.

Abū al-Khaṭṭāb said: This remained in the heart of Abū ʿUbaydallāh, the *wazīr*, and, when his death approached, he wrote this Qur'ānic verse in his testament.

According to al-Haytham b. ʿAdī: A man came in to al-Mahdī and said, "O Commander of the Faithful, al-Mahdī cursed me and called my mother a whore; either you should order me to exonerate him from his sin, or you should give me compensation and I shall ask God to forgive him." He asked why he had cursed him and the man replied, "I cursed an enemy of his in his presence and he was angry with me."

---

810. Ḥamzah b. ʿAlī contributes a few scattered narratives to the *History*.

811. Al-Tamīmī. He had been one of the original agents (*nuqabā'*) of the ʿAbbāsids in Khurāsān and had fought in the ʿAbbāsid armies beside Qaḥṭabah, so his disaffection was all the more striking.

812. *Qur'ān*, III: 18–19.

813. That is to say that the ʿAlids, not the ʿAbbāsids, were the rightful leaders of the Muslim community.

"Who was this enemy that he was angry with you for cursing him?" he asked. "Ibrāhīm b. 'Abdallāh b. Ḥasan," the man replied. "Ibrāhīm is a very close relation and most worthy of al-Manṣūr's kinship rights. If your cursing was as you allege, he was protecting his kin and defending his honor. What is wrong with someone who comes to the aid of his own cousin (*ibn 'amm*)?"[814] He said, "He was his enemy," but al-Mahdī replied, "He did not come to his aid out of hostility (to you) but because of his kinship." He silenced the man and, when he turned to go, al-Mahdī said, "Perhaps you wanted something and you were not able to find a better pretext for coming to me than this claim?" and he
[533] replied, "Yes." Then he smiled and ordered that he be given five thousand *dirhams*.

A man was brought to al-Mahdī who claimed to be a prophet and when he saw him he said, "Are you a prophet?" and the man replied, "Yes," so he asked to whom he had been sent, and he replied, "Have you left me to go to those to whom I was sent? I was despatched in the morning, and you arrested me in the evening and put me in prison." Al-Mahdī laughed at him and let him go.

According to Abū al-Ash'ath al-Kindī[815]—Sulaymān b. 'Abdallāh—al-Rabī': I saw al-Mahdī praying in a hall on a moonlit night, and I do not know whether he was more beautiful or the hall or the moon or his clothes. He read this verse: "Then it is to be expected of you, if ye were put into authority, that ye will do mischief in the land, and break your ties of kith and kin?"[816] He completed his prayers and turned to me and said, "O Rabī'," and I said, "Your servant, O Commander of the Faithful," and he said, "Bring me Mūsā," and stood up to pray. I asked (myself), "Which Mūsā, his son Mūsā[817] or Mūsā b. Ja'far?"[818] (who was imprisoned at my house) and I began to think and came to the conclusion that it was Mūsā b. Ja'far, and I brought him. Then he broke off his

---

814. Stressing the unity of the Family of the Prophet, despite Ibrāhīm's rebellion in 145/768.

815. Presumably a member of the family of al-Ash'ath b. Qays; see above, note 580.

816. *Qur'ān*, XLVII: 22.

817. The future caliph al-Hādī.

818. Mūsā al-Kāẓim, son of Ja'far al-Ṣādiq. Mūsā is held to have been killed by Hārūn in 186/802 and is venerated by twelver Shī'is as the seventh *imām*.

prayer and said, "O Mūsā I was reading this verse 'Then it is to be expected of you, if ye were put into authority, that ye will do mischief in the land and break your ties of kith and kin,' and I was afraid that I had broken the tie of kinship with you, so confirm that you will not rise in rebellion against me," and he said, "Yes," and confirmed it and he released him.

According to Ibrāhīm b. Abī 'Alī—Sulaymān b. Dāwūd: I heard al-Mahdī reciting quickly in the *miḥrāb* of the mosque in a unique chant "Hast thou not turned thy vision to those who were given a portion of the Book? They believe in sorcery and evil," in the chapter of the women.[819]

According to 'Alī b. Muḥammad b. Sulaymān—my father: I came into the presence of al-Mahdī and he was sitting for the *maẓālim*. A man from the family of al-Zubayr[820] approached him and mentioned an estate that one of the kings of the Banū Umayyah—I do not know whether it was al-Walīd[821] or Sulaymān[822]—had confiscated from his father. He ordered Abū 'Ubaydallāh to extract its record from the old *dīwān*. He did that and read the record to al-Mahdī that said that it was included among a number of them that 'Umar b. 'Abd al-'Azīz[823] had not seen fit to return. Al-Mahdī said, "O Zubayrī, this 'Umar b. 'Abd al-'Azīz, who was one of your tribe of Quraysh, do you know why he did not see fit to return it?" and he asked, "Do you approve of all the acts of 'Umar?" and al-Mahdī asked, "What acts of his do you not approve of?" "One of those was that he apportioned to the prematurely born baby of the Banū Umayyah, while in his infant clothes, a share of the most honorable *'aṭā'*[824] and apportioned an old man of the Banū Hāshim sixty." Al-Mahdī said, "O Mu'āwiyah, did 'Umar do that?" and he replied, "Yes," so he said, "Restore his estate to the Zubayrī." [534]

819. *Qur'ān*, IV: 51.

820. Ibn al-'Awwām, the Prophet's companion. The family's estates were confiscated after the unsuccessful rebellion of his son 'Abdallāh b. al-Zubayr against the Umayyad caliph 'Abd al-Malik.

821. B. 'Abd al-Malik, Umayyad caliph 86–96/705–15.

822. B. 'Abd al-Malik, Umayyad caliph 96–99/715–17.

823. Umayyad caliph, 99–101/717–20, respected by the 'Abbāsids as the only righteous Umayyad.

824. The highest level of salary.

ʿUmar b. Shabbah—Abū Salamah al-Ghifārī: Al-Mahdī wrote to Jaʿfar b. Sulaymān, who was governor of Medina, ordering him to bring a group of people who were suspected of Qadar.[825] Among them were ʿAbdallāh b. Abī ʿUbaydah b. Muḥammad b. ʿAmmār b. Yāsir,[826] ʿAbdallāh b. Yazīd b. Qays al-Hudhalī,[827] ʿĪsā b. Yazīd b. Da'b al-Laythī,[828] and Ibrāhīm b. Muḥammad b. Abī Bakr al-Usāmī.[829] They were brought in to al-Mahdī and ʿAbdallāh b. Abī ʿUbaydah among them exculpated himself to him and said, "This was the faith of your father and his belief," and he replied, "No, that of my paternal uncle Dāwūd,"[830] but ʿAbdallāh said, "No, your father was of this belief of ours, and it was his faith," and he let them go.

According to ʿAlī b. Muḥammad b. Sulaymān al-Nawfalī—his father—Muḥammad b. ʿAbdallāh b. Muḥammad b. ʿAlī b.
[535] ʿAbdallāh b. Jaʿfar b. Abī Ṭālib:[831] I saw as a sleeper sees at the end of the reign of the Banū Umayyah; it was as if I had entered the mosque of the Prophet of God and I raised my head and looked at the writing in mosaic that was in the mosque and there was what the Commander of the Faithful al-Walīd b. ʿAbd al-Malik had ordered.[832] There was a voice saying, "Wipe out this writing and write in its place the name of a man from the Banū Hāshim called Muḥammad."

I said, "I am Muḥammad and I am of the Banū Hāshim. Whose son is it?" and the voice replied, "Son of ʿAbdallāh," and I said, "I am son of ʿAbdallāh; son of whom?" and the voice said, "Son of Muḥammad," and I said, "I am the son of Muḥammad; son of whom?" and the voice said, "Son of ʿAlī," and I said, "I am son

825. A belief in human free will, which came to be considered heretical; see *EI*², s.v. "Ḳadariya."

826. A traditionist occasionally quoted in the *History*.

827. No more is known about him. It is suggested in the Addenda that the name should be Qanṭash.

828. A traditionist quoted by al-Ṭabarī who later became a valued companion of the caliph al-Hādī.

829. Not recorded elsewhere.

830. B. ʿAlī al-ʿAbbāsī; see note 430, above.

831. A descendant of ʿAlī's brother Jaʿfar; the Jaʿfarids were sometimes thought of as possible candidates for the caliphate. He and his forebears had identical names to those of the caliph al-Mahdī for five generations.

832. Umayyad caliph 86–96/705–15.

of ʿAlī; son of whom?" and the voice said, "Son of ʿAbdallāh," and I said, "I am son of ʿAbdallāh; son of whom?" and the voice said, "Son of ʿAbbās." If I had not reached ʿAbbās, I would have had no doubts that I was the lord of the affair.

I told the story of this dream at the time, and we did not know al-Mahdī and people told it, so he entered the mosque of the Prophet and raised his eyes and looked and saw the name of al-Walīd and he said, "Indeed I still see the name of al-Walīd in the mosque of the Prophet of God." He called for a chair, and it was put before him in the court of the mosque and he said, "I will not leave until it is wiped out and my name is put in its place." He ordered that workmen and ladders and the necessary equipment be brought, and he did not leave until it was changed and his name was written.[833]

According to Aḥmad b. al-Haytham al-Qurashī—ʿAbdallāh b. Muḥammad b. ʿAṭā': Al-Mahdī went out after the stillness of the night to walk around the house (the Kaʿbah) and he heard a bedouin woman by the side of the mosque, and she was saying, "My people are poverty-stricken, eyes glance at them with repugnance, debts weigh on them, famines bite them hard, their men have passed away and their wealth has gone, and their dependents have grown numerous. They have become wanderers far [536]
from home and emaciated phantoms of the road. They are God's and the Prophet's trust that he ordered to help. Is there one to order good for me? May God protect him in his journey and assist his people in his absence." He ordered Nuṣayr al-Khādim to pay her five hundred *dirhams*.

According to ʿAlī b. Muḥammad b. Sulaymān—his father: The first person to use Ṭabarī furnishings[834] was al-Mahdī. This was when his father had ordered him to settle at al-Rayy and he was given the Ṭabarī from Ṭabaristān and put ice and reeds[835] around it until canvas was introduced to them (for cooling), and the Ṭabarī was pleasant for them in it.

According to Muḥammad b. Ziyād—al-Mufaḍḍal: Al-Mahdī

833. Cf. the surviving inscription in the Dome of the Rock in Jerusalem, where ʿAbd al-Malik's name has been replaced by that of al-Ma'mūn.

834. That is, textiles from Ṭabaristān in northern Iran.

835. See the description of al-Manṣūr's coolhouse, p. 121.

said to me, "Collect for me proverbs that you hear from the *badw* and that you consider authentic." I wrote proverbs for him and accounts of the wars of the Arabs that were mentioned in them, and he gave me grants and treated me very well.

According to 'Alī b. Muḥammad: One of the descendants of 'Abd al-Raḥmān b. Samurah[836] sought to rebel in Syria and he was brought to al-Mahdī. He released him and was generous to him and brought him close in his audience, and he said to him one day, "Recite the *qaṣīdah* of Zuhayr with the rhyme in *rā'*,[837] which goes:

Whose tents are those on the mountain top of al-Ḥajr?"

and he recited it. The Samurī said, "Gone are the people who deserve to be eulogized by such poetry." Al-Mahdī was angry with him and considered him ignorant and thrust him aside but did not punish him, and the people considered him stupid.

It was said that Abū 'Awn 'Abd al-Malik b. Yazīd was ill and al-Mahdī visited him and there was a shabby house, badly built,
[537] and the arch of the *ṣuffah* was made of mud brick. There was a luxurious tent in his audience. Al-Mahdī sat down on a pillow and Abū 'Awn sat in front of him, and al-Mahdī treated him with respect and commiserated with him about his illness. Abū 'Awn said, "I hope for good health from God, O Commander of the Faithful, and that He will not cause me to die in my bed before I am killed in your service. I trust that I will not die before I show God in your service what He is entitled to, for indeed we have been succored and given succor."

Al-Mahdī expressed a very good opinion of him and said, "Request from me what you need and ask me for what you want, and I will provide for you in life and death. By God, if your wealth fails in any way, make a request and I will indeed fulfill it, whatever it is. Say and request."

Abū 'Awn thanked him and blessed him and said, "O Commander of the Faithful, my request is that you show favor to

836. B. Ḥabīb b. 'Abd Shams. Ḥabīb was a brother of that Umayyad after whom the dynasty was named.

837. In the classical Arabic ode (*qaṣīdah*) all the lines end with the same rhyme.

'Abdallāh b. Abī 'Awn and summon him, for your anger against him has lasted a long time."

Al-Mahdī replied, "O Abū 'Awn, he is on the wrong road and is against our belief and your belief. He defames the two *shaykh*s, Abū Bakr and 'Umar,[838] and uses evil language about them."

Abū 'Awn said, "He is, by God, O Commander of the Faithful, of the belief for which we rebelled and that we summoned people to.[839] If you have engendered any change, order us to do what you wish, so that we can obey you."

Al-Mahdī went away and, when he was on the road, he said to one of his children and family who were with him, "Would that you were like Abū 'Awn. By God, I did not expect that his house would be built of materials other than gold and silver. You, if you found a *dirham*, would build in teak and gold."

According to Abū 'Abdallāh—his father: Al-Mahdī preached the sermon one day and said, "Servants of God, fear God," and a man stood up and said "And you too fear God, for you are acting unjustly!" He was arrested and brought, and they set about goading him with the points of their scabbards. When he was brought into al-Mahdī, he said, "O son of a whore, you said to me when I was on the pulpit, 'Fear God!'" and he said, "How bad! If this insult [538]
came from someone other than you, I would have been appealing for your assistance against him." He said, "I think you are only a Nabaṭī," and he replied, "It is the most positive form of proof against you if a Nabaṭī orders you to fear God." He saw the man after that, and he was talking about what happened between him and al-Mahdī. My father said, "I was present with him at the time, only I did not hear the words."

According to Hārūn b. Maymūn al-Khuzā'ī—Abū Khuzaymah al-Bādhghīsī:[840] Al-Mahdī said, "Nobody seeks my help with a petition or offers an excuse that is more pressing than he, reminding me of a favor I did him so that it would be followed by its

838. An indication of 'Alid sympathies since Abū Bakr and 'Umar, the first two caliphs, were held by some to have deprived 'Alī of his rightful inheritance, the caliphate.

839. This seems to mean that the original beliefs of the 'Abbāsid movement agreed with this but that the view had subsequently been modified.

840. Neither of these is recorded elsewhere.

sister (i.e., one like it) and so good would be done to its asker because withholding of later things removes gratitude for earlier ones."

According to Khālid b. Yazīd b. Wahb b. Jarīr—his father: Bashshār b. Burd b. Yarjūkh[841] had attacked Ṣāliḥ b. Dāwūd b. Ṭahmān, the brother of Ya'qūb b. Dāwūd, in a poem when he was appointed governor of al-Baṣrah saying:

They carried Ṣāliḥ your brother onto the pulpits,
and the pulpits groaned because of your brother.[842]

Ya'qūb b. Dāwūd heard of this attack and came into al-Mahdī and said, "O Commander of the Faithful, this blind infidel has attacked the Commander of the Faithful," and he said, "Damn you, what did he say?" and he replied, "Let the Commander of the Faithful excuse me from reciting it," but he insisted on his reciting it so he said:

A caliph who fornicates with his paternal aunts
and who plays with a child's toys and polo mallets,
May God give us another in his place.
And Mūsā thrusts into al-Khayzurān's cunt.

He sent for him to be brought, and Ya'qūb b. Dāwūd was afraid
[539] that he would come to al-Mahdī and eulogize him and he would forgive him, so he sent someone to meet him in al-Baṭīḥa[843] at Kharrārah.

According to 'Abdallāh b. 'Amr—his grandfather, Abū al-Ḥayy al-'Absī: When Marwān b. Abī Ḥafṣah came in to al-Mahdī, he recited his poem in which he says: How can it be that the inheritance of the paternal uncles should pass to the sons of the daughter? This is something that does not happen.[844]

He rewarded him with seventy thousand *dirhams*, and Marwān said:

---

841. The celebrated poet; see *Aghānī*, Būlāq, III, 19; Beirut; III, 129.

842. The pulpit (*minbar*) is used here to symbolize the authority of the governor.

843. The great swamp of southern Iraq, between Baghdad and al-Baṣrah. *Aghānī* expands the text to add, "He met him and whipped him so that he killed him and threw him into the swamp at the place called Kharārah."

844. Al-'Abbās was the paternal uncle of the Prophet and, the 'Abbāsids argued, his true heir, rather than his daughter Fāṭimah, who married 'Alī.

With seventy thousand he has made me wealthy with his gifts,
and no poet before me has ever acquired as much.

According to Aḥmad b. Sulaymān—Abū ʿAdnān al-Sulamī: Al-Mahdī asked ʿUmārah b. Ḥamzah, who was most sensitive of the people in poetry, and he replied that it was Wālibah b. al-Ḥubāb al-Asadī[845] and he was the one who said:

She is sinless, but she has
love, which, like the points of spears,
Strikes fire in the heart and the bowels,
for the heart is the wounded part.

He said, "You told the truth, by God," so ʿUmārah asked, "What is stopping you from taking him as a boon companion, for he is a noble Arab and elegant poet?" and al-Mahdī replied, "What prevents me, by God, from making him a boon companion are his words:

I said to our cupbearer when we were alone
'Bring your head near mine like that.
And lie on your front for me for a while,
for I am a man who has sex with my companion.'

Do you want to be his companion on this condition?"

According to Muḥammad b. Sallām: There was in the time of al-Mahdī a foolish person who used to recite poetry in order to praise al-Mahdī. He was brought in to him and asked to recite a poem in which he said "*Wa jawārin zafarātin*," and al-Mahdī said to him, "What is the meaning of *zafarāt*?" and he answered, "Do you not know that, O Commander of the Faithful?" and he said, "No, by God," and the poet said, "And you are the Commander of the Faithful and the lord of the Muslims and the son of the paternal uncle of the Prophet of God and you do not know it? Am I expected to know it? Not at all, by God." [540]

According to Ibn Sallām—more than one person: Ṭurayḥ b. Ismāʿīl al-Thaqafī[846] came in to al-Mahdī, gave his genealogy to

845. ʿAbbāsid poet, noted for his wine drinking and pederasty, eventually forced to retire to his home town of al-Kūfah by the hostility of Abū al-ʿAtāhiyyah and Bashshār b. Burd; *Aghānī*, Būlāq, XVI, 148; Beirut, XVIII, 43.

846. A well-known poet at the court of al-Walīd b. Yazīd who died in the reign of al-Mahdī; see *Aghānī*, Būlāq, IV, 74, Beirut, IV, 304.

him, and asked if he would hear some of his poetry, and he said, "Are you not the one who said to al-Walīd b. Yazīd:

You are the son of the wide-open spaces,
and the winding track and the path through the sands are not tramped upon to reach you?

And, by God, you will never say anything like that to me. I will not hear a poem from you, but if you wish I will make you a grant."

It is said that al-Mahdī ordered a fast in the year (1)66 to ask for rain for the people on Wednesday, and on Monday night (Tuesday night in the Arabic terminology) there was a snowfall, and Laqīṭ b. Bukayr al-Muḥāribī said about that:

O Imām of right guidance, you watered us with rain,
and, because of you, hardship was removed from us.
You spent the night concerned with protecting them while the people
were sleeping, covered by the darkness.
They slept when your night grew long among them;
yours are the fear, the humble prayers, and the weeping.
Their affairs gave you concern because of the foolishness
of the crowd, who disobeyed and acted evilly.
We were watered and we had been smitten by drought, and we said,
"A severe (red) year that has become worse"
By a prayer that you sincerely offered in the blackness of the night
to God, and the call was answered
By snows that give life to the ground, so that
in the morning it was a green flower.

[541] It is said that the people in the days of al-Mahdī fasted for the month of Ramaḍān in the height of summer. Abū Dulāmah was seeking a reward for that, and al-Mahdī promised him one, so he wrote a note to al-Mahdī in which he complained of his sufferings from the heat and the fast, and in that he said:

I call on you in the name of the kinship that links us
in closeness both near and far.

I implore you to hear, you the most generous man who walked,
from a singer who hopes for the reward of a singer.
The fast has come, and I fasted it devotedly,
hoping for the recompense of the devoted faster.
I bowed in prayer until my forehead cracked
from what I imposed on myself of butting the mosque.

When al-Mahdī read the note, he summoned him and said, "What kinship is there between me and you, O son of fornication?" and he replied, "The kinship with Adam and Eve," and al-Mahdī laughed at him and ordered that he be given his reward.

According to ʿAlī b. Muḥammad—his father—Ibrāhīm b. Khālid al-Muʿayṭī:[847] I came in to al-Mahdī, and my singing had been described to him and he asked me about singing and about my knowledge of it and asked me if I sang the *nawāqīs*,[848] and I said, "Yes, and the *ṣalīb*[849] too, O Commander of the Faithful." Then he disregarded me, and I was told that he said, "Muʿayṭī, I have no need of him among those who are brought to me in my solitude and I do not like his company, and Maʿbad the singer has the [542]
nawāqīs in this poem:

Ask the abode of Laylā. Does it answer and speak?
How can the desert plain reply?
Does an abode reply that looks like a blank paper
because of its long decay and the length of its survival?"

According to Qaʿnab b. Muḥriz Abū ʿAmr al-Bāhilī—al-Aṣmaʿī: I saw Ḥakam al-Wādī[850] when al-Mahdī was traveling to Jerusalem, and he accosted him on the road. He had some little poems, and he took out his tambourine to play it and said, "I am the poet who said:

---

847. Not noticed in *Aghānī*.

848. A type of poetry but also the board on which the Christians strike to summon people to church.

849. The cross.

850. Al-Ḥakam b. Maymūn, mawlā of al-Walīd b. ʿAbd al-Malik. His father was al-Walīd's barber, and he began his career as a camel driver taking oil from Wādī al-Qurra to Medina. He sang for every caliph from al-Walīd b. Yazīd to Hārūn, in whose reign he died. See *Aghānī*, Būlāq, VI, 64, Beirut, VI, 264.

When will the bride come out?
Her confinement has lasted long.
Dawn has come near or has actually appeared,
and she has not completed her dressing."

The guard rushed to him, and he cried out and they desisted. He made inquiries about him, and it was said that he was Ḥakam al-Wādī, and he was brought in to him and he gave him a grant.

According to ʿAlī b. Muḥammad—his father: Al-Mahdī went into one of his houses one day, and there was a Christian slave girl of his and her bosom was wide and the part between her breasts was uncovered and there was a cross of gold hanging there. He thought it was very beautiful and stretched out his hand toward it and pulled it out and took it. She wept for the cross, and al-Mahdī said about that:

One day I contended with her at pulling the cross from her, and she said,
"Woe to me, Do not you think the cross licit?"

He sent for one of the poets and gave him a gift and ordered him to sing it, and he was proud about this song.

He said: I heard my father say that al-Mahdī observed a slave girl who was wearing a crown in which there was a narcissus of gold and silver, and he thought it very beautiful and said:

[543] How beautiful is the narcissus in the crown!

He was unable to continue, and he asked who at court (could complete the line), and they said, ʿAbdallāh b. Mālik,[851] so he summoned him and said, "I saw a slave girl of mine with a beautiful crown on her and I said:

How beautiful is the narcissus in the crown!

Are you able to add to it?" and he replied, "Yes, O Commander of the Faithful, but let me go out to think about it," and al-Mahdī said, "Please yourself!" He went out and sent for the tutor of one

---

851. A military man, for many years chief of police; poetry does not seem to have been his forte. For his ability as a wrestler, see above, pp. 250–51.

of his children and asked him to complete it and gave him a gift, and he said:

> on (her) brow that shines like ivory.

And he completed it up to four verses, and 'Abdallāh sent it to al-Mahdī, and al-Mahdī sent him forty thousand and he gave the tutor four thousand and kept the rest for himself, and there is a well-known tune about it.

According to Aḥmad b. Mūsā b. Muḍar Abū 'Alī: Al-Tawwazī recited poetry to me by al-Mahdī about Ḥasanah, his slave girl:

> I see water, and I am afflicted by severe thirst,
> but there is no path to reach it.
> Is it enough for you that you enslave me
> while all people are my slaves?
> If you were to cut off my hands and feet,
> I would say from excess of pleasure "O, more!"

According to 'Alī b. Muḥammad—his father: I saw al-Mahdī when he had entered al-Baṣrah by Sikkat Quraysh, and I saw him going along and in front of him was al-Banūqah between him and the chief of police. She was wearing a black cloak (*qibā*) and a sword, as pages do, and I could see some signs of her breasts on her chest.

According to 'Alī—his father: Al-Mahdī came to al-Baṣrah and passed along the Sikkat Quraysh, where our house was,[852] and the governors never used to go along there when they arrived. They used to think it an evil omen; scarcely a governor who passed along it remained in office except for a short time before he was deposed, and no caliph ever passed along it except al- [544]
Mahdī. They used to go along the Sikkat of 'Abd al-Raḥmān b. Samurah, which ran parallel with the Sikkat Quraysh. I saw al-Mahdī going along and 'Abdallāh b. Mālik, who was in command of the police, was going in front of him with the *ḥarbah* in his hand, and his daughter al-Banūqah went before him, between him and the chief of police, dressed as a young man with a black cloak

---

852. 'Alī b. Muḥammad al-Nawfalī was a Qurashī, which is why he lived in that street.

and belt and Shāshiyyah, wearing a sword, and I saw that her breasts had raised the cloak by their swelling.

Al-Banūqah was brown, of beautiful stature, and charming and, when she died, in Baghdad, al-Mahdī showed grief the like of which has never been heard of. He sat for the people to offer their condolences, and he gave orders that no one should be kept away from him and large numbers of people came to offer their condolences and they made great efforts with their eloquence. Some of the people there were criticized by those with knowledge and literary education (*adab*), but they agreed that they had never heard of condolences more succinct or more eloquent than those of Shabīb b. Shaybah, who said, "O Commander of the Faithful, God is better for her than you, and the rewards of God are better for you than her, and I ask God not to make you sad and not to torment you."

According to Ṣabbāḥ b. ʿAbd al-Raḥmān—his father: When al-Banūqah, daughter of al-Mahdī, died, Shabīb b. Shaybah came in to him and said, "May God give you recompense, O Commander of the Faithful, for what you have been deprived of and follow you with fortitude. May He not wear out your courage by adversity or deprive you of the benefits of the reward of God, which is better for you than her, and the mercy of God, which is better for her than you. It is more worthy to be given patience for what cannot be returned."

Bibliography of Cited Works

Primary Sources: Texts and Translations

Agapius of Manbij. *Kitāb al-'Unwān*. Ed., with French translation, A. Vasiliev, in *Patrologia Orientalis*, vol. VIII (Paris, 1911).

al-Aghānī; see al-Iṣfahānī.

al-Azdī, Abū Zakariyyā' Yazīd b. Muḥammad. *Ta'rīkh al-Mawṣil*. Ed. A. Ḥabībah (Cairo, 1387/1967).

al-Balādhurī, Aḥmad b. Yaḥyā. *Futūḥ al-Buldān*. Ed S. Munajjid (Cairo, 1957). English translation, P. K. Hitti and F. C. Murgotten, *The Origins of the Islamic State*, 2 vols. (New York, 1916–24).

Caskel, W. *Ǧamharat an-Nasab. Das genealogische Werk des Hišām ibn Muḥammad al-Kalbī* (Leiden, 1966).

al-Dhahabī, Muḥammad b. Aḥmad. *Tārīkh al-Islām* (Cairo, 1967–69).

Fihrist; see Ibn al-Nadim.

Freytag, G. W. *Arabum Proverbia*, 3 vols. (Bonn, 1838–43).

Gardīzī, 'Abd al-Ḥayy b. al-Ḍaḥḥāk. *Zayn al-Akhbār*. King's College, Cambridge, ms. 213.

al-Hamadhānī, Muḥammad b. Isḥāq, known as Ibn al-Faqīh. *Kitāb al-Buldān*. Ed. M. J. de Goeje (Leiden, 1885).

Ḥamzah al-Iṣfahānī. *Tarīkh sinī al-mulūk al-arḍ wa'l-anbiyā*. Ed. Y. al-Maskūnī (Beirut, 1961).

Ibn al-Athīr, 'Izz al-Dīn. *al-Kāmil fī'l-Tārīkh*. Ed C. J. Tornberg; 13 vols. (Leiden, 1866–71; reprint, Beirut, 1965–67).

Ibn Hishām, *Sīrah Rasūl Allah*. Ed. F. Wüstenfeld (Gottingen, 1858–60). English translations, A. Guillaume, *Life of Muhammad* (London, 1955).

Ibn al-Kalbī; see Caskel.
Ibn Khallikān, Aḥmad b. Muḥammad. *Wafayāt al-Aʿyan*. Ed. I. ʿAbbās (Beirut, 1968–72). English translation, McGuckin de Slane, *Ibn Khallikan's Biographical Dictionary*, 4 vols. (Paris, 1842–71).
Ibn al-Nadīm, Muḥammad b. Isḥāq. *Kitāb al-Fihrist*. English translation, *The Fihrist of al-Nadīm*, 2 vols. (New York, 1970).
Ibn Sallām, Muḥammad al-Jumaḥī. *Ṭabaqāt Fuḥūl al-Shu'arā'*. Ed. M. M. Shakir (Cairo, 1952).
al-Iṣfahānī, Abū'l-Faraj ʿAlī b. al-Ḥusayn. *Kitāb al-Aghānī*, 20 vols. (Būlāq, 1285–86/1868–70); 23 vols. (Beirut, 1375–80/1955–60).
———. *Maqātil al-Ṭālibiyyīn*. Ed. A. Saqr (Cairo, 1949).
al-Jāḥiẓ, ʿAmr b. Baḥr. *Manāqib al-Turk*. Ed. G. van Vloten, in *Tria Opuscula Auctore Abu Othman Amr b. Bahr al-Djahiz Basrensi* (Leiden, 1903).
al-Jahshiyārī. Muḥammad b. ʿAbdūs. *Kitāb al-Wuzarā'*. Ed. M. al-Saqqa et al. (Cairo, 1938).
al-Khalīfah b. Khayyāṭ. *Tārīkh*. Ed. S. Zakkar, 2 vols. (Damascus, 1967–68).
al-Khaṭib al-Baghdādī. *Tārīkh Baghdād* (Beirut, 1967).
al-Kindī, Muḥammad b. Yūsuf. *The Governors and Judges of Egypt*. Ed. R. Guest (Gibb Memorial Series, XIX; London, 1912).
Mālik b. Anas. *al-Muwaṭṭā'*. Ed. Muḥammad Fu'ād ʿAbd al-Baqī (Cairo, 1951).
Muḥammad b. Ḥabīb. *Kitāb al-Muḥabbar*. Ed. I. Lichtenstädter (Hyderabad, 1949).
Pseudo Dionysius of Tell-Mahré. *Chronique*. French translation, J. Chabot, (Paris, 1895).
al-ʿUyūn wa'l-Ḥadā'iq. Ed., M. J. de Goeje (Leiden, 1869).
al-Wāqidī, Muḥammad b. ʿUmar. *Kitāb al-Maghāzī*. Ed. M. Jones (London, 1966).
al-Yaʿqūbī, Aḥmad b. Isḥāq. *al-Buldān*. Ed. M. J. de Goeje (Leiden, 1892). French translation, G. Wiet, *Les Pays* (Paris, 1937).
———. *al-Tārīkh*. Ed. M. T. Houtsma (Leiden, 1883).
Yāqūt, Yaʿqūb b. ʿAbdallāh. *Mu'jam al-Buldān*. Ed. F. Wüstenfeld, 5 vols. (Leipzig, 186–73; Beirut, 1955–57).

Secondary Sources and Reference Works

Adams, R. M. *The Land behind Baghdad* (Chicago, 1965).
Ahsan, M. M. *Social Life under the Abbasids* (London and New York, 1979).
Barthold, V. *Turkestan Down to the Mongol Invasions* (London, 1928).

Bosworth, C. E. *Sistan under the Arabs* (Rome, 1968).
Brooks, E. W., "Byzantines and Arabs in the Time of the Early Abbasids," *English Historical Review*, XV (1900): 728–47.
Cahen, C. "Fiscalité, Antagonismes sociaux en Haute-Mesopotamie au temps des premiers Abbasides d'après Dénys de Tell-Mahré," *Arabica*, I (1954): 136–52.
Creswell, K. A. C. *Early Muslim Architecture*, 2 vols. (Oxford, 1932–40).
Crone, P. *Slaves on Horses* (Cambridge, 1980).
——— and M. Hinds. *God's Caliph* (Cambridge, 1986).
Daniel, E. L. *The Political and Social History of Khurasan Under Abbasid Rule* (Minneapolis and Chicago, 1979).
Dietrich, A. "Das politische Testament des zweiten 'Abbasidenkalifen al-Mansur," *Der Islam*, XXX (1952): 133–65.
Groom, N. *Frankincense and Myrrh* (London and New York, 1981).
Honigmann, E. *Die Ostgrenze des byzantinischen Reiches* (Brussels, 1961).
Kennedy, H. "Central Government and Provincial Élites in the Early 'Abbasid Caliphate," *Bulletin of the School of Oriental and African Studies*, XLIV (1981): 26–38.
———. *The Early 'Abbasid Caliphate: A Political History* (London and Totowa, 1981).
Lane, E. W. *An Arabic–English Lexicon*, 8 vols. (London, 1863–93; reprint, Cambridge, 1984).
Lassner, J. *The Shaping of 'Abbāsid Rule* (Princeton, 1980).
———. *The Topography of Baghdad in the Early Middle Ages* (Detroit, 1970).
Le Strange, G. *Baghdad during the Abbasid Caliphate* (Oxford, 1900).
———. *The Lands of the Eastern Caliphate* (Cambridge, 1905; reprint, London, 1966).
———. *Palestine under the Moslems* (London, 1890; reprint, Beirut, 1965).
Morony, M. *Iraq after the Muslim Conquest* (Princeton, 1984).
Omar, F. *The Abbasid Caliphate* (Baghdad, 1969).
Shaban, M. A. "The Political Geography of Khurasan and the East at the Time of the Arab Conquest," *Iran and Islam*, ed. C. E. Bosworth (Edinburgh, 1971).
Sourdel, D. *Le vizirat 'abbāside*, 2 vols. (Damascus, 1959–60).

Index

For the purposes of alphabetization the abbreviations *b.* (for *ibn* "son") and *bt.* (for *bint* "daughter") have been disregarded.

N

P

Q